New Orleans

New Orleans
The Making of an Urban Landscape

Second Edition

Peirce F. Lewis

CENTER FOR
AMERICAN
PLACES

Santa Fe, New Mexico,
and Staunton, Virginia

PUBLISHER'S NOTES: *New Orleans: The Making of an Urban Landscape, Second Edition* was published in March 2003 in an edition of 300 clothbound and 2,200 paperbound copies, with the generous financial assistance of a Friend of the Center for American Places. A second paperback printing of 2,000 copies, complete with minor updates and corrections, was issued in May 2005. The first edition of *New Orleans* was published in paperback only in 1976 by Ballinger Publishing Company, of Cambridge, Massachusetts (a subsidiary of Harper & Row, Publishers, Inc.), as part of the *Comparative Metropolitan Analysis Project* of the Association of American Geographers, Washington, D.C., John S. Adams, research director, Ronald Abler, associate director and atlas editor, and Ki-Suk Lee, chief cartographer. The first edition was supported by a grant from the National Science Foundation, and a modified version appears as *Book One* in this second edition. For more information about the Center for American Places and the publication of *New Orleans: The Making of an Urban Landscape, Second Edition*, please see page 200.

The Center for American Places, Inc.
P.O. Box 23225
Santa Fe, New Mexico 87502, U.S.A.
www.americanplaces.org

Distributed by the University of Virginia Press
P.O. Box 400318
Charlottesville, VA 22904, U. S. A.
www.upress.virginia.edu

9 8 7 6 5 4 3 2

Library of Congress Cataloging-in-Publication data can be obtained directly from the publisher.

ISBN 1-930066-09-0
ISBN 1-930066-10-4 (pbk)

Frontispiece: The New Orleans skyline and Mississippi River, looking upstream past the central business district, circa 2000. Most of the high buildings are hotel and office complexes, erected since the early 1970s. Photograph by Donn Young, Board of Commissioners for the Port of New Orleans. (Used by permission.)

Cover: A postcard image of a Mardi Gras celebration in the early twentieth century.

For Felicia

A town is saved, not more by the righteous men in it
than by the woods and swamps that surround it.

—Henry David Thoreau, 1854

It is not entirely a disadvantage to be born a member of a small isolated metropolis
instead of a great central one. If the seed of its population be good and strong,
if the geographical situation be a fortunate one, if the detachment from,
and the connection with, the civilized world be nicely adjusted, the former being
definite and the latter difficult (and surely these conditions were met with a century
and a half ago on the banks of the Mississippi), there follows for the smaller metropolis
a freedom of development with a resultant cleanness of character,
which is as great a gain for a city as for an individual. In such a smaller mother-city,
individual acts assume an importance, individual lives an intrinsic value,
which it would be absurd to attribute to inhabitants of a great centre;
our gods seem closer to us, our fates more personal . . .

— Grace King, 1904

Because we [Southerners] started later,
and because we were poorer than our fellow city dwellers in the North,
we have had neither the time nor the money
to immortalize — in concrete —
quite as many of our mistakes as they did.

—Joel L. Fleishman, 1972

In its passion for politics, the Gret Stet of Loosiana, as southern Louisianans refer to it, resembles most closely the Arab republic of Lebanon, but in its economy it is closer akin to the Arab sheikdoms of the Persian Gulf. The Gret Stet floats on oil like a drunkard's teeth on whiskey. "Oil is to Louisiana, what money is to a roulette game [Leibling quotes an acquaintance as saying]. It's what makes the wheels go round."

New Orleans resembles Genoa or Marseilles, or Beirut or the Egyptian Alexandria more than it does New York, although all seaports resemble one another more than they can resemble any place in the interior. Like Havana and Port-au-Prince, New Orleans is within the orbit of a Hellenistic world that never touched the North Atlantic. The Mediterranean, Caribbean and Gulf of Mexico form a homogenous though interrupted sea. New York and Cherbourg and Bergen are in a separate thalassic system.

—A. J. LIEBLING, 1961

...and while neither Atlanta nor New Orleans yet vies seriously with New York, Chicago, Los Angeles as irreclaimable disaster sites, they are trying hard and cheerfully, and, given time, may well succeed.

—REYNOLDS PRICE, 1972

The future of our city . . . cannot be foretold by looking to other places. It is to be found by looking at what we've been and what we are . . . I know politicians are not supposed to wonder about these things. I'm a politician, but I'm also a New Orleanian, and that means I'm different.

— MOON LANDRIEU, MAYOR OF NEW ORLEANS, 1972

CONTENTS

Apologia and Acknowledgments
for Book One (1976)

I ACCEPTED JOHN ADAMS'S AND RON ABLER'S INVITATION to write this "vignette" about New Orleans in large part to satisfy personal curiosity—I wanted to know more about New Orleans and about myself. I saw a chance to educate myself about a legendary part of America—a place which was terra incognita to me and, judging from the dearth of scholarly writing about New Orleans, not very well known to most other American geographers either. I was also curious to know whether one could "learn" a big city in a short time—not perfectly, of course, for even old-timers cannot do that, but well enough to explain how a city's gross patterns of internal geography get to be the way they are, and to explain how they relate to their neighboring areas. Above all, I wanted to see if one could draw a holistic picture of a place such as New Orleans, where romance and reality are so cheerfully interchanged—on the one hand recognizing the romance without wallowing in it, on the other hand recognizing the hard economic realities of urban life without treating the city as an economic machine. I had been telling students for a long time that all these things were possible; it was time to put up or shut up.

The reader must decide whether I have succeeded, for I am too close to this venture to judge, and I have grown too fond of New Orleans to be very dispassionate. (I have learned, if nothing else, that it is possible to fall in love with a city on short notice, even if one may not understand it perfectly.) To the degree that I have succeeded, however, it is less my success than the success of the throng of people who helped me, supported me, and educated me during my encounter with New Orleans. I owe the most to Sam and Joyce Hilliard, of Louisiana State University's Department of Geography, who nourished me in mind and body, and whose kindness I shall never be able to repay; to James Lewin of the New Orleans City Planning Commission, who showed me his adopted city and why he had fallen in love with it; to Dr. Milton B. Newton, Jr., of LSU, who argued me through the redneck country beyond New Orleans; and to John Chase, that extraordinary and literate gentleman (can one say more?) who helped me more than he may know.

I also owe a great debt to Captain Paul Vogt, and his fellow bar pilots at Pilottown, who showed me the amazing business of getting ships in and out of the Mississippi River and showed me once again that southern hospitality to strangers still thrives; to John and Ann Fluitt of the University of New Orleans; to Dr. Ronald Lockman of the Geography Department at the University of New Orleans; to Ada Newton and Joyce Nelson for access to the excellent archives of the geography department's map room at LSU in Baton Rouge; Mrs. Connie Griffith and Mr. William Cullison, III, of the Special Collections Division of the Tulane University Library; and Mr. Colin B. Hamer, Jr., of the Louisiana Division of the New Orleans Public Library. All gave me free access to invaluable archival material. Captain Albro Mitchell, Jr., of the bar pilots, essentially loaned me his entire library on the port of New Orleans.

I am also indebted to the officials of the remarkably hospitable public bodies of the New Orleans area: Dr. Gordon A. Saussy, assistant director of the Division of Business and Economic research, UNO; Mr. Alfred C. Nichols, public relations and advertising manager of the greater New Orleans Tourist and Convention Commission; Mr. William Smollen of STAR/NASA at Michoud; Mr. Robert Smith, manager for news and publications for the Board of Commissioners of the Port of New Orleans; Dr. David Slusher, state soil scientist for Louisiana; the geologists of the New Orleans District of the U.S. Army Corps of Engineers; Mr. Hugh N. Ford, director of the Jefferson Parish Planning Department; Mr. Peter J. Nogueria, research analyst for the Chamber of Commerce of the New Orleans Area; and Mr. Thomas W. Schnadelbach, Jr., senior planner of the New Orleans Regional Planning Commission. Special thanks go to Mr. Hugh G. Lewis for cartographic help, and to Mrs. Colleen Kristula for long hours of typing and retyping manuscripts. Richard Ormrod, Helen Chelius, and Fred Kniffen all called my attention to things I would have not otherwise noted. None of these kind people, of course, are responsible for my errors.

I owe a particular debt to those who read the entire manuscript, and whose careful criticisms helped me find and hopefully eliminate some of my more egregious blunders: John Chase and Maurice Ries of New Orleans; Donald Deskins of the University of Michigan; James E. Vance, Jr., of the University of California at Berkeley; Donald Meinig of Syracuse University; and John S. Adams of the University of Minnesota at Minneapolis.

Finally, I am grateful beyond measure to my wife, Felicia, and to Miss Malvina Evans, who endured my day to day crotchets and eccentricities without reproach. The same goes for the people of New Orleans—a fine folk.

Peirce F. Lewis
University Park, Pennsylvania
November, 1973

Preface and Acknowledgments
to Book Two (2003)

WHEN PAUL GROTH SUGGESTED bringing out a second edition of *New Orleans: The Making of an Urban Landscape*, I reacted with enthusiasm. The book, originally published in 1976, had been allowed to go out of print by an indifferent publisher, and I had thought that was the end of it. But as the 1970s rolled into the 80s and 90s, I kept getting calls and letters from urbanists and Orleanophiles who had learned about the book by word of mouth and wanted to get a copy. Since the original press run had long been exhausted, it seemed to me that a second edition would be a good idea.

But too much time had elapsed to let the 1976 edition stand as it was, and I didn't want merely to republish a period piece. So I went to New Orleans in early 2001 to find out what had happened to the city in the intervening twenty-five years, and to see what kind of updating would be needed. I had expected to find changes in New Orleans; a quarter of a century, after all, is a long time in the life of an American city.

But I had not expected to find that New Orleans had been shaken by a seismic upheaval. The city's economy, society, and politics had all been turned on their heads. The population had shifted drastically. It even seemed that the city's rather self-satisfied vision of itself might be coming loose from its moorings. And, of course, the city's landscape had also changed — so much that parts of New Orleans were unrecognizable to me, after the passage of twenty-five years. In short, I found the city transformed, and in many ways that were neither expected nor welcome. (Happily, I found a large part of the city very much intact. For all its warts and blemishes, New Orleans remains one of America's great urban treasures.)

A second edition of *New Orleans* could not accommodate such dramatic change with a few cosmetic amendments to the original text. The transformed city demanded brand new text, and a substantial amount of it. Although I decided to leave the original text much as it had been written in 1975, I did correct typographical errors, make some necessary modifications throughout to reflect contemporary word usage, and the like, and provide essential updates and revisions as warranted. That original text, here titled "Book One," had sought to explain how the city had come to be the way it was over a period of more than two and a half centuries, and how, over the years, the city had been bent to fit a very difficult geographic site. There seemed no need to repeat that story. A new "Book Two" would aim to explain how and why the city had been transformed during the last quarter of the twentieth century, and to help readers understand the dramatic consequences of that transformation.

Acknowledgments

When I undertook my research for the new Book Two, I went about it the same way I had in the early 1970s. In the conventional academic manner, I set out to find and read everything that seemed relevant to the state of the city. During my bibliographic search, I found that one thing had not changed: the voluminous writing about New Orleans was sadly lacking in solid reliable material that described how the city had evolved, and how it worked. An unseemly volume, however, consisted of literary treacle which oozed over New Orleans and apparently had drowned most serious efforts to understand the city. An example of that genre appeared unblushingly in a publication of the city's Tourist and Convention Bureau, where an ecstatic promoter described New Orleans as "one part fantasy, one part mystical metropolis, and several parts sweet romance." It would take another Mark Twain to relegate such glutinous stuff to its proper container.

Happily, however, there were shining exceptions, and they helped me enormously. Richard and Mariana Campanella's *New Orleans, Then and Now*, published in 1999 (see the *Bibliography to Book Two*) is an excellent evocation of the city's changing landscape, described in lucid intelligent prose, and illustrated by a wonderful range of old and new photographs, including a large number of very useful aerials. The School of Business at the University of New Orleans continues its careful and serious research into the city's economy and demography, and many of the findings are published in *The Louisiana Business Survey*. And the Friends of the Cabildo had published a splendid five-volume series about the city's neighborhood architecture. But, as with my earlier researches in the 1970s, I discovered that my best sources of information and insight came from the experience of a few savvy Orleanians, who had been paying careful attention to the goings-on in their beloved but beleaguered city.

In 1973, I had the great good fortune to meet John Chase, the legendary cartoonist for the *New Orleans States-Item* and the writer of authoritative and witty books about the city and its history. We had a good deal in common, it turned out, and we became good friends. John Chase introduced me to all sorts of knowledgeable people, and he taught me vastly more about New Orleans than I ever learned from books. John Chase died in 1985, and I still mourn him. It is doubtful we will see his like again.

John Chase was a journalist and an exceptionally good one. In my experience, good journalists are among the keenest and most perceptive observers of what the world is like, and how it works. As a geographer, I have always felt a special affinity for journalists; after all, both professions have the job of describing the world lucidly and accurately. The main difference, I think, is that journalists have shorter deadlines than geographers.

So, on my visit in 2001, I sought out journalists once again, and I was lucky enough to make the acquaintance of two bright and talented staff writers for *The New Orleans Times-Picayune*, the main daily newspaper for the metropolitan area. Both men caused scales to fall from my eyes in great cluttering heaps. One was Keith Darcé, a correspondent who covers business affairs and especially the Port of New Orleans. Keith also follows the doings of the city's large gay community, and its growing economic and social impact on the city's fortunes. The other (whom I actually met via e-mail) was Coleman Warner, a staff writer on the city desk who covers the changing scene in the city's myriad neighborhoods—as well as the general condition of planning (such as it is) in southern Louisiana. Both men were openhanded in sharing with me their rich and extensive knowledge of New Orleans, and I am indebted to them both. For any serious scholar of New Orleans, I commend them to the writings of both Keith Darcé and Coleman Warner.

I also owe a particular debt to two other hospitable and well-informed Orleanians. One is Mark Tullis, an attorney by profession, a bibliophile and closet academic by inclination, who early on had written to me and urged me to republish *New Orleans*. In addition to giving me his enormous insight into the doings of his native city, he loaned me a good share of his collection of Orleaniana, and was unsparingly generous with information, ideas, and time. Mark spent hours in a variety of New Orleans libraries, searching out information on my behalf, and before the manuscript was finished I came to regard him not only as a kind and benevolent friend, but as a valued academic colleague as well.

My other benefactor was Richard Campanella, whose wonderful book about New Orleans I have already mentioned. Rich possesses a knowledge of New Orleans akin to that of Mark Tullis and John Chase, and I came to rely on him for knowledge and ideas that I would otherwise never have discovered. Rich is a card-carrying geographer and Assistant Director for Environmental Analysis in Tulane University's Center for Bioenvironmental Research. Rich led me on several eye-popping tours of New Orleans, and he also bestowed on me his very considerable talents as expert in GIS (Geographic Informations Systems) and computer cartography. He is a generous man, and made several of the maps in Book Two, based on some exotic computer programs from the 2000 census. I am very grateful.

I must also acknowledge several other kind people, without whom this new book would have been immeasurably more difficult to complete. Charlene Woodcock, of the University of California Press, was an ever-present source of comfort and help during the creation of Book Two. I owe her a debt of gratitude that I will never be able to repay. Ronald Abler, executive director of the Association of American Geographers, along with John Adams, professor of geography at the University of Minnesota, helped me untangle the book's very knotty copyright problems. William Borah, a widely respected New Orleans attorney, environmental activist, and co-author of *The Second Battle of New Orleans*, helped me understand why planning and preservation have traveled such a rutted road in New Orleans. Peg Culligan, chief of protocol for the Board of Commissioners for the Port of New Orleans (a.k.a. the "Dock Board"), spent hours explaining the intricate workings of New Orleans's maritime activities, and then took me on an unforgettable tour of the port which ended at a dizzying height above the Mississippi River atop one of Nashville Avenue's new state-of-the-art gantry cranes. Donn Young, the talented photographer for the Dock Board, graciously made his photographs available without fuss or fee—among them the photograph which serves as this book's frontispiece. And I was fortunate to acquire the considerable cartographic and computer skills of Henry J. Rademacher of Pennsylvania State University, who re-drew several important maps and graphs.

I also thank Jonathan Raisz for allowing me to use a portion of the wonderful *Map of the Landforms of the United States* by his gifted and famous grandfather, Professor Erwin Raisz of Harvard University (Figure 1). Thanks also go to my fellow geographers—Karl Raitz of the University of Kentucky, Charles Aiken of the University of Tennessee, and Sam Hilliard, emeritus professor of geography at Louisiana State University—for reactions to my questions about the demographic history of New Orleans. I am also indebted to my old friend, Dr. Paul Groth, a professor in the departments of architecture and geography at Berkeley, for prodding me to undertake this enterprise.

My special thanks go to Richard Campanella, Keith Darcé, Mark Tullis, and Coleman Warner for spending long hours reading and criticizing the final manuscript, pointing out errors and infelicities that I had not noticed. I must, alas, take responsibility for those that remain. And I am enormously grateful to George F. Thompson, an old friend and president and publisher of the Center for American Places, for his enthusiastic reception and sensitive handling of my manuscript and the ultimate production and publication of the whole enterprise.

It is customary, I know, for authors to thank their spouses for help and support in their writing. I will not violate that tradition. Without Felicia's help, encouragement, and considerable personal sacrifice, this book would have never happened. Thanks is too weak a word to express my gratitude to her. I again dedicate this book to her with my love.

PEIRCE F. LEWIS
State College, Pennsylvania
February, 2003

BOOK ONE

The Shaping of New Orleans, from Its Beginnings to 1975

Chapter 1
THE ECCENTRIC CITY

AMERICANS HAVE RARELY been very fond of their own cities. Poets, states-men, and armies of crackerbarrel philosophers have repeatedly told us that virtue resides in rural places, while cities are dens of vice and iniquity. Thus, when headlines cry scandal in city governments; when city streets are fouled with garbage and air corrupted by smog; when we learn that people are fleeing the crime-ridden city for the green lawns of suburbia—we shake our heads in disapproval, but we are not surprised. Although the United States is one of the most urbanized countries on Earth, its cities are not very successful creations. Most Americans know it, and many accept it as inevitable.

But there are exceptions — a select company of big American cities beloved by their residents and praised by visitors. This book is about one of them—New Orleans, a city that has been admired perhaps as enthusiastically and as persis-tently as any other American city. Nor has New Orleans gained its reputation by boosterism, either. Unlike Los Angeles, Houston, New York City, and other boastful places, New Orleans has rarely thought it necessary or seemly to broad-cast its virtues to the world. Ordinary Orleanians assume that everyone else shares their admiration for their native city—assume that outsiders envy their own happy condition and would instantly move to New Orleans if they only had the chance. From time to time, other Americans — especially those in upstate Louisiana who live outside the magic circle—have found this Orleanian attitude smug and have said so loudly. But it no more distresses an old-time Orleanian to be called smug than it does a native of Boston or San Francisco—two other American cities that resemble New Orleans in civic self-assurance. Orleanians know very well that their native city occupies a special niche in America's small chamber of urban delights. It has been so for two and a half centuries.

Obviously, any city with a million people in its metropolitan ambit will possess defects, and New Orleans has more than a few.[1] Furthermore, the flaws are not merely cosmetic blemishes. Nobody who knows New Orleans, for example, would urge other cities to imitate its dreary record of chronic political rascality, its ominous racial affairs, the egregious quality of its public school system, or even the homicidal way its expressways are designed. But one can admire Paris without endorsing living standards in Parisian garrets. It is the same with New Orleans: we need not approve every particular to know that, in its elusive *genre de vie* (what we inelegantly render in English as "lifestyle"), New Orleans is almost in a class by itself.

It is tempting, then, in this era of urban decay, to hold up New Orleans as a model—a place for other American cities to admire and, perhaps, to imitate. New Orleans serves that function imperfectly, however. In the first place, it is by no means certain that New Orleans can long retain its most delectable qualities. Sins of the past are catching up, as they have with other American cities, while increasingly the city is pressed by economics and by fashion to remodel itself in a more conventional image. Furthermore, many of the things that make New Orleans special and admirable cannot be duplicated by other urban places in the United States: many of its most important attributes spring from a history and a geography that are eccentric to the mainstream of American urban experience. (Indeed, the cities that might profit most from a study of New Orleans are not American ones, perhaps, but those old cities in preindustrial countries that seek to retain traditional virtues but find it hard to make a living in the modern world at the same time.) And, finally, New Orleans is not even an easy place to study. For a city of its size, age, and prominence, there is an uncommon scarcity of serious scholarly work on the city. To be sure, there are studies of certain aspects of New Orleans, and some—notably in local architec-

---

[1] More precisely, the 1970 census counted 1,046,000 people in the New Orleans SMSA (Standard Metropolitan Statistical Area) of Orleans, Jefferson, St. Bernard, and St. Tammany parishes. (A "parish" is the Louisiana equivalent of a county elsewhere in the United States.) The SMSA boundaries are highly artificial, however, and it would be more accurate to say that the population lay somewhere between 1.0 and 1.1 million in the city and its contiguous suburbs.

ture and history—are distinguished and entrancing. But serious comprehensive studies of the contemporary city are hard to come by; published works about New Orleans too often tend to be narrow in scope, esoteric in topic, or dripping in saccharine—sometimes all three. This special quality of scholarship about New Orleans is no accident, however, for it stems from the special qualities of the city itself.

A Romantic Sort of Place

From the outset, New Orleans was a foreign city, and it has never completely lost its foreign flavor. If Americans have never been very good at understanding cities, they have been even worse at understanding foreigners. Furthermore, when Americans bought the city in 1803, it was no mere frontier village, but a robust place with a mature personality. By standards of the time, it was a good-sized city: the 1810 census counted New Orleans as the fifth largest city in the country—a position it maintained off and on until shortly before the Civil War. Clearly it was big enough to resist assimilation into the American mainstream for a long time, and to keep its foreign ambience.[2]

These Orleanians, furthermore, were a different breed of foreigners than Americans were accustomed to dealing with. The American East Coast gentry, of course, had plenty of experience in dealing with foreigners, but all obviously of a rather inferior kind—half-naked "foreign" Indians, wretched Africans in chains, and a good many Europeans who came as indentured servants and the like—supplicants who no more merited esteem than Indians and Negroes. But the Creoles of New Orleans were another sort, prouder even than Bostonians.[3] They considered their Franco-Spanish civilization obviously superior to that of England, and

---

[2] French was spoken by a good many Orleanians until well into the twentieth century. When Louisiana seceded from the Union in 1861, the articles of secession were published in both French and English—as were all of Louisiana's laws.

[3] The word "Creole" is widely used in two quite different senses. It derives from the Spanish word *crillo*, "a child born in the colonies"—according to John Chase *(Frenchmen, Desire, Good Children)*. In this context, it came to designate native-born white Orleanians of Spanish and French ancestry. Over the years, however, the word took on broader meaning, to include anybody or anything that is native to New Orleans or is associated with traditional New Orleans. Thus, in spite of stiff-necked whites, many light-skinned New Orleanian blacks call themselves Creoles, and with pride. In the same sense, a much-loved variety of southern Louisiana tomato is a "Creole tomato" and the assemblage of traditional New Orleans cooking practices combine to form the famous Creole cuisine. A Creole skyscraper, on the other hand, is unthinkable; although a Creole might own one or even build it, modern things just can't be Creole.

planets apart from the unwashed Kentuckians who landed, spitting tobacco, on the Mississippi levee. As H.W. Gilmore put it much later on, it was "the only case of its kind in American history . . . when the spreading American frontier ran into a culture which, on the basis of manners and fine appearance at least, was superior to its own."

While the Creoles were revolted by the Americans, the Americans were stunned by the finery of this transplanted Mediterranean city, and it seems doubtful if they, or generations of successors, really expected to understand the place. From the Creole's standpoint, the more misunderstanding the better, since social intercourse with barbarian Anglo-Americans was a loathsome prospect. Both parties invented their own mythology, sometimes by accident or whimsy, sometimes through malice, but a city which was different enough to begin with became shrouded in an almost impenetrable fog of romance and fable. (Scholars evidently found the atmosphere excessively gassy, and fled.) The Civil War, which speeded the process of cultural convergence in many other parts of the nation, only made understanding New Orleans more difficult. After all, New Orleans was by far the largest city of the South, and it was easy to believe that the wrongs inflicted at the hands of those same barbarian northerners were more cruel and more numerous than the wrongs suffered by lesser places. So went the mythology, and so it grew. Whether the tales are true or not is quite beside the point; at the end of Reconstruction, New, Orleans lay far outside the mainstream of American urban society and was quite content to remain there—in image if not in fact.

The City Looked Different

For visitors, already prepared to believe that New Orleans is different, seeing the city is likely to confirm their convictions, for a good share of the city looks like nothing else in North America. It was so from early times. The urban historians Glaab and Brown remark that "by the 1840's travelers found a monotonous similarity in the appearance of American cities, particularly those that had been newly built in the West." Having made that statement, they immediately hasten to note that New Orleans was different—a foreign-looking city which most visitors found entrancing.

Part of the difference in appearance—and in the city's image—is simply the result of climate. New Orleans is a tropical city or nearly so; indeed, until fairly recently, the only tropical city of any consequence in the United

States.[4] This very fact enlarged New Orleans's image, for all Americans know that the tropics are both romantic and faintly corrupt. Visitors who came looking for an atmosphere of mildew and lassitude were quick to find it, especially in the summertime before air conditioning, when Orleanians quite sensibly paused for lengthy midday siestas in the shade. Outsiders even blamed the long hot summer for the fetid condition of New Orleans's politics, which had presumably rotted in the steaming heat. But visitors seldom failed to mention and admire the luxuriant vegetation, especially in the fashionable districts of the city, and even the slums looked somehow less slummy in a setting of banana plants and crepe myrtle. Many visiting authors seemed almost inspired. Even the misanthropic Mrs. Trollope, who entered the United States by way of New Orleans in 1827 and found nothing much to her liking, was "cheered . . . by the bright tints of southern vegetation." When somebody took her for a walk in the nearby woods, "the eternal forests of the western world," they made her feel "rather sublime and poetical." (From what she wrote later on, one guesses she contracted spleen and vapors in the swamp.)

Mrs. Trollope was not the last of the literati to be inspired by the combination of foreignness and tropical setting. According to C. Vann Woodward, Lafcadio Hearn, who later won fame by celebrating the spooky romance of feudal Japan, found New Orleans enchanting, meantime pledging himself "to the worship of the Odd, the Queer, the Strange, the Exotic, the Monstrous." His books about New Orleans added considerably to the city's eccentric reputation, but did little to provide a dispassionate portrait of the city. With each additional author, the miasma grew thicker.

New Orleans's buildings were foreign and eccentric, too. It was not just the pastel stucco and cast iron of the French Quarter, nor just the flamboyant mansions of the Garden District, so celebrated in architectural literature. Even the

---

[4] By strict standards, most climatologists would call New Orleans subtropical, not tropical. In January, the coldest month, the average day ranges between a low temperature of 45° F and a high of 64° F, and the weather bureau on one terrible February day a few years ago recorded a temperature of 7° F, the lowest in thirty years and one which produced real suffering. But winter is short, and "cool" would be a more accurate description than "cold." Summer, by contrast, is sweaty and seemingly endless; temperatures in the nineties are recorded from March through early November, with drenchingly high humidity much of the time. The vegetation reflects the climate more tellingly than statistics— bougainvillea, bananas, sugar cane, and citrus all grow in and around the city. And, as in much of the humid tropics, there is no dry season at all. (For a fuller description of New Orleans's climate, see the U.S. Department of Commerce, Environmental Data Service's *Climatic Atlas of the United States* [Washington, D.C.: U.S. Government Printing Office, June, 1968].)

modest houses of ordinary citizens (both white and black) were unusual. Part of the architectural flavor had descended through the Creoles from French and Spanish ancestry. Much more was imported from the Caribbean, where an early marriage of African and European ideas had given birth to picturesque houses that afforded maximum ventilation and shade. And more than a few stylistic quirks consciously aped changing European fancies, especially the more florid varieties which adorned the times of Victoria and Napoleon III. But standard American models were not much favored by the New Orleans elite, who generally set styles for the whole city. In architecture, New Orleans was foreign, not just in small areas, but for miles. If the mixture did not resemble any particular foreign city very much, it resembled the ordinary North American city not at all.

The Flavor of Salt

New Orleans's romantic differences are compounded by the fact that it is a seaport. All ports, of course, enjoy a certain worldly quality that comes from the constant mingling of products and people from far-off places, but again New Orleans is not even ordinary as a port. First of all, the port of New Orleans is big—ranking second only to New York City in volume and value of cargo handled. Unlike New York, however, which does a good many things beside handling cargo, New Orleans embraces marine commerce with the same single-minded enthusiasm as Detroit makes automobiles. Manufacturing, by contrast, plays a relatively insignificant role in the city's economic life, and even that limited industry is mostly associated with the port—shipbuilding and the like.

This heavy dependence on the port has occasionally proved dangerous, for if the port is unhealthy, the city is in serious economic trouble. But shipping is a business that pays reasonably well, especially if that business is located at the entrance to the richest river valley on Earth. Most of the time, New Orleans has stayed economically healthy, meantime thoroughly relishing its bigamous marriage to the river and the ocean. Obviously, going down to the sea in ships was a good deal more enjoyable than pouring pig iron or slaughtering hogs. There are still more poems written about Old Man River and the briny deep than about making machine tools or assembling transistor radios.

An Old Important Place

Even if New Orleans had not been a romantic place, Americans would have found the city difficult to ignore, especially in the early days of the Republic when so many of America's national attitudes were forged and hardened. New Orleans occupied an extraordinarily important geographic location (never mind the romance), the possession of which was viewed as indispensable for America's national well-being. Its command of the entrance to the Mississippi was like Québec's command of the St. Lawrence, and both cities were seen as gatekeepers to the continental interior. The possession of both cities by foreigners was threatening to merchants and frontier farmers—maddening to all red-blooded patriots. American rage grew more furious after the Revolution, when permanent settlers began flooding into the upper reaches of those two great rivers. Despite several formal and informal raids on Québec, it presently emerged that America could not have it, and the national dudgeon subsided after the Erie Canal proved a better entry to the Great Lakes anyhow.

But New Orleans—as usual—was different. No imaginable canal could substitute for the Mississippi, which with its tributaries constituted a magnificent system of natural highways in the roadless territory that the newly independent Americans were about to occupy. While Québec was dangerous in imagery—a stone fortress brooding over an isolated river—New Orleans was a menace in fact, for in foreign hands it could throttle the commercial life of half the national territory. Ironically, the most succinct description of the city's importance came from that classic enemy of cities in general, Thomas Jefferson: "There is on the globe one spot, the possessor of which is our natural and habitual enemy. It is New Orleans. . ."

Thus, New Orleans was important in myth and important in fact—indeed, in the company of American cities, uniquely so. Moreover, Orleanians have always known it and hastened to capitalize on the combination by deliberately surrounding the city with as much additional mythology as they could conjure. H. Brandt Ayers, the noted Alabama newspaper editor, has remarked that "you can't eat magnolias." Orleanians might disagree, for magnolias have paid the city handsomely. In early times, the image of Paris-in-the-Wilderness helped promote Creole separatism and was frequently used as a basis for claiming special treatment for New Orleans at the hands of state and national government. More recently, New Orleans has found that romance is a salable commodity and has built a tourist industry which ranks second only to the port in the city's economy. To read the brochures, New Orleans offers the tourist a variety of the less deadly sins, crusted with an antique patina, and smelling strongly of gardenias. If the metaphor is mixed, it causes little concern. It is the nature of romance to be inconsistent.

It is hardly surprising that this extraordinary city has spewed a prodigious outpouring of writing, by native Orleanians and visitors alike. As might be expected, some of it is very good: Lafcadio Hearn's gothic prose proved as much, as did the novels and essays of George Washington Cable. Even today, the works of such native authors as John Chase, the gifted cartoonist and historian, can be sensitive and engaging. Equally, the majority of writing about New Orleans is very bad. A typical species is the semiliterate Victorian pseudopoetry that Mark Twain so loved to lampoon, and which was lamentably slow to expire in the swamps of the lower Mississippi. But good or bad, New Orleans's writers have paid more attention to gumbo and hoopskirts, to scarlet women and duels at dawn, than to the harder realities of economics, geography, political science, or demography.

If Orleanians thought about this imbalance—and most of them surely did not—it must have seemed only reasonable. After all, New Orleans is a different sort of place, and what is more natural than to pay attention to eccentricities, especially when they are colorful and entertaining? After all, what other American city possesses a genuine indigenous cuisine—and, as Richard Collin vividly demonstrates, one of such variety and excellence? What other city, especially a southern city, exhibited such tolerance to sin, or such an easygoing attitude toward race relations? What other American city is so strongly flavored with Mediterranean Catholicism, with carnivals that bridge the chasm between sacred and profane with such élan? Whose society was so brilliant, so exclusive, and so elusively foreign? What other city had such an illogical and dangerous site, but insouciantly went about its mixed business of commerce and fun in defiance of threats from pestilence, flood, and hurricane? Above all, what other city was so extravagantly charming?

Even scholars could convince themselves that New Orleans was different from other American cities in fundamental and important ways. What other southern city had a demographic history like New Orleans—in fullest bloom while most of America was still rural, only to fall on evil days at the very moment that the country was being transformed into an urban nation? How had New Orleans managed to escape many of the racial tragedies of the 1960s, this despite its hateful history as the place to which slaves were sold down the river and despite the fact that the New Orleans metropolitan area contained a higher percentage of blacks than any other city in the nation? Indeed, until the rise of Atlanta, what other big city did the South possess at all?

It is a useful and healthy thing for a city to be proud of its heritage, to possess a sense of peculiar identity to cherish and preserve. But it is easy for Orleanians—too easy, in fact—to leap to the conclusion that their splendid ghost-haunted city is so aberrant that the ordinary laws of nature do not apply to it. It may be worthwhile to study conventional cities—the Chicagoes, the Pittsburghs, even the eccentric Los Angeles, that wave of the urban future. But the argument continues: there is scarcely any point for a scholar to study New Orleans, particularly if the scholar is predisposed to study cities in search of general urban theories. After all, if ordinary norms do not apply, then the city is not going to make any sense a priori. Equally unrewarding to aspiring scholars, whatever they discover about New Orleans remains particular to New Orleans and cannot be used as a reliable basis for the study of other places. It is enough to turn any scholar into other, more productive undertakings, and apparently it did.

The argument is much too pat, of course. Romance and curiosity are fine things, but a million people cannot survive by eating magnolias. New Orleans is an unusual city, but it is still a city: people live and work there and, as in less exotic places, cause traffic jams when they travel to and from work. White and black people live in different parts of the city, and the geographic distribution of the races is not random. Many of the problems which afflict the "inner" parts of northern cities also afflict New Orleans, and just as white northerners are fleeing to the suburbs of Detroit and Omaha, so are white southerners doing it in New Orleans, albeit in somewhat different patterns. And so it goes. In many important ways, New Orleans is not unique, and it does not serve the city well to perpetuate the myth that it is. As the perceptive A. J. Liebling remarked in 1961: "I realized that New Orleans might be exotic in some respects but that in others it was exactly like everyplace else."

On the other hand, New Orleans is not the average American city by any stretch of the imagination, and one may be grateful that it is not. Simultaneously unique and not unique, New Orleans has much to learn from the rest of the nation's cities, even if it is nothing more than learning what not to do. Correspondingly, it may have a good deal to teach the rest of the nation as well, especially in the creation of gentle and humane urban environments.

The Island City

We shall have no "hyphenated Americans," Theodore Roosevelt used to say. Roosevelt, of course, was expressing both official policy and a deeply rooted national xenophobia. Foreigners are simply intolerable as permanent residents of the United States, and this country over the years has invented various ways to persuade or force foreigners to assimilate. One of the few ways that a foreign group can avoid being swept into the mainstream of American life is to find some island, some isolated nook where it can continue to grow, as some exotic plant might grow undisturbed on some far-off Pacific atoll. (Thus, the Mormons survived and flourished as an exotic culture in their Utah oasis.) It is true for cities as it is for national groups, and New Orleans has preserved its exotic individuality because it is a cultural island. And, as we shall presently see, the city is a cultural island in part because it was first a physical island.

The cultural insularity of New Orleans persists at several different scales, much as a physical island might be located in several bodies of water at the same time—in a small estuary, which is the arm of a bay, which opens off a gulf, which in turn is an extension of the ocean. From least to greatest, New Orleans is an island in Cajun southern Louisiana, an island in the state of Louisiana, an island in the South, and an island in the nation. Each kind of insularity has affected the city's character and colored its urban personality.

Island among Cajuns

Just as New Orleans began as a French city, much of southern Louisiana is French in ancestry. The city, however, is not just an extension of the countryside, as one might consider Wichita a creature of the Kansas prairies or Charlotte a creature of the Carolina Piedmont.

Rural southern Louisianians trace their ancestry mainly to French-Canadians, expelled by the British from New Brunswick and Nova Scotia in the mid-eighteenth century. These are the people from Acadia, and their descendents in Louisiana are called "Cajuns," a corruption of the word Acadian. Like their French-Canadian ancestors, the Cajuns are still a profoundly rural people, which the urbane Creole Orleanians emphatically were not, and are not now.

Outsiders often confuse Creoles with Cajuns, since French names dominate both groups, both are overwhelmingly Roman Catholic, and both have peculiarities of architecture and diet which set them apart from northern Louisiana and the rest of the South. But similar peculiarities also set them apart from one another. To take but one example, Cajun and Creole cuisine resemble each other as the country cooking of the French provinces resembles the *haute cuisine* of Paris; both are splendid, but they are not the same thing. So, also, the people—although both have French forebears, Creoles and Cajuns are entirely different species.

To Orleanians, Cajuns are hicks from the swamps, hillbillies without hills. These country bumpkins are tolerated for their wildly accented jokes and tall tales, which are widely circulated by radio and on phonograph records. Otherwise, Cajun influence on the cosmopolitan city is negligible. Nor has the city had much impact on the ordinary swamp Cajun; the main Cajun city in Louisiana, judging from names in the telephone directory and food on the restaurant tables, is not New Orleans at all, but rather Lafayette, 150 miles west.

Indeed, the Cajuns themselves are isolated; they could not have survived otherwise as a discrete ethnic group. The Mississippi Delta, where many of them live, is an area where transportation is extremely difficult by land, and not so easy by water either. For example, it is forty-eight airline miles from the small town of Grand Isle into New Orleans; it is 109 miles by road, and until fairly recently there was no road. Even closer places such as Lafitte and Delacroix sit amid swampland at the end of devious dead-end roads. They are not en route anywhere, and unless travelers are inextricably lost, they are unlikely to pass through either town by accident. Thus, as the Cajuns began their career in Louisiana as a profoundly nonurban people, two centuries of isolation did little to urbanize them. To the degree that they have joined the national mainstream, it is national television that has done it and not the influence of New Orleans. Meantime, New Orleans sits grandly aloof, occasionally patronizing the Cajuns, but usually ignoring them.

Island in Louisiana

If New Orleans is an urban island in rural Cajun Louisiana, the city is an armed fortress in the context of Louisiana as a whole. In many American states, of course, there is considerable hostility between the rural and small town folk, as opposed to the people of the state's largest city. This, of course, is the traditional "upstate-downstate" split which has set Chicago against the rest of Illinois, Detroit against Michigan, and New York City against upstate New York. In Louisiana the split is exaggerated to yawning proportions, for the difference is not merely between city and country, but between two disparate cultures.

Upstate Louisiana is the extension of what the late Professor Kniffen of Louisiana State University called "the Upland South," the traditional South to most Americans, the South of Faulkner and Truman Capote. Its white ancestry is Anglo-Saxon, and heavily Scots-Irish, with almost no traces of ethnic groups outside the British Isles. Its religion is Protestant with a strong fundamentalist strain, and its home has been the complex of small dirt farms, hamlets, and small towns that dot the eroded piney hills where cotton once was king. The area is poor—dirt poor—and if it has lost some of its poverty in recent years, it is because many of the poorest farmers have given up and left their wretched little plots.

Politics in northern Louisiana have a strong Populist bias, stridently and colorfully represented by such figures as Huey Long, a shrewd and sophisticated man who advertised himself to the public as an uncouth redneck and the mortal enemy of city slickers and big money capitalists. For Long, and the northern Louisiana constituency that reared him, New Orleans was wickedness incarnate, bad enough for its wealth and arrogance, but doubly detested for its Popery and foreign ways. When Long made occasional liaison with the New Orleans political machine, he loudly announced how he disliked the job but had no other choice. (Long's private views were something else again. Once he had been safely elected governor, he set up permanent residence in New Orleans, where his sybaritic enjoyment of the city became something of a public scandal.)

The political antagonism is further complicated by the Cajuns, who are allied to New Orleans by religion and ethnicity, but linked to northern Louisiana in poverty and rurality. Even when Cajuns voted with their fellow Catholics in New Orleans, southern Louisiana has only recently had the population to win statewide elections. As a result, New Orleans was often a political underdog and the subject of malevolent attentions from northern Louisiana legislatures and governors. For a long time, however, the city possessed a formidable political machine known as the "Old Regulars," which held a balance of power in the state whenever factions of northern Louisianians went to war among themselves. Since such warfare was chronic in northern Louisiana, the North more often sought some kind of accommodation with the city, ordinarily with no particular regard for legal niceties. Thus, while Southern politics have a reputation for picturesque chicanery, Louisiana is in a class by itself, in large part because it was the only Southern state that had to contend with a big exotic city.

The results have been lurid in the extreme. V.O. Key, Jr., one of the closest observers of the Southern political scene, subtitled his study of Louisiana politics "The Seamy Side of Democracy." The most vigorous description, perhaps, comes from T. Harry Williams, Huey Long's biographer, who quotes "an impressed twentieth-century critic" (A.J. Liebling) as writing: "Louisiana politics is of an intensity and complexity that is matched, in my experience, only in the Republic of Lebanon." According to Williams, "he decided that the state as a whole, but especially its southern section, was part of the Hellenistic Mediterranean littoral . . . the western-most of the Arab states. Its people had a tolerance of corruption not found elsewhere in America . . . " Williams continues: "Some [observers] have gone so far as to suggest that Louisiana is not really an American state, but a 'banana republic,' a Latin enclave of immorality set down in a country of Anglo-Saxon righteousness. . . . It is understandable that Louisianians have always had a non-American attitude toward corruption. They have accepted it as a necessary part of political life, and they have even admired it when it is executed with style and, above all, with a jest."

A good many Orleanians, however, are not amused. The "toleration of corruption," they suggest, is not unrelated to the fact that the Mafia first found American roots in New Orleans, even before it had landed in New York City. Then, too, corruption is grossly wasteful, perhaps helping to explain Louisiana's chronically low ranking when compared with other states in quality of schools and other public services. Nor can one overlook the fact that the New Orleans public is justifiably suspicious of government qua government, with the result that a good many civic ills go unattended because the public is unwilling to support governmental attempts to correct them. It is true that most Americans distrust politicians, but in New Orleans that distrust reaches almost pathological levels.

Island in the South

The very fact New Orleans is a city, of course, makes it a foreigner in the South—a region which has been nonurban in fact and antiurban in sentiment. (Populism has been endemic in the South in large part because the South has been traditionally the least urbanized area in the nation.) Indeed, one can argue with some justice that the South had no real cities until recently, that the true metropolises—Baltimore, Cincinnati, Louisville, St. Louis, Dallas, Houston, and even Miami, that exotic outpost of New York City—were located in the rim of the South, like a row of spectators standing on the brink but not daring to come in. The Nashvilles, the Chattanoogas, the Montgomerys, the Little Rocks have (as of this writing in 1975) been small, sleepy, and largely lacking in the kinds of urban atmosphere that one associates with big cities. Even the densities of population within Southern cities have been low, with houses sitting on plots of ground that often look more like small farms than urban lots. That situation is changing now, and that is why metropolitan Atlanta and "the Atlanta spirit" are correctly viewed as revolutionary in the context of southern culture.

of urbanization has been an essential southern trait, then one suspects
may be wrong to call New Orleans southern at all, that the city really
to the outer rim. That may be true. In the fundamental things that set
people apart from one another culturally—how they speak, eat, drink, dress,
shelter themselves, and even how they view sex—Orleanians do not seem like
southerners. The New Orleans accent, for example, often sounds more like
Brooklyn than like Vicksburg, and scholars have noted that New Orleans is like
New York City in having a number of distinct regional accents. The rich and
cosmopolitan Orleanian cuisine is a world apart from the "hogmeat and hoecake" of the Upland South that Professor Sam Hilliard of Louisiana State
University has described so artfully. As for drinking, Orleanians may be no
more bibulous than upland southerners, but they drink different things and
under different circumstances. In its sexual mores, New Orleans has a reputation for permissiveness that may be undeserved, but is of long standing, as an
1853 gazeteer makes clear when it compares the "insalubrity of the climate"
with "the morals of the city." The gazeteer goes on in a tone of indignation:
"From certain flagrant features of open abandonment . . . among a population
so little American in its composition, it is not strange that an impression
extremely unfavorable to the morals of the city should be produced." Today, the
reputation of "open abandonment" is carefully nourished by bartenders,
innkeepers, and other interested parties. That reputation is responsible for
drawing libidinous conventioneers into town from great distances, and may
help explain the disproportionate number of emancipated youths who wander
the streets of the French Quarter at night, seeking adventure.

The Island as a World City

But the insularity of New Orleans emerges most obviously when the city is
compared with other big American cities and, indeed, with most other big
cities in the world. The ordinary big city in the United States—especially one
that relies on commerce for a livelihood—serves (and is served by) a hinterland which surrounds it and largely determines its character. Most of the midcontinental cities are obviously colored by their rural hinterlands, even those
that are heavily industrial. Chicago, for example, as Carl Sandburg and Louis
Sullivan have both said in their own ways, is a Midwestern prairie city, just as
Denver is a compound product of plains and mountains, and Seattle is an offspring of the Pacific Northwest. The key to the economic and social character
of each of these cities—as to a host of lesser places such as Tulsa, Des Moines,

or Indianapolis—is the social and economic character of the territory which lies immediately adjacent to the city.

This is not true of New Orleans. To be sure, New Orleans serves as market town for the Cajun Mississippi Delta, and even for parts of Anglo-Saxon Louisiana and Mississippi that lie north of the city across Lake Pontchartrain—but that market is quite incidental and unimportant. New Orleans has a larger role: to link the distant and unimaginably rich interior of North America with the ocean.

Such phraseology may seem merely a pompous way of saying that New Orleans is a big seaport, but it is more than that. The richest part of the New Orleans hinterland is the *upper* Mississippi River valley, not the lower valley, and that was true even before the boll weevil effectively wiped out the cotton belt of the old South—even while the bales still stood high on the levees at the foot of Canal Street. A large part of the agricultural and industrial products of the Midwest find their way to market by way of the port of New Orleans, and the port is the city's most important source of income.[5] That wealth, because it comes from very far away, has allowed the city to ignore adjacent areas and even to ignore other ports which might potentially compete with it.

Phrase it in different terms: the hinterland of the ordinary inland city is shaped like an amoeba, spreading off into the surrounding countryside with fuzzy boundaries and uncertain impetus, but with a roughly circular shape. New Orleans's hinterland, by contrast, is shaped like a lollipop, with the city at the tip of the stem. Economically, the valley of the Mississippi River is like a funnel, and New Orleans controls the outlet. Orleanians know it very well and see little reason for the city to concern itself with areas nearby, since they are irrelevant to its economic well-being. Indeed, their very poverty and lack of sophistication merely reminds New Orleans that the city is an especially favored place. If nearby people gnash their teeth in rage at Orleanians' smug belief in their own superiority, it does them no good. New Orleans is rich, it is superior, and its nearest competitors are half a continent away.

Despite New Orleans's rather parochial pride, it is not unique, for there are other cities like it, both in the United States and elsewhere in the world. But to list those cities merely reaffirms the eccentric brilliance of New Orleans, for the list includes some of the greatest and most glittering cities on Earth. New

---

[5] That was true in 1975, when this was first written. By the end of the twentieth century, however, tourism had overtaken the port as an employer and as a source of New Orleans's income. See, also, Chapter 7, "The New Tourism."

York City is like New Orleans, connected to the wealth of the Great Lakes by the umbilical cord of the Hudson and Mohawk valleys, its harbor open to Europe and the world, but scorning nearby New Jerseyites and other lesser breeds without the law. San Francisco is like New Orleans, commanding the Golden Gate, through which the Babylonian treasures of the interior West pour out to the Pacific and the world beyond—but culturally closer to Hong Kong and Singapore than to Fresno. The great colonial capitals—Calcutta, Alexandria, and Shanghai—were like New Orleans, each secure in its marshy wilderness, each extending its tentacles into an unbelievably rich hinterland, while scorning the groundling masses who huddled nearby. So, too, the great imperial seaports—St. Petersburg in the Neva marshes; Venice on its islands at the foot of the Alpine passes; and Byzantium commanding from its Golden Horn the Mediterranean to one side, the vast plain from the Vistula to the Caucasus on the other. Carthage was like New Orleans, on the edge of the desert, but demanding tribute from the trade between the eastern and western basins of the Mediterranean.

All of these cities are ports, to be sure, but that obscures the point. In a larger sense they were oases such as Samarkand and fabled Karakorum, which never depended on the area around them, but instead defied and scorned them. The wealth of these cities rested on distant, foreign, and romantic places.

Such environments may breed great and rich cities, but they breed neither humility among a city's inhabitants nor a tendency toward introspection. If Orleanians think of their city in comparative terms, they usually make comparisons with other cities they believe to be competitors—Mobile, perhaps, or the upstart Houston. The comparisons, quite naturally, are invidious. They rarely think of comparing New Orleans with Byzantium or Samarkand, and, perhaps, it is just as well. They have enough to nourish their self-confidence already.

Chapter 2
A Place on the River

The Impossible but Inevitable City

When one glances at a small-scale map of the United States, it is obvious that there had to be a city at the mouth of the Mississippi River. Common sense demanded one, and so did experience. Common sense also tells us that the location helped determine the kind of place New Orleans was to become.

Although the location of New Orleans is obvious on a small-scale map, it is far from obvious when one examines a detailed map of the swamp where the Mississippi debouches into the Gulf of Mexico and even less obvious when one visits the area. The Mississippi Delta is a fearsome place, difficult enough for building houses, lunacy for wharves and skyscrapers. Nor have environmental problems disappeared under the onslaught of modern technology. Yellow fever was eradicated around 1900, but flooding remains a constant threat. Foundation materials are the consistency of glue in many parts of the city, and there are few old buildings or sidewalks that have not settled or broken since they were built. Most dreaded are the hurricanes that boil out of the Gulf with random ferocity, pushing floodwaters of the Gulf of Mexico ahead of them.

Yet the city is still there. The apparent paradox between excellent location and miserable location merely illuminates the distinction between two terms—"site" and "situation"—which urban geographers use to describe the location of cities. Site is the actual real estate which the city occupies, and the site for New Orleans is wretched. Situation is what we commonly mean when we speak of a place with respect to neighboring places. New Orleans's situation is its location near the mouth of the Mississippi, and the fact that a million people work and make a living on this evil site only emphasizes the excellence of the situation. There is no contradiction. If a city's situation is good enough, its site will be altered to make do.

That is precisely what happened in New Orleans. The situation guaranteed prosperity for New Orleans, but the site also guaranteed that the city would be plagued by incessant trouble: yellow fever, floods, and unbearable summer heat. And because it was so difficult, the site also guaranteed that the form of the city's physical growth would be shaped by local environment to a far greater degree than in most other American cities.

In a word, New Orleans was shoehorned into a very constricted site. It is scarcely surprising that the shoe has pinched from time to time. Nor is it surprising that the city has taken some very strange shapes as a result. Further, some of the city's most important internal patterns—the distribution of black population to name but one of many—can be explained directly or indirectly by the difficulties and curiosities of local environment.

River, Delta, and City

To understand how these patterns evolved, to understand the extraordinary difficulties of building and maintaining a city here, one must understand what the immediate physical site of New Orleans is like. That site, like the personality of the city itself, is an offspring of the Mississippi River, a direct result of the river's behavior in its lower courses over the last several thousand years. Like the city it nourishes, however, the Mississippi is unusual—quite different, indeed, from any other large North American river. And the difference is not just a matter of size.

To begin with, the Mississippi is unusual because it has a delta. Not only do most North American rivers lack deltas of any kind, but also their mouths are *embayed*—that is, the sea has entered the river mouth and flooded it. Nearly every river in the world is that way, and the reason is the same. During glacial times—most recently about 25,000 years ago—sea level dropped because considerable ocean water was locked up in huge sheets of continental ice. At the glacial maxima, when sea level was lowest, rivers cut down to meet the new low sea level, and then, when the ice melted and sea level rose again, their valley mouths were flooded to form the estuaries that line the coast of North America today.

Finding a site for a city at the mouth of an embayed river poses no special difficulty. A host of big port cities—such as London, Hamburg, and old Québec—grew up quite naturally at the narrow inland neck of the estuary—the first place where ships were forced to use the same channel and the first place where land traffic could conveniently cross the river. But there is no embayment on the Mississippi, which is uniformly wide for hundreds of miles upstream. Correspondingly, south of Cairo, Illinois, where the Mississippi Valley opens out into its great deltaic plain, no place on the river is much easier or harder to cross than any other, and bridges were out of the question until fairly recently. Nor is there any well-defined head of navigation until one reaches the falls of St. Anthony at Minneapolis; indeed, the shallowest and most treacherous water in the lower Mississippi is across sand bars at the mouth of the river in the Gulf of Mexico. (To locate a city there, where the highest point is a tussock of salty grass, would be insanity.) In fact, there is no high ground on the lower Mississippi below Baton Rouge, more than 200 miles upstream from the Gulf. In sum, the Mississippi River demands a city at its mouth, but fails to provide any place for one.

To make matters worse, the Mississippi's delta projects into the Gulf of Mexico and causes trouble both for seagoing ships and coastal vessels. Because the several mouths of the river are flanked by extremely low land—little more than grassy sandbars or mudflats—the river mouths are extremely hard to find, and equally easy to confuse with a myriad of bayous that lead into the coastal marshes and then fade away. Furthermore, there is no way to get into the river by water except through the mouths, and no way for coastal ships to cross the upstream river. As a result, coastal vessels from a place such as Pensacola, heading for Lake Charles, Galveston, or even New Orleans itself, would necessarily leave the sheltered coastal waters and head out into the dangerous Gulf, either to round the delta or, optimistically, to find the mouth of the river. For shallow-draft coastal vessels to embark into the stormy Gulf, the detour was, at best, risky and, at worst, suicidal.

Thus, from the very beginning, mariners had three basic questions, each bearing on where ships and boats could go, and in turn where a city could logically be expected to prosper:

1. Could the river be reached by deep-water vessels in any way other than by entering the mouths of the river far out in the Gulf of Mexico? (Masters of north-south ships were interested in the answer to this question.)

2. Could longshore shipping find its way through the delta by some sheltered

inland route, and thus avoid crossing the open water of the Gulf? (This question applied to ships traveling east-west via coastal waterways.)

3. Was there any place in this featureless, slimy plain where goods could be off-loaded and stored for a time without risk of flooding?

The answer to all these questions was a qualified "yes." And, in a faltering sort of way, they pointed to the place where New Orleans was ultimately to grow and flourish. To understand how that happened, and simultaneously what sort of site the city was to occupy, it is necessary to turn the clock back and see what the river has been doing over the past few thousand years, and what sort of delta it has been building.

EVOLUTION OF THE SITE OF NEW ORLEANS

Foundations of the Delta: What Lies Beneath

From Cairo, Illinois, southward, the Mississippi River generally follows a broad downwarp in the earth's crust. That downwarp, called the Mississippi Embayment, has allowed the ocean periodically to invade the continent as far north as southern Illinois. The southern end of the embayment in the New Orleans area is still sinking at a perceptible rate; an average figure, often cited, is about three inches per century. In some places, however, subsidence is considerably faster, and there are places in the delta where sugarcane fields, cultivated by eighteenth-century farmers, are now completely under water.

All other things being equal, this crustal subsidence should have put all of southeastern Louisiana under water with an arm of the Gulf reaching north at least as far as Baton Rouge and perhaps much farther. If that had happened, of course, there would be no delta as we know it, and no New Orleans. What made the difference was continental glaciation.

Although the ice spread over much of the continent at least four successive times, it never came within 500 miles of the site of New Orleans. It did two things to the Mississippi River system, however, which ultimately made New Orleans possible and which was to shape its development as sculptors shape their clay. First, the ice wiped out a number of preglacial drainage systems in the Midwest and rerouted drainage toward the Mississippi. As a result, the Mississippi River system was much enlarged. Second, the ice carried an enormous volume of miscellaneous debris, while simultaneously generating windstorms which deposited blankets of silt all across the upper and lower Mississippi basin. As the glaciers melted, both iceborne debris and windblown silt eventually found their way into the river. The combination—an increased flow of water and an increased burden of material—caused the Mississippi to begin extending its delta at a rapid rate, filling the southern end of the embayment even as it was sinking.[1]

Thus, if one imagines a cross section cut through the delta from east to west, it would resemble a saucer made of preglacial bedrock filled with layer upon layer of deltaic material—silt, clay, lenses of sand, and a large bulk of soupy organic matter which results from the decomposition of swamp and marsh vegetation. The underlying bedrock which forms the floor of the saucer dates back to the Pleistocene geologic epoch, a million or so years ago, but is not really rock in the conventional sense. Rather, it varies between semicompacted clay, silt, and silty sand. Altogether, the cross section rather resembles a shallow clay saucer filled with layer upon layer of warm jello.

North of Lake Pontchartrain, the Pleistocene "rocks" crop out at the surface to form a low bluff which parallels the lakeshore; north of the bluff the material has been eroded into low hills, now covered with spindly pines—a region so totally different from the flat delta around New Orleans that it seems another world. Although it is thirty miles and more from downtown, this rolling Pleistocene country is much beloved of New Orleans's real estate dealers, who are luring exurbanites into the hilly woods with the enticement of inexpensive "quarter-acre estates," with no foundation problems and freedom from danger of flood. With Interstate 10 now completed from downtown New Orleans, the southern edge of the Pleistocene in St. Tammany Parish and in Hancock County, Mississippi, is beginning to look like Suburbia-in-the-Woods, and the sleepy country villages of Slidell, Louisiana, and Picayune, Mississippi, are turning into hives of land speculation.

The bluff on the northern edge of Lake Pontchartrain is caused by a group of faults, and the Pleistocene material has been dropped below the surface of the shallow lake, where it continues to dip gently southward below New Orleans. Under the city, it lies seventy to 100 feet below the surface of the delta. This fact is of great importance to builders of skyscrapers and other heavy structures,

---

[1] The Mississippi, like all rivers, sorted material at the same time it was depositing that material. The coarsest material deposited by the melting ice—boulders, cobblestones, and gravel—were mainly left in the upper river, far to the north. Thus, by the time the Mississippi neared the Gulf of Mexico, only fine materials were left—sand, silt, clay, and even smaller particles. Gravel and stone are so scarce in the vicinity of New Orleans that building contractors and cement manufacturers must have the materials shipped in by barge. Many children in New Orleans have never seen a rock.

for the deltaic material is usually too weak to support much weight. If builders have large-scale ambitions, they must be prepared to sink pilings a minimum of seventy feet to gain solid footing on the Pleistocene, unless they are lucky enough to find an old buried sand bar of the Mississippi on which to rest the foundations. Either way, it is a chancy and expensive business, and one important reason why skyscrapers and big bridges were late in coming to New Orleans.

The Surface of the Delta

Although the detailed geologic history of the Mississippi delta is very complicated, the general mechanics of delta formation are well understood, and have been lucidly described by Professors Fisk, Russell, and other geologists from the Coastal Studies Institute at Louisiana State University, as well as geologists Kolb, van Lopik, and Saucier of the Waterways Experiment Station of the U.S. Army Corps of Engineers in Vicksburg. At a general level, however, these mechanical principles are fairly straightforward, and it is helpful to understand them, since they help explain minute but systematic differences in elevation within the city, as well as differences in subsurface material.

These may sound like trivial matters, but in New Orleans they are not. Except for levees and artificial hills, no part of New Orleans is more than fifteen feet above sea level, a good part lies within five feet of sea level, and much of it is below sea level. Under such conditions, even a few inches of elevation can determine whether a particular area is habitable or not. Differences in material are equally important. Silt, for example, drains well and makes a reasonable foundation. Clay and organic material, by contrast, drain badly and generally make wretched foundations. In sum, the river's geologic history helps explain the city's human history, and its contemporary patterns of growth and internal development.

Old Distributaries and New Land

A river such as the Mississippi builds delta land in two quite different ways, and the New Orleans metropolitan area contains both kinds. The first is by depositing material where the river empties into the sea. Often, such deposits take the form of sand bars or mudbanks which occur just off the river's mouth and often impede the channel. If these deposits accumulate substantially, an island will form and the river will be split into two or more distributary channels. The contemporary Mississippi is doing that today about twenty miles below Venice, Louisiana, where it divides into three major distributaries called, respectively, Pass à l'Outre, South Pass, and Southwest Pass. The latter two are the main deep-water ship channels into the Mississippi, with the Southwest Pass carrying by far the larger volume of traffic because it is deepest.

Obviously, where the river separates into several courses, no pass contains the scouring power of the main river upstream. Although the Mississippi is a very deep river in its main channel—with one pool opposite the French Quarter in the neighborhood of 200 feet deep—the passes are much shallower and have the disconcerting habit of silting up. In time the river may abandon them completely. Such silting in the distributaries occurs constantly and unpredictably, both in the channels and over the bars; indeed, the difference in behavior between the distributaries and the sinuous main river has a certain official sanction. The pilots, who guide ships from the Gulf up to New Orleans, are divided into two independent organizations: the "bar pilots," responsible only for piloting over the passes and Gulf bars; and the "river pilots," who take over at Pilottown and guide vessels upriver to the city. The division point is where the river changes character.

Keeping the river open, furthermore, is a serious full-time concern of Orleanians, for the health of the port depends on maintaining a deep channel. Significantly, one of New Orleans's folk heroes is Colonel James Eads, who is nationally known for building the Eads Bridge at St. Louis in the 1870s—the first big trans-Mississippi bridge ever to be built. His fame in New Orleans, however, rests with the "Eads Jetties," which he built at the opening of South Pass to force the river to scour a reliable, deep-water channel for oceangoing ships. (By 1879 the jetties were in place, and the old sand bars were gone forever.) In contemporary times, the job of keeping a clear channel of forty-foot draft belongs to the U.S. Army Corps of Engineers, which is also responsible for building flood control and navigation works in the metropolitan area, as elsewhere along the Mississippi. The Corps has come in for acerbic criticism in many parts of the nation for alleged sins against nature, but it enjoys considerable popularity in New Orleans and—not surprisingly—wields considerable political influence.

Just as the river is making and abandoning distributaries today, so it made them in the past. Two abandoned distributaries meander through the New Orleans area, and both have left important marks on the city. One of them wandered away from the Mississippi at Kenner Bend, about twenty miles above the French Quarter, and strayed eastward toward the Gulf in a sinuous path roughly parallel to the river and north of it. When the river abandoned the distributary, it was left as a discontinuous sluggish bayou west of town called Bayou Metairie, its eastern section variously called Bayou Sauvage or Bayou Gentilly. (In Louisiana patois a *bayou* is any stream or small river.) Although the Metairie-Gentilly Bayou was never important to Europeans as a route of water transportation, it is paralleled by a belt of fairly well-drained ground which provided a flood-free *land* route into the city—from the west via Metairie Road; from the east via Chef Menteur Highway and Gentilly Boulevard. Metairie Road for most of its history was a rather bucolic path (*métairie* = farm), since there is another route into the city from the west, leading along the riverbank from Baton Rouge—the so-called River Road. Gentilly "Ridge," however, has always been the main road into New Orleans from the east, carrying both national highways (U.S. 90) and the main line of the Louisville and Nashville Railroad.

The other distributary—Bayou Barataria—is less important, if more colorful, since it heads south into the swamps where nobody except a few Cajuns and the pirate Lafitte ever lusted to go. More recently, however, real estate developers have been pushing their suburbs into the swamps by way of Bayou Barataria's banks.

Natural Levees, Crevasses, and an Undependable River

The river's other method of making delta land is more spectacular and considerably more important to the evolution of contemporary New Orleans. It involves nothing less radical than the Mississippi River abandoning its lower course for tens or hundreds of miles at a time and lunging out to sea by an altogether new route. When the river does this—as it does regularly every several hundred years—it leaves great gashes across the delta and, in combination with the sea, redistributes geography in a wholesale way. Consider how it happens and what it has done to the site of New Orleans.

Begin with the river meandering across its floodplain to the sea. Most of the time, the river does little work; that is done at flood time, when fast-moving water picks up additional material that is normally untouched. Where the muddy river rises and spills over its low banks, its velocity is abruptly reduced, partly because the spillover is shallow and turbulent, partly because the current is checked by the friction of dense thickets of vegetation. Consequently, the coarsest material is abruptly dropped to collect in a belt along the riverbank. (In the lower Mississippi, "coarse" material is mainly silt, since the coarser sand and gravel have mostly been left behind upstream or are moving down the bed of the river by traction.) Farther back from the river, as the overbank flow is slowed, finer and finer material is dropped, until almost nothing is left but nearly microscopic particles of clay that may take days or weeks to settle.

The result is immediate and straightforward. The river systematically raises up its banks, higher and higher with each successive flood. The French word is *levée*—meaning "raised up"—which is exactly what a levee is. One should not confuse the *natural levee* with the artificial levees later built atop them. An artificial levee may be thirty feet high and faced with concrete or rip-rap; it is one of the most prominent features in the landforms of New Orleans. The natural levee, by contrast, is so subtle that many Orleanians are unaware of its existence. At New Orleans, the crest of the natural levee is ten to fifteen feet above sea level and a mile or two wide. Obviously, with such dimensions, its slope away from the river is extremely gentle (a bicycle rider is scarcely aware of the slope), and its inner boundary where it merges with the backswamp can be defined only arbitrarily. From the ground, one must strain to see the natural levee, but from the air it is the most striking feature of the landscape aside from the river itself. It is a simple fact that the natural levees of the Mississippi and lesser streams provide the only well-drained areas in the whole of southeast Louisiana. Nearly all settlement, both urban and rural, is located on natural levees—partly because for a long time the river provided the only reliable transportation in this watery wilderness, but mainly because the natural levees provided the only place that was reasonably safe from flood and the only easy place to build roads and buildings.

For the first 200 years of New Orleans's history, the city was chiefly confined to the natural levee of the contemporary Mississippi or, as we have seen, along Bayous Metairie, Sauvage, and Barataria—natural levees of abandoned distributaries of the river. The hideous alternative was to build in the backswamp: the low, perenially flooded area back from the river a mile or two—during most of the city's history a pestilential morass whose most polite description was "back of town." Less politely, these swampy fringes of the city were called variously "Crawdad-town" or the "Quarter of the Damned." With most of the silt and much of the clay already left behind, the floodwaters had only submicroscopic material left to deposit—ooze, to put it charitably. There was plenty of vegetation, however, and, as centuries passed, rotting organic material would accumulate to great depths. In time, the material would become peat and eventually soil, but as David Slusher, a Louisiana state soil scientist, pointed out, one cannot dignify most it by calling it soil—not yet, at any rate. It is simply a black, slimy material that varies in consistency between thin soup and dense glue. In sum, the backswamps are not very attractive places to build cities, and for most of New Orleans's past not even the most poverty-stricken inhabitants would venture to live there. The city simply came to a sullen stop at the edge of the backswamp.

Although backswamps are generally odious places, New Orleans's are particularly so, especially in the Uptown end of town. ("Uptown" generally means "upriver"; see *Appendix A*.) The reasons are simple and deadly. The Mississippi rounds the Uptown area in a great semicircular meander, with the result that the Mississippi's natural levees bound the area on three sides. The side to the north, however, is also blocked by the lower but continuous natural levees of the abandoned Metairie distributary. In all, the middle of the Uptown area, later to be dubbed "Mid-City," is surrounded completely by natural levees which have turned it into a shallow bowl whose center lies below sea level. At best it was wet, but after heavy rains or a flood it filled up with water, most of which stayed to form a noisome swamp. Within the twentieth century the city has found ways to pump the water out and make Mid-City habitable, but in prehistoric times, when water rose high enough in the bowl, it spilled northward over the lowest place in the Metairie levees. That low place eventually turned into a channel— a small, sluggish, but profoundly important stream called Bayou St. John. This miserable stream, flowing into Lake Pontchartrain, was one of the main access routes into early New Orleans. We shall return to it presently.

As the river builds its natural levees, however, it is also extending those levees into the Gulf. The combination sounds innocent enough, until one recalls that the river *requires* a certain gradient, no matter how slight, in order to maintain a current. If the current slackens too much, material is deposited in the riverbed, which literally lifts itself by its own bootstraps. Thus, as a matter of simple geometry, as the river's mouth extends farther and farther, any particular upstream stretch imperceptibly rises higher and higher with each new flood and each new increment to the natural levees. In time, the river will stand some considerable elevation above the adjacent floodplain.

That is the reason why small streams in southern Louisiana do not flow into the Mississippi as tributaries, but instead flow away from it, or parallel to it, always avoiding the natural levees of the larger stream. (The same is true of the whole lower Mississippi valley.) For the same reason, intracoastal shipping could not be taken through the Mississippi Delta in a simple sea-level canal, but had to wait for the building of locks—not completed until 1909. At New Orleans the river is about ten to fifteen feet above sea level and above the city, and that is exactly why the city that is nourished by the river also lives in dread of it. To puncture the natural levee, whether by natural or artificial means, would invite a flood of Noachic proportions.

To be sure, a river perched on a ridge is in an unnatural and unstable condition. With a river the size of the Mississippi, flowing between ridges over ten feet high at New Orleans, about double that height at Baton Rouge, the instability is very great and highly dangerous. Any large flood can cause the river to break through its natural levee and vomit out into the backswamp. Such a rupture in the levee—locally known as a "crevasse"—was dreaded above all things by the early settlers. The natural levee, after all, was the only farmland worth owning, and a crevasse in one's farm could literally erase one's holdings and dump them into the backswamp as a sheet of mud.[2] The river roads, which always followed the crest of the levee, would instantly be cut, and since the river roads were the sole dependable means of land transportation in the delta, a crevasse could paralyze the whole tenuous road network.

But to the Orleanian, a major crevasse posed two other overriding threats. First, of course, was the danger of a break in the levee near the city. The last time the Mississippi burst into the city out of control was in 1849 via Sauvé's Crevasse, and it was a serious inconvenience. (Since then, the city has seen no general uncontrolled floods, which demonstrates that artificial flood control has worked fairly well.) But above all, and most to be feared, was the very real prospect that, once the river got out of its banks into the backswamp, there would be no getting it back. The river would have changed its course for good.

The map of Louisiana shows multiple evidence that the river has done just that many times. The last 5,000 years have left geologic evidence of numerous old channels, each with its own delta. Three of them can be seen on any good road map, and their location determines the patterns of roads and rural settlement in the whole of southeast Louisiana.

The westernmost and oldest course that is still plainly visible is now occupied by Bayou Teche, now an insignificant stream which traces a path from Opelousas southward to the Gulf of Mexico. (Just as the city of Lafayette is the urban heart of Cajun Louisiana, the natural levees of Bayou Teche form its main artery, and such Techeside towns as St. Martinsville, Breaux Bridge, and New

[2] If a riverside farmer was quarreling with his neighbor, it was not unknown for him to take revenge during flood time by cutting the neighbor's levee, creating an artificial crevasse, and thus flooding him out. Such behavior ranked on a par with arson and horse thievery, and armed guards customarily patrolled the levee when the river was high. Paradoxically, though, the formation of a crevasse might eventually redound to the benefit of a landowner. A thick deposit of river mud could easily convert a useless backswamp into highly valuable farmland.

Iberia are still overwhelmingly Cajun in population and general flavor, remarkably "foreign" places in the context of contemporary America.[3]) About halfway between the Teche and New Orleans is a more recent ancestor of the Mississippi, Bayou Lafourche, whose natural levees apparently mark the Mississippi's course in its penultimate stage, just before it jumped its banks to adopt its present course near the town of Donaldsonville. Perhaps the best marked of the three deltas—although not the best marked channel—is the so-called St. Bernard Delta east of New Orleans. Drowning and alongshore currents have damaged the St. Bernard Delta less than the others, and its tattered bird's-foot outlines forms the coast of Louisiana in the eastern part of the New Orleans metropolitan area. As for the present river course, the Mississippi has occupied this location for several hundred years, with only minor changes.

It is easy to think of this chronicle as mere geologic antiquarianism, with nothing to do with the present condition of New Orleans. That idea would be wrong for two vital reasons. First, as we have seen, there is almost no human habitation in southeast Louisiana except on old natural levees of the Mississippi or its distributaries. And since old river courses run parallel to each other, separated by swampy troughs, the roads do, too—a fact which helps to explain why travel in and through the Cajun country is so impossibly difficult and why for most of history the Cajun area has been so ill-connected with New Orleans. Second, and of more immediate importance to New Orleans, the Mississippi was on the verge of jumping its traces again, just as Americans arrived on the scene. If the river were to change course *below* New Orleans, it would be awkward, to put it mildly, requiring an entirely new navigation system from the Gulf of Mexico. That problem could be handled, however, even through it would be expensive. A diversion *above* New Orleans would spell nothing less than catastrophe, since the Port of New Orleans would no longer be located on the Mississippi River, but instead on a stagnant bayou.

Diversions were imminent in two areas, and both were prevented in the nick of time. One diversion was threatening the east bank of the river about thirty

[3] Nowadays, many Cajuns fear that their ancient culture will soon disappear, overwhelmed by the wealth and glitter of twentieth-century English-speaking America. One can drive through St. Martinsville, symbolic center of Cajun tradition, and see bumper stickers urging residents to speak French, not English. Meantime, however, English-speaking tourists are invited to bring their money to Cajun country and visit crawfish festivals at Breaux Bridge, the Tabasco factory on Avery Island, and—of course—the Evangeline Oak at St. Martinsville, where Longfellow's heroine pined for her lost amour. It seems doubtful whether the Cajuns can have their tourists, however, and speak French at the same time.

miles above New Orleans at a place called Bonnet Carré. Indeed, floodwaters had more than once broken through and formed a crevasse which took great volumes of river water and mud from the Mississippi directly into Lake Pontchartrain. Happily, the crevasse had been stopped up, but the situation remained dangerous. At that location, the river floods at about twenty feet, and Lake Pontchartrain is essentially at sea level. If the river had gotten loose, it would have poured directly into the Gulf by the way of lakes Pontchartrain and Borgne and the Rigolets, instead of taking 130 miles by way of its present route. Meanwhile, the new channel from Pontchartrain to the Rigolets would rapidly have begun to fill up with deltaic mud.

Two other diversions were even more serious, since they were located not only above New Orleans, but also above Baton Rouge. The pair of weak spots lay along the west bank of the river—one slightly south, the other slightly north of the Mississippi state line. The southern diversion lies close to the small town of Morganza. The northern diversion was located close to the juncture of the Mississippi with the Red River from Texas and Oklahoma. There, in 1831, Henry Shreve, "a consummate riverman,"[4] had caused an artificial channel to be cut across the neck of a large Mississippi River meander, in order to shorten the river's course and improve navigation. The abandoned rivercourse was named, appropriately, Old River. Had the Mississippi broken through either at Old River or Morganza it would have poured into the slot between the present natural levees of the Mississippi and the ancient levees of Bayou Teche. This slot, a swampy wasteland about twenty miles wide, was occupied by a sullen slough called the Atchafalaya River, which led grudgingly but more or less directly to the Gulf. The Atchafalaya route would have saved the Mississippi about half its distance to the sea, and if the main river had jumped into the Atchafalaya, it might well have stayed there. The entire Mississippi below St. Francisville would have become an abandoned distributary, just as bayous Teche and Lafourche had been abandoned in earlier geologic time. And New Orleans, no longer on the Mississippi, would have lost its *raison d'être*.

The job of averting such calamities fell to the U.S. Army Corps of Engineers, which set about with its usual energy to build new control structures at all three weak spots—and so to guarantee New Orleans an indefinite future free from river flooding. (Congress had assigned to the Corps the mammoth job of controlling floods on the entire Mississippi after the catastrophic flood of 1927,

[4] The words are John McPhee's. See footnote 5.

which had devastated a good share of the Mississippi River valley.) The Corps built great concrete floodgates both at Morganza (finished in 1954) and at Bonnet Carré (finished in 1931), which prevent breaching of the levee, but which can be opened temporarily to allow water to escape into great concrete channels if a flood crest approaches New Orleans. Thus, if the city is threatened, the Bonnet Carré Spillway could be opened to allow part of the surplus to pour into Lake Pontchartrain, thus lowering the flood crest at the city itself. Bigger floods could be handled by opening floodgates at Morganza and at Old River. Bonnet Carré was opened for the first time in the flood of 1937, and the diversion turned out to work very well, leaving New Orleans flood-free.

But to make the situation even more complicated, the Atchafalaya had been receiving most of the Red River's considerable waters via the Old River channel, in addition to which the Mississippi had been leaking water into the Atchafalaya. These additional waters considerably energized the Atchafalaya at Old River, causing it to erode its bed to a point where serious observers forecasted the day when the Mississippi would tear through its levees and route itself down the Atchafalaya. After a series of destructive floods, where the Mississippi came close to doing that, it became increasingly apparent that, if something drastic were not done, that day was not far away. So, during the 1950s, the Corps built an elaborate system of interconnecting floodways at Old River, called "the Old River Control Structures," with two purposes in mind. One was to allow Mississippi River water to be diverted into the Atchafalaya on a routine basis— with the result that the Atchafalaya became, in effect, a distributary of the great river, taking about a third of the Mississippi's natural flow to the Gulf and converting the Atchafalaya from an insignificant bayou into one of the nation's largest (and shortest!) rivers. The second purpose was to serve as an emergency spillway, like Bonnet Carré and Morganza, so that Mississippi floods could be diverted into the Atchafalaya before they reached Baton Rouge or New Orleans.

The whole operation worked—but barely. The record-breaking flood of 1973 forced the Corps to open not only Bonnet Carré, but also Morganza for the first time, and contemporary observers suggested that the river would have opened Morganza itself, with or without the permission of the Corps. And, during the same flood, unprecedented volumes of water severely undermined the 200,000-ton Old River Control Structure, and very nearly carried it away.[5]

---

[5] For an engaging account of the epochal struggles of the Corps with flood control at Old River and nearby points, see John McPhee's essay, "Atchafalaya," originally published in *The New Yorker*, but more accessible in his fascinating collection of essays, *The Control of Nature*.

The Corps set about to correct the situation, and, at great expense, it managed to do so—or so it seemed at the time. The Mississippi continued to flow where it was—confined to its course by the traditional combination of natural and artificial levees, reinforced by increasingly elaborate spillways, floodways, and control structures. And, while confining the Mississippi within its banks seemed obviously to be a good thing for the welfare of New Orleans, the long-term effects were far from good. By the end of the twentieth century, the levee-building projects of the Corps would lead ineluctably to one of the most hair-raising threats that New Orleans had ever faced. That story is told in Chapter 8, "The Rising Waters."

The Catalogue of Difficulties

A summary of what is wrong with the site for New Orleans makes a formidable list:

1. The main and oldest part of New Orleans is built on natural levees of the Mississippi, rarely over fifteen feet above sea level. The most solid material on the levee is silt.

2. Most of the contemporary city lies at or below sea level. The Mississippi River normally flows at ten to fifteen feet above sea level and floods at about twenty.

3. Behind the city, at sea level and below, was a half-flooded swamp, with no foundation material worth mentioning and, until about 1900, a breeding ground for malaria. After heavy rains or river floods, there was and is no way for the water to get out except by evaporation or by pumping it out.

4. Bedrock for foundation material consists, at best, of compacted clays, but one must dig a minimum of seventy feet below the surface muck to find them.

5. The only overland avenues into the city until recently were by way of the natural levees. In flood time, the levee could be cut almost anywhere by the sudden and unpredictable formation of a crevasse. At best, the city had poor highway access to the outside. During floods, it might have none at all.

6. Until recently, there was serious risk of the Mississippi changing course upstream, thus leaving New Orleans isolated on a dead-end bayou.

7. Most of the adjacent areas of southern Louisiana are unpopulated, thus depriving the city of a nearby hinterland. Nearly all the scanty population lives

on natural levees of old rivercourses, which are separated by belts of back-swamp which slice the delta into north-south strips. The backswamps are barriers to east-west land transportation, and the natural levees are barriers to east-west water transportation.

8. The entrances to the Mississippi are 120 miles downstream from the city. Until artificially removed, mud and sand bars made navigation hazardous, at best, and sometimes threatened to block it completely.

9. Hurricanes periodically strike the Gulf Coast from the south and drive very high tides ahead of them. Areas high above sea level are safe, but most of contemporary New Orleans is substantially below the safety level.

10. The entire city is built on land which is gradually sinking, and some of the city is built on land which is rapidly sinking.

The geologists Kolb and Van Lopic epitomized the area by calling it "a land between earth and sea—belonging to neither and alternately claimed by both." Mrs. Trollope, typically, was less kind: "I never beheld a scene so utterly desolate as this entrance to the Mississippi."

The Successful Site

But a million people inhabit a city in this desolate and dangerous place and, judging from what they say about it, a large literate proportion of the citizenry is delighted with its fate. Inevitably one must ask, what impelled the building of a city at this particular spot and what permitted it to succeed amidst a sea of environmental troubles?

It is not enough to say that the city's founders were ignorant of local site conditions. That simply is untrue, for they understood the Mississippi Delta a good deal better than many of New Orleans's contemporary real estate dealers. Rather, one must scan a map of the lower Mississippi much as the early explorers must have scanned it. (Many early maps were surprisingly good, and they had to be, for lives depended on them.) They were looking for high ground, of course, but that meant going to the site of Baton Rouge, the last and southern-most point along the river where the banks are free of flooding. It was a tempting target, and for a while early explorers had convinced themselves that the site could be reached by entering Lake Borgne from Mississippi Sound, continuing through either Chef Menteur Pass or the Rigolets into Lake Pontchartrain, thence via Pass Manchac into Lake Maurepas and up the Amite River to the back side of the natural levee near Baton Rouge. Thence a short portage led across the levee to the Mississippi.

This route was used sporadically for a long time, but it was mainly important as a political boundary. The Amite defined the northern limit of the "Isle of Orleans" (the Mississippi was its southern boundary), the area that President Thomas Jefferson wanted to buy from Napoleon in his original 1803 negotiations. It also served as the boundary between British and Spanish-French possessions. Since most settlers circumspectly kept to their own sides of the Amite, it became one of the sharpest cultural boundary lines in the United States—and remains so today: to the south are French Catholic Cajuns; to the north Scots-Irish Protestant upland southerners.

But Baton Rouge was an inconvenient distance upstream for oceangoing ships.[6] And the sluggish Amite was an awkwardly out-of-the-way route for coastal vessels to gain a Mississippi portage. If there were an easier route, it would obviously be better.

That route was found early in the game, shown to Bienvile and Iberville in 1699 by the Choctaws, who had been using it for a long time. From the Gulf Coast the route began the same as the way to Baton Rouge—from Mississippi Sound and Lake Borgne through the passes into Lake Pontchartrain. Instead of continuing west to Lake Maurepas, however, the little shallow-draft vessels turned south into Bayou St. John, which flows into Lake Pontchartrain directly off the backslope of Bayou Metairie's natural levee. Bayou St. John is only about four miles long, but from its "headwaters" it is only a two-mile portage to the Mississippi itself, mainly across the well-drained land of the natural levee. In sum, it was by far the easiest way to get into the great river from either the Gulf of Mexico or the sheltered waters of the Gulf Coast. It was at the place where the portage met the river that the French decreed that their city would be founded—the capital of New France on the Mississippi, and the fortress that would command the wealth of North America's interior. Le Blonde de la Tour's city plan today delineates the French Quarter of New Orleans. It was, to put it mildly, a successful choice.

---

[6] The Army Corps of Engineers now maintains a dredged forty-foot channel to Baton Rouge, which is thus the head of oceangoing navigation on the Mississippi. Despite this high-sounding title, the Port of Baton Rouge is no challenge to New Orleans. The main effect of the deep channel is to make the riverbank accessible to oil and chemical tankers and oceangoing barges, which draw up alongside the levee to load and unload cargo. As a result, the picturesque old Cajun farmsteads on the river are being replaced by refineries and chemical plants. The day is not far off when the seventy miles of river between New Orleans and Baton Rouge will be an unbroken line of heavy industry.

One can protest, of course, that this explanation is too facile, that it is one thing to found a city, but quite another to make it survive, much less flourish. Early settlement does not guarantee long-run success. Tadoussac, for example, predated Québec, just as Mackinac predated Detroit, and Plymouth predated Boston. Clearly, too, the Bayou St. John portage is utterly unimportant in New Orleans's later life—marked only by a ruined fort, a few historical markers, and two streets with picturesque names (Bayou Road and Grand Route St. John). Bayou St. John itself is channelized along the edge of City Park and serves largely decorative purposes. What made the difference was that, below Baton Rouge, the banks of the lower Mississippi were almost uniformly obnoxious, although a purist might argue that they grew slightly more repulsive as one moved downstream. What Bienville did, with the faltering support of the French government, was to create an oasis. When slight "improvements" were made—in the form of a church and a three-foot artificial levee to keep out the worst floods—early New Orleans was light years better than the horrid swamps that surrounded it, and travelers on the Mississippi headed for it like a haven of the refuge, which indeed it was. Thus, while the term "Isle of Orleans" technically refers to all land between the Amite, the Mississippi, and the Gulf, the real isle was the city itself—an island of civilization in an ocean of wilderness.

One should not then feel too sorry for New Orleans, either in its early days or now, despite its appalling site. The very awfulness of that site gave the inhabitants a certain cheerful *ésprit de corps*. They had conquered the swamp and were clearly pleased with themselves. This special feeling was not limited to the city either, and New Orleans gained a reputation not merely as a city in the wilderness, but as a beacon which shone with special brilliance, a prize most eagerly to be sought. Once that happened—only shortly after the founding of the city—no other place had any hope of competing with New Orleans for command of the Mississippi and what it represented.

Thus, it was that New Orleans began its career, a cultural island in large part because it was first a physical island. Paradoxically, too, it was a place which was miserably connected with its immediate surroundings, but superbly connected with the rest of the world. An outpost of high civilization on a challenging shore, it is no wonder New Orleans felt itself a special kind of place.

Gallery

MAPS AND ILLUSTRATIONS
OF NEW ORLEANS
AND ITS SURROUNDINGS

(WITH AN INDEX AT THE END OF THE GALLERY)

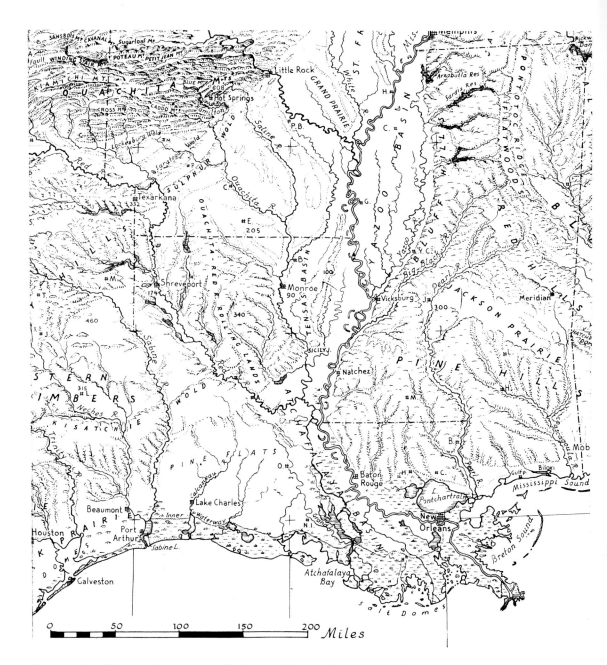

Figure 1. **Landforms of the lower Mississippi River valley.** Many of the river's important peculiarities are shown in this portion of Erwin Raisz's superb *Map of the Landforms of the United States* (1957). The Mississippi's alluvial plain is enormous, extending more than 500 airline miles north from the Gulf of Mexico, well beyond the northern margin of this map. During the recent geologic past, the river has changed its course repeatedly, leaving behind abandoned channels and vast swampy areas, so that access to the river is difficult except in the few favored places where flood-free land abuts the river. Memphis, Vicksburg, Natchez, and Baton Rouge are all located in such places. Natural levees of the Mississippi, present and past, form north-south strips of "high" land, preventing the Mississippi's tributaries from joining the main river, and forcing them to flow parallel to it for hundreds of miles. East-west transportation is extremely difficult across the alluvial plain with its alternation of swamps and natural levees. Access to New Orleans from the outside world is much easier by river or from Lake Pontchartrain; overland routes from the Upland South are difficult and costly. Note that the Mississippi's "bird's-foot" delta extends far out into the Gulf of Mexico; were it not for human-made levees, the Mississippi in flood would long since have spilled out to the Gulf by way of the Atchafalaya Basin, leaving New Orleans stranded, a river port without a river. See, also, figures 24 and 25. (Copyright Erwin Raisz, used by permission of the publisher.)

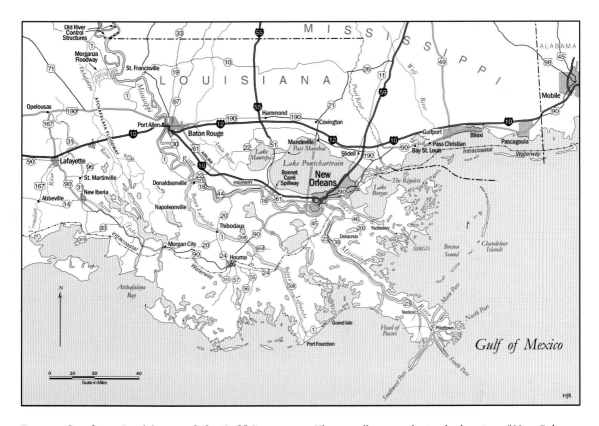

Figure 2. **Southern Louisiana and the Gulf Coast, 2002.** The map illustrates the insular location of New Orleans, and its isolation from the well-drained uplands north and east of Baton Rouge. Within the delta itself, only the natural levees are sufficiently well-drained to support towns and farms. Where roads depart from the natural levees (such as I-10 and the Lake Pontchartrain Causeway), they must be thrust at great expense across lakes and uninhabited swamps, an enterprise feasible only within the recent past. Natural levees of abandoned Mississippi River courses are traditional loci of a Cajun population, especially Bayou Teche (Lafayette to Morgan City) and Bayou Lafourche (Donaldsonville, Thibodaux, and Port Fourchon). Many roads in the delta are dead-ends. (Map by Henry J. Rademacher, Geography Department, Pennsylvania State University.)

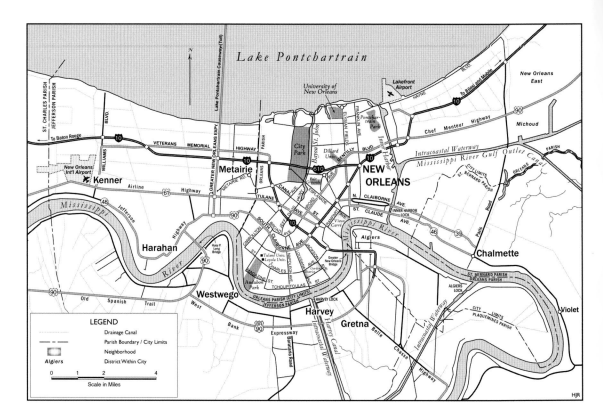

Figure 3. **New Orleans and vicinity, 2002.** Note the relationship of well-drained natural levees and ill-drained backswamps away from the Mississippi; the fine lines on the south side of the river are drainage canals, carrying rainwater from the natural levees into the backswamp, and generally following old French property lines, perpendicular to the river. Main highways into the city formerly followed the natural levees (e.g., Jefferson Highway), whereas modern highways (e.g., I-10, West Bank Expressway, and the Lake Pontchartrain Causeway) ignore topography, but at a huge cost. Airline Highway (now U.S. 61), the brainchild of Governor Huey P. Long, was designed as a straight-line route between New Orleans and Baton Rouge, defying swamps and balanced budgets. It was a typical Long project—vastly expensive and hugely popular among Louisiana's voters. (Map by Henry J. Rademacher, Geography Department, Pennsylvania State University.)

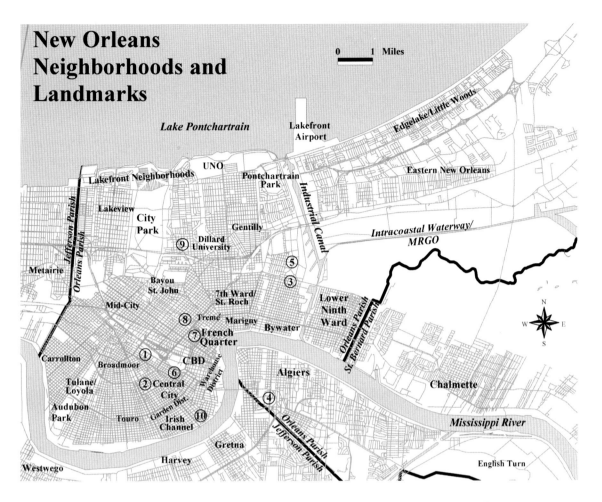

Figure 4. **Neighborhoods and landmarks of New Orleans, 2001.** (Map by Richard Campanella.)

The numbers in the map locate the city's main public housing projects:

1. B.W. Cooper

2. C.J. Peete

3. Desire (demolished in 2001)

4. Fischer

5. Florida

6. Guste

7. Iberville

8. Lafitte

9. St. Bernard

10. St. Thomas (demolished in 2001)

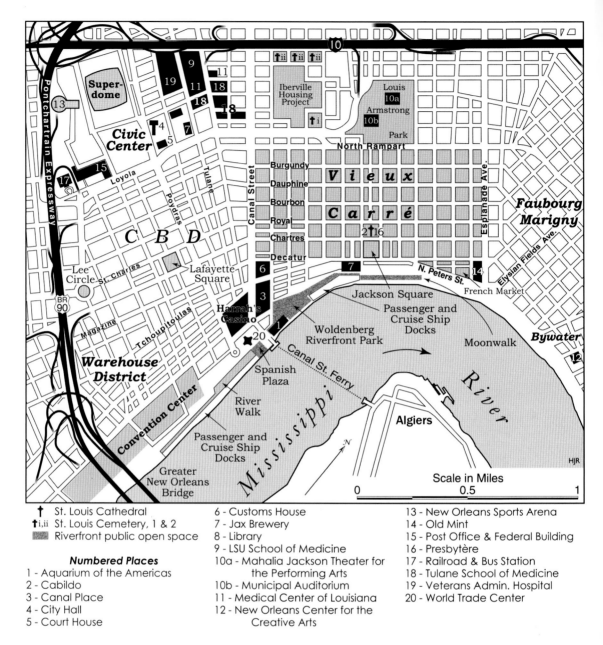

Figure 5. **The French Quarter and CBD (central business district) of New Orleans, 2002.** The Vieux Carré, with its European grid, stands out clearly on any street map of New Orleans. Canal Street, the Quarter's western boundary, marks the division between French and American cities. The present CBD is the core of the old American city. Lafayette Square was intended as the Anglo-Saxon counterpart of the French *Place d'Armes,* later renamed Jackson Square. (Map by Henry J. Rademacher, Geography Department, Pennsylvania State University.)

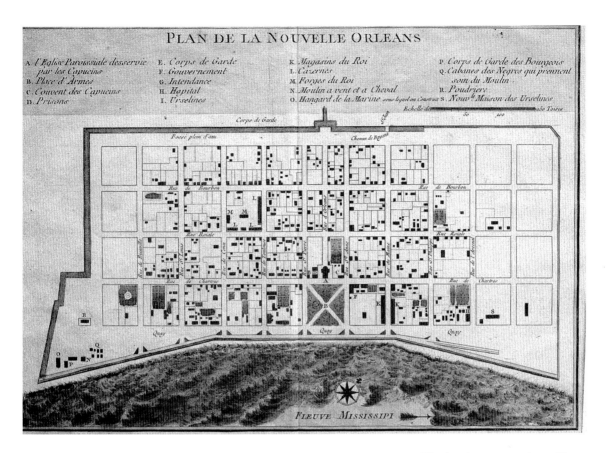

Figure 6a. Jacques Nicholas Bellin's *Plan de la Nouvelle Orleans,* **1746.** This handsome map shows New Orleans's gridiron pattern without pretentious walls and only about half-occupied with buildings. This area, now the French Quarter (Vieux Carré), however, was a statement of classic intention. (From Bellin's "Le Petit Atlas Maritime reçueil des cartes et plans des quartres parties du monde," Paris, 1764. Courtesy of the Louisiana Collection, Special Collections Division, Tulane University Library.)

Fig. 6b. New Orleans, a symbol as well as a city. This highly stylized print shows a well-scrubbed classical city, with some highly imaginary hills in the distance. (Ambroise-Louis Garneray, *Vue de la Nouvelle Orleans, c. 1830.* Aquatint. Courtesy of the Louisiana Collection, Special Collections Division, Tulane University Library.)

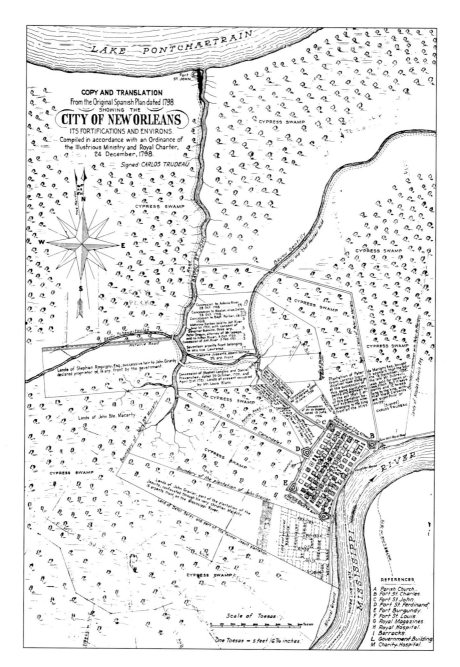

Figure 7. **Carlos Trudeau's** *Plan of the City of New Orleans and the Adjacent Plantations,* **1798,** was drafted just before the Louisiana Purchase of 1803 caused the transfer of New Orleans from France to the United States. This famous map shows how New Orleans commands the portage from the Mississippi River to the spindly headwaters of Bayou St. John and thence by water to Lake Pontchartrain. The lake is essentially at sea level, and connects directly to the Gulf of Mexico via Lake Borgne and the Rigolets. The present-day Bayou Road follows the old route of the portage. The map shows how the building of Canal Carondelet improved the portage by allowing shallow-draft boats to penetrate the swamps as far as the inland walls of the French Quarter. The turning basin of the canal can be seen just below the rampart labeled "D" on the city's walls. (Just as the rampart would give its name to Rampart Street, so, also, the now-defunct turning basin would lend its name to Basin Street, famed in the history of jazz.) Peter de Marigny's estate, just downriver from the Quarter, was still not subdivided. "Alluvial Gravel" along the riverbank is the *batture*. Bayou Gentilly, an old distributary of the Mississippi, possesses its own natural levees, and these explain the swath of "well-drained" land that slashes southwest-northeast across the map, midpoint between the Mississippi and Lake Pontchartrain. (Courtesy of the Louisiana Collection, Special Collections Division, Tulane University Library.)

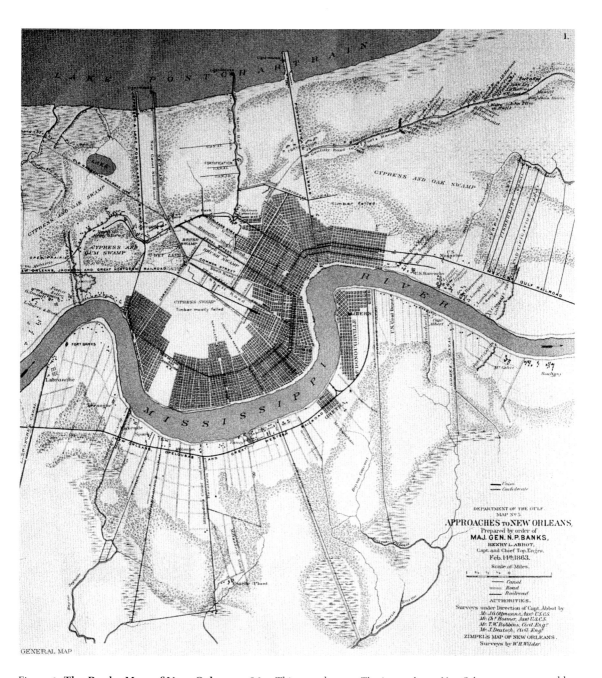

Figure 8. **The Banks Map of New Orleans, 1863.** This superb map, *The Approaches to New Orleans*, was prepared by the Union Army for military purposes. It is one of the best nineteenth-century maps of New Orleans. Note how closely the city is confined to the natural levees of the Mississippi. "West Bank" (south of the river) is still rural, but farms, roads, and villages are also confined to the natural levees. The only other permanent settlements are located along Bayou Metairie-Gentilly, an old distributary channel of the Mississippi with its own small natural levees. Note that military defenses are necessary in only a few places, because there are only a few places whereby the city can be approached —via the natural levees, via the river, or via the canals from Lake Pontchartrain. (Courtesy of the Louisiana Collection, Special Collections Division, Tulane University Library.)

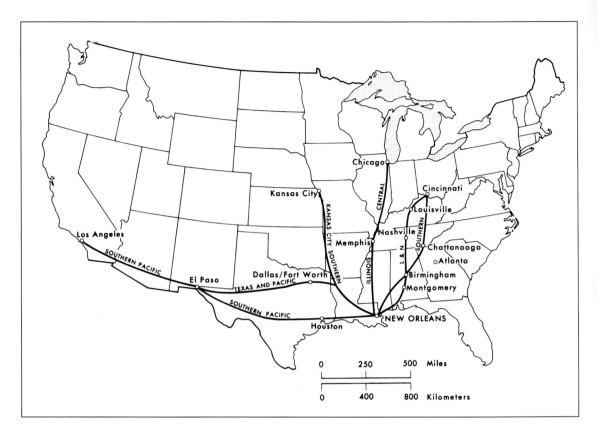

Figure 9. **Mainline railroads into New Orleans, c. 1975.** Main lines are shown where New Orleans is a major terminus (all routes are generalized). Note the excellent connections with the Midwest, especially via the mainline Illinois Central. Note, also, the absence of main lines to the eastern South, where Atlanta dominates.

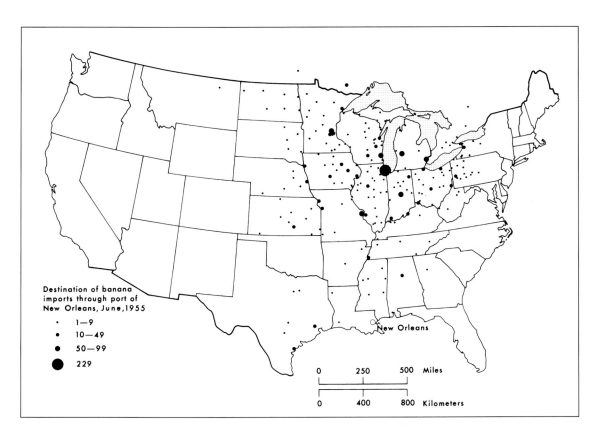

Figure 10. **Banana imports through New Orleans, June of 1955.** This apparently exotic map is an indirect geographic measure of New Orleans's critical role as a link between Latin America and the interior of the United States. Source: Donald J. Patton, *Port Hinterlands: The Case of New Orleans* (College Park: The University of Maryland, February, 1960).

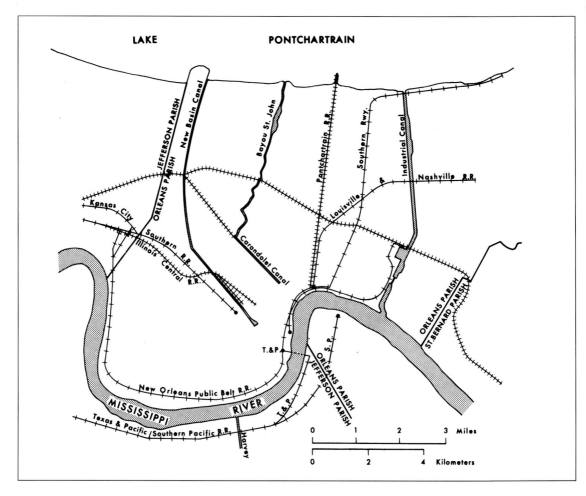

Figure 11. **Main rail and canal lines through New Orleans, c. 1926.** Line names are modernized to avoid confusion. Note the absence of a central railroad station. Also note the close correspondence between the modern expressway system and the earlier rail system. (After a map prepared by the City Planning and Zoning Commission, Harland Bartholomew & Associates. Courtesy of the Louisiana Collection, Special Collections Division, Tulane University Library.)

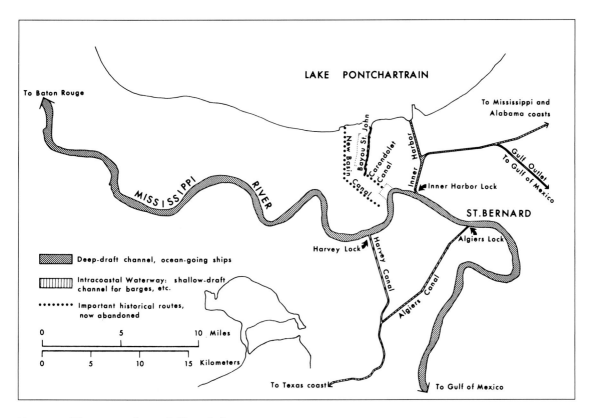

Figure 13. **New Orleans's urbanized area in 1890.** As a part of the U.S. Geological Survey's "New Orleans Quadrangle," this is the first map of the city made to the exacting standards of federal surveyors. The city is still compact, and largely confined to the natural levee of the Mississippi. (Compare with Figure 8). The French Quarter's rigidly rectangular pattern is easily recognized on the northwest side of the river's sharp bend from north to east. Note that the upriver "American" part of the city has expanded much more than has the downriver Creole section. Most streets back of the city are imaginary. Note, also, Audubon Park in Uptown, the site of the 1884-85 World's Fair, and that the streets, following old French lot lines, seem to converge in the center of the city, but in fact converge in the still-uninhabited Mid-City backswamp. The old course of Bayou Metairie is shown by contour lines just east of Kennerville, on the western margin of the map. (The eighteenth-century plantation lines are visible in Figure 7.)

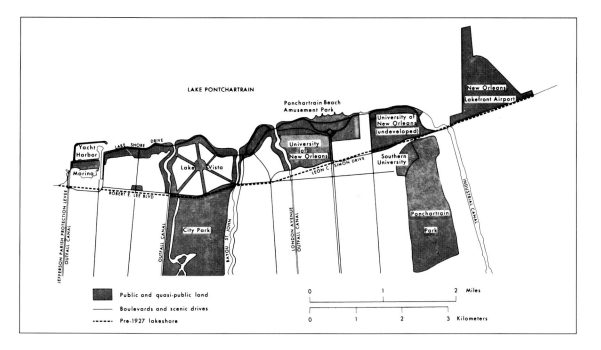

Figure 14a. **Lakefront New Orleans, 1926 and after.** The natural shoreline of Lake Pontchartrain was a smooth curve (see the dashed line). All land north of the line is fill, nearly all since 1927. Bayou St. John, once the main entrance to French New Orleans, now serves decorative purposes. Unshaded areas are mainly private residential, including some of the most affluent parts of the city, sold by the Levee Board to help pay for the project. The area around Pontchartrain Park is an isolated upper-middle-class black neighborhood.

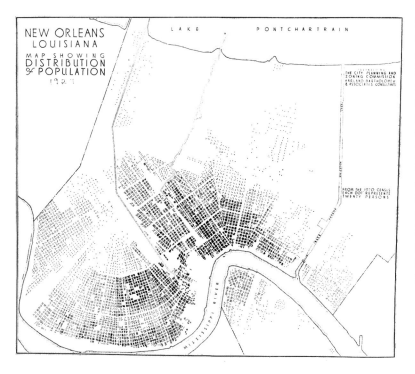

Figure 14b. **Population distribution of New Orleans, c. 1920.** The pumping system had just begun to allow people to live in the backswamp. Note the high densities in the old Creole part of the city between the Vieux Carré and Bayou St. John, and in the emerging backswamp ghetto, just west of the central business district. Ill-tempered Lake Pontchartrain still kept the lakeside part of New Orleans uninhabitable. (Courtesy of the Louisiana Division, New Orleans Public Library.)

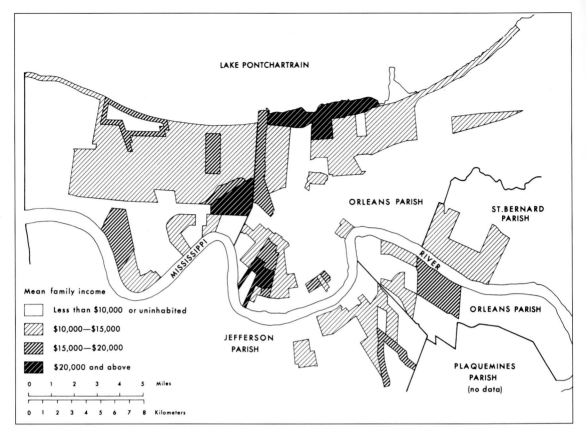

LAKE PONTCHARTRAIN

ORLEANS PARISH

ST. BERNARD PARISH

MISSISSIPPI

RIVER

ORLEANS PARISH

JEFFERSON PARISH

PLAQUEMINES PARISH (no data)

Mean family income

Less than $10,000 or uninhabited

$10,000—$15,000

$15,000—$20,000

$20,000 and above

0 1 2 3 4 5 Miles

0 1 2 3 4 5 6 7 8 Kilometers

Fig. 15a

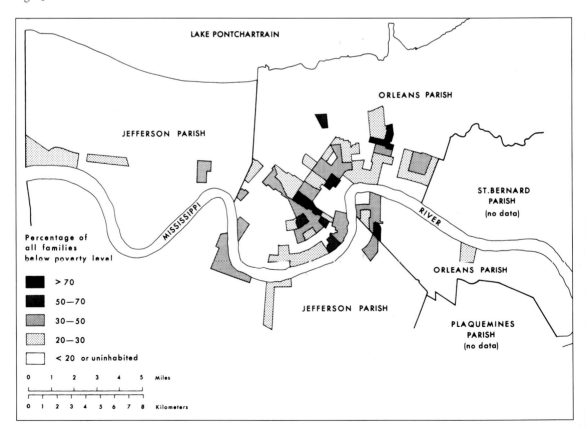

LAKE PONTCHARTRAIN

ORLEANS PARISH

JEFFERSON PARISH

ST. BERNARD PARISH (no data)

MISSISSIPPI

RIVER

ORLEANS PARISH

JEFFERSON PARISH

PLAQUEMINES PARISH (no data)

Percentage of all families below poverty level

> 70

50—70

30—50

20—30

< 20 or uninhabited

0 1 2 3 4 5 Miles

0 1 2 3 4 5 6 7 8 Kilometers

Fig. 15b

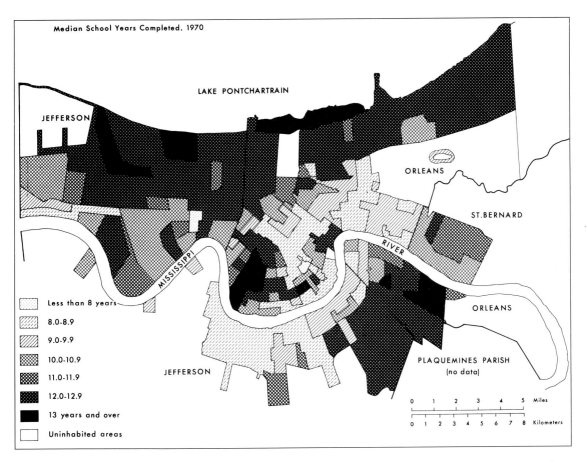

Figure 16. **Education in metropolitan New Orleans, 1970.** High educational levels obviously occur near Tulane University, Loyola University, and the University of New Orleans, but high levels elsewhere reflect wealth and prestige, especally in the new affluent suburbs, the Garden District, and the Vieux Carré. Low education is associated with blacks and blue-collar workers: for example, in the Ninth Ward, downriver from the Vieux Carré; West Bank Jefferson's shipbuilders; and dockworkers who live near the river in Uptown New Orleans. (Courtesy of Hugh G. Lewis.)

opposite page

Figure 15a. **Affluence in metropolitan New Orleans, 1970.** Extreme wealth occurs mainly in middle-aged suburbs: Lakefront dating from the late 1930s; Old Metairie from the late 1920s; the University-Audubon Park district along upper St. Charles Avenue. Affluence in the older part of the city is confined to the Garden District and French Quarter, although figures appear low because census tracts also include poor areas. The large swath of upper-middle-income on the north side of the city is post-World War II white suburbia. Essentially all affluent areas are white. Source: U.S. Census of Population, 1970.

Figure 15b. **Poverty in metropolitan New Orleans, 1970.** The map shows the percentage of households in each census tract whose income falls below the poverty level, as defined by a federal interagency committee. The poverty threshold was set in 1969 as $3,743 for a family of four and is adjusted to take into account family size, sex and age of the head of the family, number of children, etc. Given the definitions, this map obviously shows the city's big areas of serious hard-core poverty. Note the close correlation between poverty and black population, especially in public housing. Note, also, the low incidence of poverty in suburban areas which developed after 1950 and in fashionable areas of the old city—the Vieux Carré, the Garden District, and the University District.

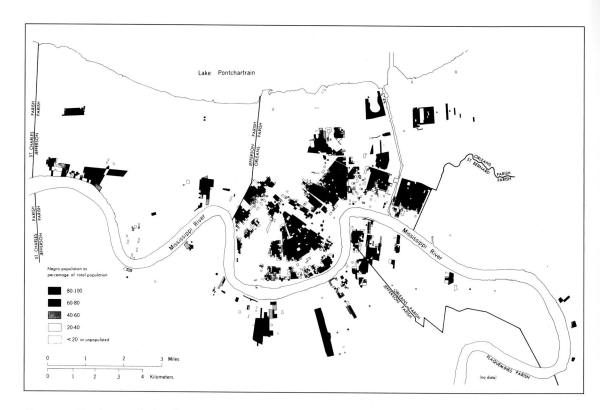

Figure 17. **Black population in metropolitan New Orleans, 1970.** This is an extremely important and revealing map—showing New Orleans just at the beginning of massive "white flight" to the suburbs. It is also important for the very fine detail that it depicts. Data for this map come from the U.S. Census Bureau's Census of Housing, which records racial data by individual city block—and not the large census "tracts" from which Figures 15a, 15b, and 16 were plotted. Note that black ghettos have not yet begun to grow together into the "superghettos" which would develop later.

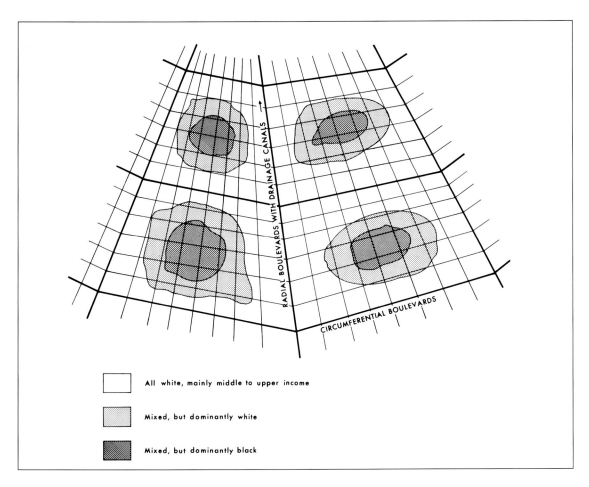

Figure 18. **An idealized neighborhood in Uptown New Orleans, c. 1970**, in which affluent whites live along boulevards, or near them. To the rear, black population increases in proportion and density, so that each "superblock" is a separate nucleus of black population. Cores of superblocks are rarely all black, although boulevards are usually all white.

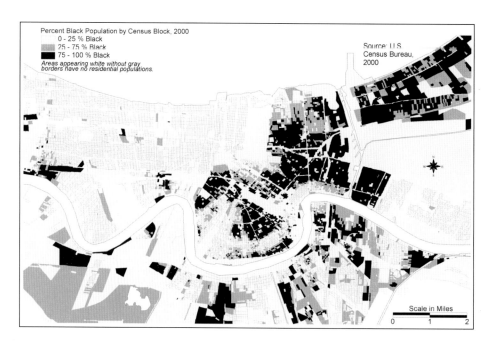

Figure 19. **Black population in Orleans Parish and part of Jefferson Parish, 2000.** Compare this map with one from 1970 (Figure 17). Neither map shows much sign of racial integration. But the fragmented black ghettos of 1970 have merged by 2000 to form a kind of superghetto that occupies most of Mid-City and spreads in a lakeside direction from City Park eastward. Eastern New Orleans (east of the Industrial Canal) had originally been colonized by whites, who were subsequently replaced by blacks who are generally more affluent than those who inhabit the old city. It is one of the few black suburbs in the city's metropolitan area. Data are mapped by block. (Map by Richard Campanella, used by permission.)

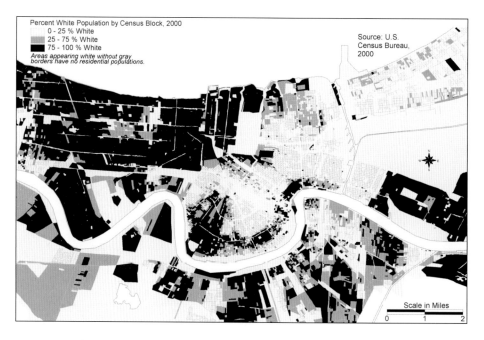

Figure 20. **White population in Orleans Parish and part of Jefferson Parish, 2000.** The main white bastions are, first, the old district from the University District, connecting with the French Quarter and Faubourg Marigny by way of the St. Charles Avenue corridor. Note the white domination of the upriver fringes of the CBD (central business district), including the Warehouse District and lower Garden Districts. Note, also, that Bywater and the Irish Channel districts, once solidly black, are now mixed, the result of the downriver and upriver thrusts of gentrification. The other large white territory is Lakeview, uptown (west) from City Park and riverside (south) to Bayou St. John and the southern extremity of the park. Data are mapped by block. (Map by Richard Campanella, used by permission.)

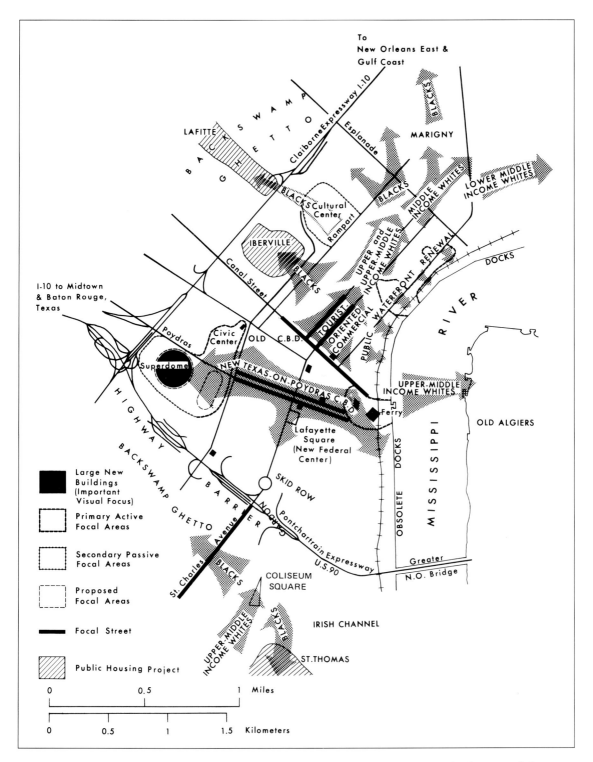

Figure 21. **Center-city New Orleans in transition, 1973 and after.** Arrows suggest the direction of changes in downtown New Orleans, largely prompted by revival of the Vieux Carré and the symbiotic revival of lower Canal Street. In the Quarter one can observe an index of who is able to pay rents at various levels: blacks ejected by middle income-whites, in turn ejected by upper- and upper-middle income whites, in turn ejected under pressure from tourist-oriented commercial uses. Upstream from Canal Street, the new Texan CBD is pushing into skid row, while upper-income whites move into the lower Garden District from other directions. Again, typically, blacks are pushed into less desirable areas with lower rents.

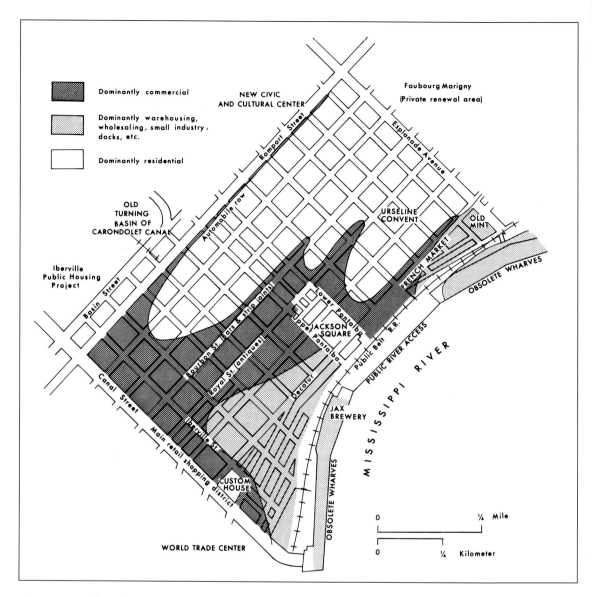

Figure 22. **Land use in the French Quarter, 1968.** Contrary to common belief, the Quarter is neither homogeneous in use nor uniformly picturesque in appearance. Note the rind of commercial and warehousing on three sides and infusion of more commerce from Canal Street. (Generalized from map in *Plan and Program for the Preservation of the Vieux Carré* [New Orleans: Bureau of Government Research, 1968].)

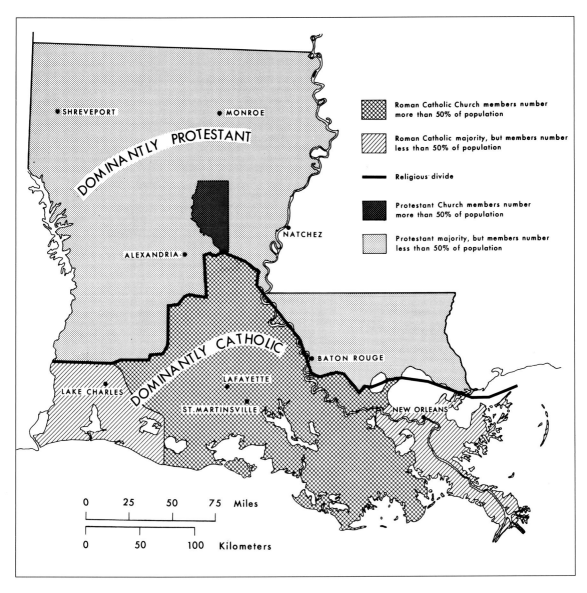

Figure 23. **Religion in Louisiana, c. 1957.** The sharp line between Protestant North and Catholic South is the most important social-cultural cleavage in Louisiana. Its earliest recognized boundary was the Amite River, the ancient northern boundary of the Isle of Orleans. Note that metropolitan New Orleans is heavily Catholic, but not as overwhelmingly so as the more rural and isolated Cajun areas to the west. Data are mapped by parish. Source: National Council of Churches Division of Home Mission. 'Churches and Church Membership in the United States," series C., no. 45, figure 64 (New York, 1957).

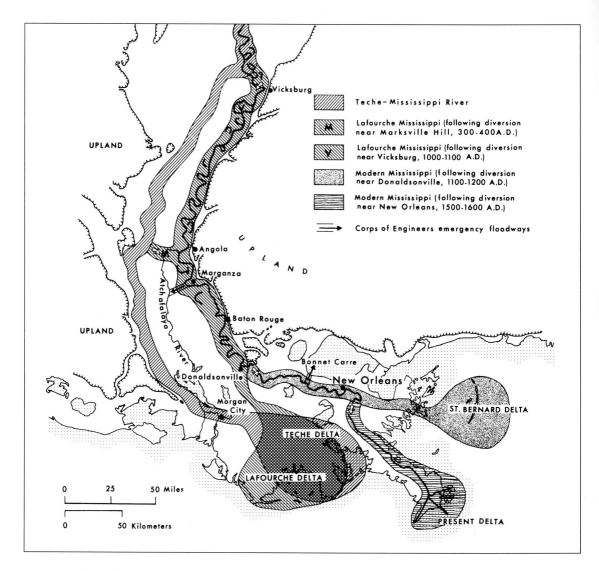

Figure 24. **The ancient deltas of the Mississippi River.** Until recently, all signs pointed to the probability that the Mississippi was on the verge of jumping out of its present course, either into Lake Pontchartrain at Bonnet Carré or, more probably, into the Atchafalaya at Morganza, or Old River, near Angola. Either course would have proved disastrous to New Orleans, and the U.S. Army Corps of Engineers has built controlled spillways at both locations to permit overflow in time of flood, meanwhile keeping the Mississippi from leaving its contemporary course. (H.N. Fisk, *Geological Investigation of the Atchafalaya Basin and the Problem of Mississippi River Diversion* [Vicksburg: Mississippi River Commission, 1952]. Modified by William D. Thornbury in *Regional Geomorphology of the United States* [New York: John Wiley, 1965], p. 61. Used with permission of the author and publisher.)

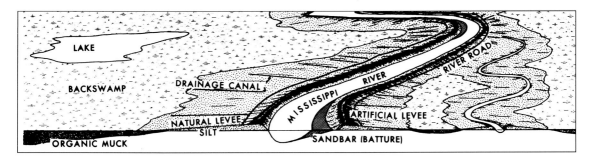

Figure 25. **An idealized cross section of the Mississippi River**, showing the relationship of the river to natural levees, backswamps, and human settlement. In flood, the river deposits silt along its banks, creating very low broad ridges called "natural levees." Behind the natural levees, standing water creates habitats for swamp-loving vegetation. Organic material accumulates in these low wet places, producing mucky undrained "backswamps." Farms, roads, and towns traditionally were built along the natural levee and shunned the backswamps. The natural levees were made more habitable by digging drainage canals perpendicular to the river, which carry excess rainwater off into the backswamp, and by building artificial levees atop the natural levees. Where the river meanders, the current is swiftest and the water deepest on the outside of the bends. On the inside of meanders, the water is slack, and fine material such as sand and silt accumulates in the form of bars, called *battures*. In low water, these *battures* are exposed. Note that the distributary channels also have natural levees, and these connect with the main river levees to form enclosed swampy basins. Mid-City New Orleans is such a basin.

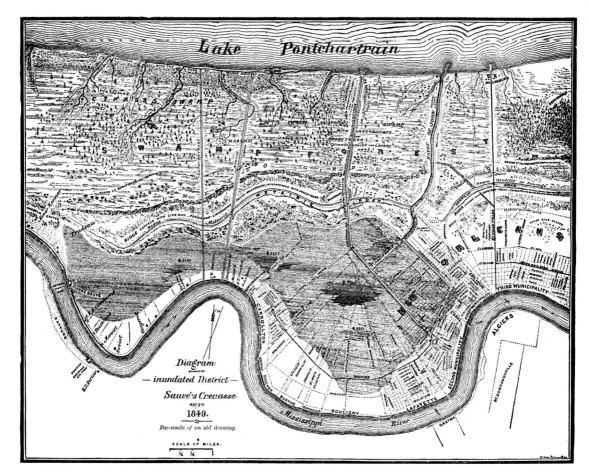

Figure 26. **New Orleans after the breaching of Sauvé's Crevasse, May 3, 1849.** Natural levees of the Mississippi River and Bayou Metairie remain unflooded. Present-day "Mid-City"—at the convergence of plantation property lines—is under nine feet of water. Note, also, that Bayou St. John connects with Carondolet Canal into the back side of the French City (First Municipality)—which the newly built "New Orleans Canal" (New Basin Canal) links Lake Ponchartrain to the American City (Second Municipality). The Third Municipality was a low-income area. The Village of Carrollton was a separate suburb, created by a horse railway along Nayades (St. Charles) Avenue. (Report on the Social Statistics of Cities, U.S. Census Office, 1887.)

Figure 27. **The Inner Harbor Lock, 2001**, looking toward the Industrial Canal and Lake Pontchartrain. Built in the early 1920s to accommodate smaller vessels of that time, the Inner Harbor Lock is the main bottleneck that has not only prevented large container ships from the Mississippi River (behind the photographer) to gain access to the Industrial Canal, but also forced the Dock Board to create new container facilities along the River. The U.S. Army Corps of Engineers would like to triple the size of this lock, but that is many years and many millions of dollars away.

Figure 28. **An oblique aerial photograph of metropolitan New Orleans, probably in the early 1970s,** looking northwestward across the Mississippi toward Lake Pontchartrain. See Figure 29 for a key to locations. (Photograph by Sam R. Sutton, courtesy of the Board of Commissioners for the Port of New Orleans.)

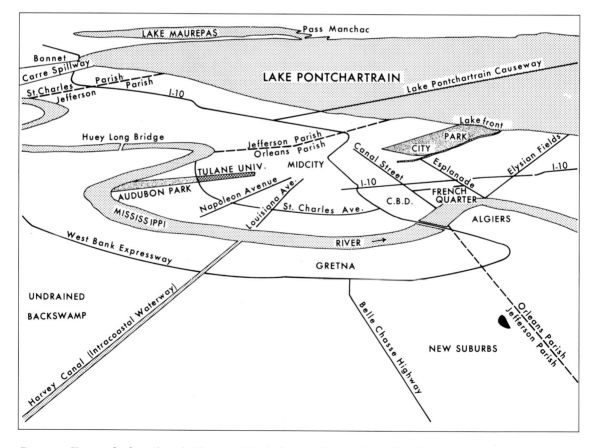

Figure 29. **Key to the locations in Figure 28.** Only the main landmarks are identified.

Figure 30. **An oblique aerial photograph of metropolitan New Orleans from Uptown, probably in the early 1970s,** looking downriver across the CBD (central business district) and the Vieux Carré toward New Orleans East and the Gulf Coast. (See Figure 31 for a key to locations. (Photograph by Sam R. Sutton, courtesy of the Board of Commissioners for the Port of New Orleans.)

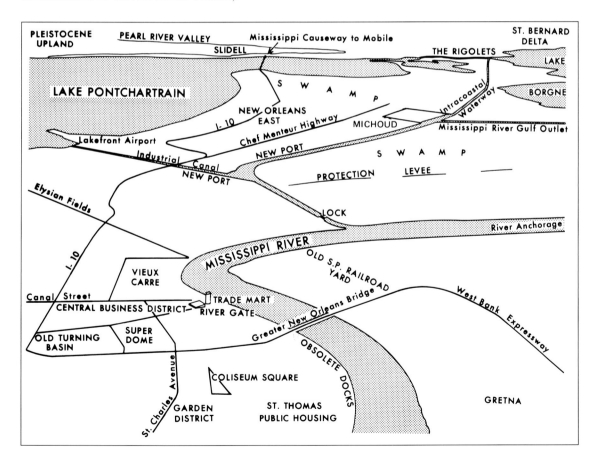

Figure 31. **Key to the locations in Figure 30.** Only the main landmarks are identified.

Figure 32. **Interstate 10, heading eastward through the swamps, 1973**, toward the Lake Pontchartrain Bridge and the Mississippi Gulf Coast. Ostensibly, I-10 was built to allow people to get into the city quickly; the actual effect was to promote a suburban ("white flight") exodus out of the city. The swampland to the right and left of the highway is shown on drawing boards as becoming one of the largest planned residential areas in the United States. Previously, the area was thought unfit for human habitation. The water in the ditch at the right marks the surface of the water table under "normal" conditions. Recent hurricanes have put this and nearby areas under several feet of water.

Figure 33. **Planned development east of New Orleans, 1973.** Interstate 10, to the left, and conspicuously shown on the billboard, has triggered this growth. The footings of the billboard are about five feet below sea level. Much of this area was heavily inundated during hurricanes Betsy (1965) and Camille (1969).

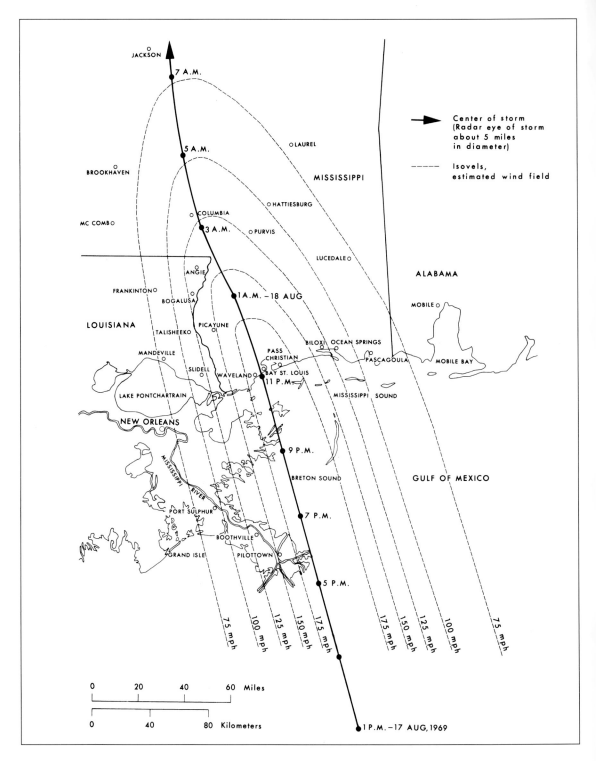

Figure 34. **The path and windfield of Hurricane Camille, August, 1969.** This category 5 hurricane was the most destructive storm to hit the Gulf Coast in historic time. New Orleans was fifty miles away from the center of the storm—a critically important distance, it turned out. Several Mississippi coastal towns were practically obliterated. (U.S. Army Corps of Engineers, New Orleans Engineers District.)

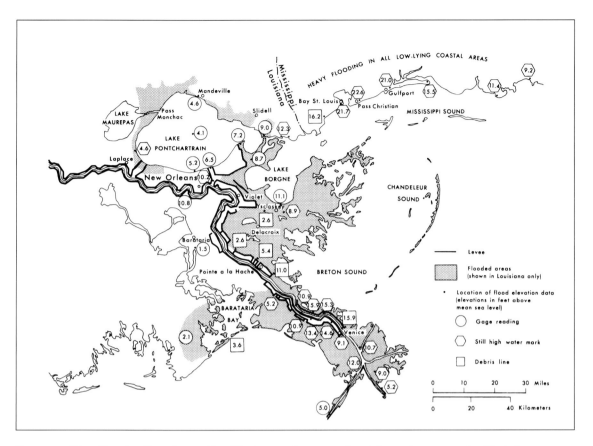

Figure 35. **Flooding by Hurricane Camille in southeastern Louisiana, August, 1969.** Shaded areas were inundated. Numbers denote depth (in feet) to which the surface was flooded. Note: the depths of high water are shown in Mississippi, but not the extent of flooded areas. In Louisiana, areas protected by levees were mainly flood-free. Elsewhere, flooding was ubiquitous. (U.S. Army Corps of Engineers, New Orleans Engineers District.)

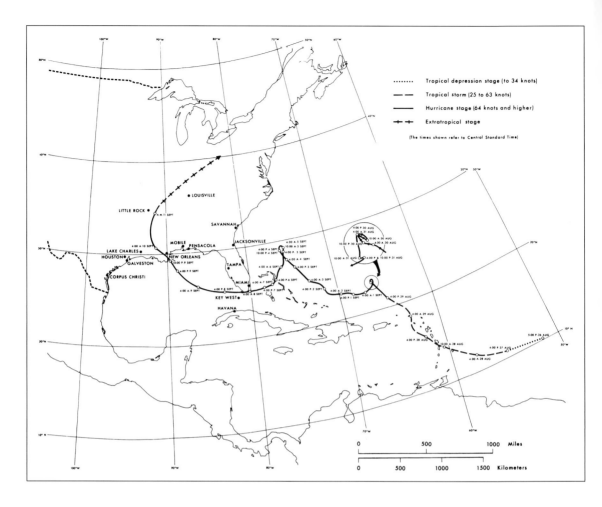

Figure 36. **The Path of Hurricane Betsy, 1965.** Hurricanes do not always oblige forecasters by following predictable paths. Up until three days before Hurricane Betsy hit the Louisiana coast in early September, 1965, the storm was of only academic importance to Orleanians. Compare this map with Figure 34, and note that Betsy passed New Orleans to the west by about the same distance that Camille passed the city to the east four years later. (U.S. Army Corps of Engineers, New Orleans Engineers District.)

Figure 37. **Hurricane evacuation route, Paris Road, 1973.** Paris Road, near New Orleans East, is a hurricane evacuation route. The signs are ominous, but the fine print in the engineers' report is even more so: "in the heavily developed areas of metropolitan New Orleans . . . prestorm evacuation in most cases is not feasible."

Figure 38. **The I-10 bridge and causeway, 1973**, across the east end of Lake Pontchartrain, looking toward New Orleans. All major arterial highways into the city cross great watery wastelands such as this and remind one forcibly that New Orleans is an island. Such bridges have made the city newly accessible, but the road goes both ways: it has also enabled suburban growth to explode into heretofore inaccessible areas. Behind the photographer from this viewing point, suburbanization is rapidly invading the Pleistocene upland around Slidell in St. Tammany Parish on the north side of Lake Pontchartrain.

Figure 39. **The middle of the French Quarter, probably in the mid-1960s**, looking down Orleans Street from Bourbon Street toward St. Louis Cathedral. The Mississippi River is beyond the cathedral, out of sight. Most buildings here postdate the fire of 1794 and predate the Civil War. The street pattern is the ideal late-eighteenth-century European gridiron. Buildings directly on the street, with private spaces within, hearken back to medieval times. The absence of modern high buildings at that time results from the Vieux Carré Commission's architectural controls. (Courtesy of the Greater New Orleans Tourist and Convention Commission.)

Figure 40. **Brennan's Restaurant on Royal Street** is famous for its delicious and lucullan breakfasts. Here tourists record their genuinely New Orleans experience to show the folks back home. The photo was taken in 1973, but might well have been taken yesterday, except for the attire. In New Orleans there are certain eternal verities.

Figure 41. **The Moonwalk, 2001**, is lonely on a cold March day. It is much less so on a warm day during the tourist season. To the left is the Mississippi, and in the distance, left, the International Trade Center. This whole area, now open to the river, was densely built up with wharves and warehouses until the mass clearances of the 1970s and 80s. On the right is the Riverfront streetcar, used largely by tourists. The French Quarter is out of sight to the right, beyond the parking lot. The Marriott Hotel and other high-rise buildings, in the distance on the right, are situated on Canal Street. Creation of the Moonwalk was a major step in returning New Orleans's riverfront to the city's citizens.

Figure 42. **Looking downriver toward the French Quarter, 2001**, near Canal Street. On the left is Decatur Street, the official riverside boundary of the Vieux Carré, which begins across the street. Tourists bring money, but they also bring automobiles, which need to be parked somewhere. So, also, the numerous tour buses that bring visitors to the Quarter. The Vieux Carré may breathe romance, but it also breathes exhaust fumes. This scene reflects a drastic change from the mid-twentieth-century landscape of riverfront New Orleans. Until the late twentieth century, most of the parking lot's area had been occupied by derelict industry, commerce, and warehousing. In the early part of the century, this had served as an important part of New Orleans's "sugar district." The derelict four-story brick building in the right foreground was part of that sugar complex, built c. 1900; it is now unused but is protected from demolition by historic preservation laws. The spire of St. Louis Cathedral, in the left middle-ground, is the heart of the Vieux Carré. To the right, along the river is Woldenberg Riverside Park. The Mississippi River floodwall is visible between the railroad tracks and the parking lot. The Jax Brewery (1895), part of the old industrial district and now a retail/restaurant complex, sits at the far end of the parking lot, across Decatur from the Cathedral. The white colonnaded building, in the left middle-ground, was a group of shops, c. 1870, associated with the sugar and molasses trade, remodeled in 1987 with a newly "historic" façade for tourist-oriented retail shops and restaurants.

Figure 43. **Antebellum mansion in Garden District, c. 1973**, at the corner of Prytania and Fourth Streets. Setting houses back from the street was an American practice, although the word "Garden" is from British English, where a "garden" means a landscaped lawn. The cornstalk iron fence allegedly was uprooted from the Vieux Carré, and is one of the few "approved tourist attractions" outside the French Quarter and CBD (central business district). (Courtesy of the Greater New Orleans Tourist and Convention Commission.)

Figure 44. **Springtime visitors to New Orleans, March, 2001.** Although tourists bring little money to the Garden District, they often come with serious intent.

Figure 45. **Lower Canal Street in 1973**, from the top of the International Trade Mart, looking toward Lake Pontchartrain and the towers of Jefferson Parish's "Fat City" in the far distance. Canal Street was the dividing line between the old Creole French Quarter, to the right, and the commercial American city, on the left. With its wide "neutral ground" (now used for buses), Canal was long New Orleans's main street; Maison Blanche, the city's traditional "big" department store, is the large light-colored building, partly hidden by the high-rise hotel. The whole area is in transition: main businesses are moving uptown (to the left), while tourism, symbolized by the slick new 1,000-room Marriott Hotel, puts heavy pressure on the Quarter. On the lower right is the old Custom House, 1849, the point from which distances in New Orleans are measured, and the scene of many events of symbolic importance in the city's history.

Figure 46. **Lower Canal Street in 2001**, from the top of the International Trade Mart, looking up Canal Street toward Lake Pontchartrain. The scene is considerably changed, reflecting new investment in real estate on lower Canal Street. On the upriver side of Canal (the left side of the photo), from left to right, the high-rise buildings are Place St. Charles, an office building, and the Sheraton Hotel. The large building dominating the right foreground is the multistory Canal Place office building with upscale retail shops on the ground floor. Behind it, farther up Canal, is the Marriott Hotel, the city's first high-rise hotel (1971). Harrah's Casino (1995), with its sprawling postmodern roof, dominates the lower left; the French Quarter begins a block or so to the right. New streetcar tracks are being laid in the neutral ground (New Orleans's argot for a median strip), one of several measures to exhume the once-lively commercial spirit of Canal Street. Note the light-colored medium-rise building in the middle distance, on the right side of Canal; that building was home to the famous Maison Blanche Department Store, now defunct and converted to become the Ritz-Carlton Hotel, the priciest hostelry in the city. When the photo was taken, the hotel was having financial trouble, in part, perhaps, because of its marginal location on a now unfashionable segment of Canal Street.

Figure 47. **Decatur Street, the riverward margin of the French Quarter, 1973**, looking Uptown. The magnolia tree at the right is in Jackson Park. Behind it is the Upper Pontalba building. To the left, the Jax Brewery is part of a commercial rind that cuts most of old New Orleans off from the Mississippi, just left of the picture. In the distance along Decatur are old warehouses and seedy seamen's bars. The large high building on the right is One Shell Square, finished in the early 1970s and the visible symbol of Texification, naturally the highest building in New Orleans. To the left of Shell is the Marriott Motor Hotel, 1,000 rooms and symbol of an efficient new tourist industry, seen by many old-timers as a threat to the French Quarter.

Figure 48. **Lower Canal Street on the margin, 2001.** Although the Ritz-Carlton is across the street to the right, off camera, much of Canal Street has slid downhill from its former eminence. The new street trees, new pavement, and new street furniture reflect the city's attempts to reverse the process. Pawn shops and security bars suggest that the upturn has yet a way to go.

Figure 49. **Looking upriver toward the Greater New Orleans Bridge, 1973**, from the International Trade Mart Tower on Canal Street. This part of the New Orleans waterfront was a purely working landscape. Wharves, docks, warehouses, and the Public Belt Railroad separate Uptown New Orleans from the Mississippi. Even at the time this photo was taken, the buildings along the riverside were deemed obsolete, because of inadequate marshaling space for modern containers. Note thunderheads in the distance, typical of New Orleans's steamy summer weather. The dredge in the river is removing sediment deposited on the inside curve of the river's meander. Although the photo is taken upriver, owing to the convolutions in the river, this view looks due south. (See Figure 3 for orientation.)

Figure 50. **Looking upriver toward the Greater New Orleans Bridge, 2001**, from the International Trade Mart Tower on Canal Street. The radical difference in landscape signals a turnaround in New Orleans's economy. The docks and warehouses are gone, replaced by high-rise hotels and tourist attractions, a cruise-ship terminal, and a gigantic convention center (obscured by the high-rise Hilton Hotel at the right). An ocean-going cruise ship is moored just short of the GNO Bridge. This is overwhelmingly a tourist's landscape. The mid-rise building close to the riverbank is One River Place, a complex of upscale condominiums, and beyond it (the long, low, white-roofed building) is the upriver portion of James Rouse's Riverwalk Marketplace. The low-rise buildings, in the left foreground, are the riverfront portions of the Riverside Hilton Hotel whose tower can be seen at the right. All that remains of the working landscape from 1973 are the two spans of the Greater New Orleans Bridge (a.k.a. The Crescent City Connection), railroad tracks that double as a streetcar line for tourists, and in the distance, on the extreme right, the two tall stacks of a power plant. Even it is now defunct.

Figure 51. **The traditional method of handling general cargo**, here cotton and barreled products, perhaps oil. The photo could have been taken any time before the 1970s. The congested docks are colorful but highly inefficient, and were put out of business by the container technology that now dominates the docks of any modern port. Note that the cranes are located on the ship—not on the shore—revealing the fact that the ship's owners expect it to do its own loading and unloading at any port in the world, no matter how primitive the dockside facilities might prove to be. That is not the case with container loading, which is inevitably managed from huge cranes alongshore. (Courtesy of the Greater New Orleans Tourist and Convention Commission.)

opposite page:

Figure 52a. **Loading cargo by container, c. 1973.** Standardized large-scale transfer of goods is cheaper and more efficient than traditional methods, but requires costly special equipment and huge dockside areas. Most of New Orleans's waterfront, at the time, was obsolete as a result. (Courtesy of the Board of Commisioners for the Port of New Orleans.)

Figure 52b. **The New Orleans skyline, 2001**, across the container storage lots of the refurbished Nashville Avenue wharves in the Port of New Orleans. The photo is taken from atop one of the port's giant gantry cranes, which loads and unloads cargo from ships on the Mississippi, located just behind and many feet below the photographer. The Superdome is visible just to the left of the skyline, which is still dominated by One Shell Square, the highest building in the city since the early 1970s when it was built. The large vacant area in the right foreground is the site of the demolished Napoleon Avenue wharves, which will presently arise like Phoenix to duplicate and complement the Nashville Avenue facility. In the distance, to the extreme right, are the approach ramps for the Greater New Orleans Bridge. The containers in the foreground reflect the genius of simplicity and the economy of scale. Cargo of all kinds can be "stuffed" into any of several standard-sized containers, and then offloaded onto trucks, especially designed to carry those containers. Conversely, the containers can be trucked alongside a "container ship" and then lifted aboard by a huge shore-based gantry crane, designed expressly for that purpose. Only modern ports, equipped with such specialized (and expensive) cranes, can hope to compete in the world of big-time maritime commerce.

Figure 52a

Figure 52b

Figure 53a. **The California bungalow**, hugely represented in the house on the right, was the Golden West's first major contribution to American domestic architecture. With big porches and overhanging shade-giving eaves, it was enthusiastically adopted throughout the South, an architectural signal, perhaps, that the South was again ready to join the Union. 1920s New Orleans is full of them.

Figure 53b. **Late Victorian styles of architecture** were flamboyant and widespread in New Orleans. Note the elevation of the main floor, originally a precaution against flooding. The big, shady verandah has disappeared with rising building costs and air conditioning after World War II. Cement pots and lawn furniture are endemic throughout middle-aged parts of New Orleans.

Figure 54a. **A prototypical shotgun house, 1971**: one-story high, one-room wide, and relatively long, making it well-suited to New Orleans's long narrow lots. The shotgun house is thought to be the only folk house-type to originate in Africa. The idea seems to have come from Africans who had been brought as slaves to Haiti, but had subsequently fled to New Orleans during and after the bloody colonial wars of the 1790s. Many shotgun houses of the Deep South are crude and rudimentary, inhabited by the poorest of the poor. This one is considerably more upscale, equipped with louvered front doors and floor length windows. These are typically Caribbean features, affording ventilation before air conditioning. Next door is a two-family bungalow—essentially a double-barreled shotgun, split down the middle. In the old parts of New Orleans, these are middle-class dwellings.

Figure 54b. **A typically Orleanian mélange of** *fin-de-siècle* **house-types, 1973.** The houses to left and right are typical, sprawling bungaloid houses, popular in affluent white neighborhoods throughout the Deep South in the early years of the twentieth century. To the rear, across an invisible street, is a shotgun house, efflorescent with Victorian gingerbread. Once dismissed as *infra dig*, the shotgun house has recently been identified as "quaint" by high-style renovators, so that gentrified shotguns are not uncommon in fashionable areas of New Orleans.

Figure 55. **A camelback house, 1973**, evidently dating from that late nineteenth century. The origin of this unusual house form is uncertain, but may have resulted from tax laws which assessed the value of a house according to its height along the streetfront, but paid no attention to how high it rose at the rear. Whatever its origin, the camelback form can be found in river towns along the Ohio and Mississippi River valleys as far away as Louisville—mute testimony to New Orleans's long-standing cultural connections along the highways of the continental interior. Domestic architectural eccentricities such as this occupy huge areas of pre-World War II New Orleans and contribute heavily to the city's picturesque un-American look. At the time this photo was taken, the house evidently was in an early stage of restoration. The dilapidated condition of this house was presumably temporary, as witnessed by the scaffolding seen on the rear of the house. Such houses as these are prime candidates for gentrification in New Orleans.

Figure 56. **Wedge-shaped blocks** result when radial streets fan out from a convex curve of the river, and/or when grid patterns do not exactly accord with old property lines. St. Roch Street, to the left, is part of the Fauberg Marigny grid; Franklin Avenue, to the right, is part of the Ninth Ward grid. As of 1973, this was a blue-collar, heavily Italian neighborhood. Architecture is typically varied—early-twentieth-century to the right, mid-nineteenth-century southern commercial arcade to the left. The house behind Sal's Plumbing and Heating is a very common, two-family Creole cottage, probably well over 100 years old. The cross street is Chartres Street. The Mississippi River levee is about two blocks behind the photographer.

Figure 57. **A backswamp ghetto, 1973,** just inland from Faubourg Marigny. Low-profile, semidetached houses are common in New Orleans; straight-pitched overhanging roofs are nineteenth-century Creole design. Although the city has obviously done little to encourage streetside amenity (poor pavement and lack of trees are typical), population densities here are much lower than in comparable parts of big northern ghettos.

Figure 58. **Gentrification in Bywater, 2001.** The process of restoration is considerably less elaborate than in the Quarter or Faubourg Marigny, whence the residents here may well have come. Despite deviations from pure-bred architectural styles, the New Orleans ambience is still here, now equipped with new pillars and fresh paint.

NUEVA ORLEANS

Aquí navegan todavía para usted Los Viejos Vapores.

Venga a pasear por el Mississippi en los antiguos vapores como aquellos que conoció Huckleberry Finn. (Claro, ahora tienen aire acondicionado.)

Visite las bellas plantaciones de antaño. Conozca la Bahía de Nueva Orleans.

Aquí tenemos toda una variedad de tours para que usted y su familia se diviertan. Desde un recorrido por el Barrio Francés hasta estos paseos en vapor por el Mississippi... Y todo esto está a sólo dos horas de México. Consulte a su Agente de Viajes.

Venga a oir el jazz - el verdadero jazz que nació aquí en Nueva Orleans. Los mejores músicos tocan para usted dondequiera que vaya.

Venga a saborear los platillos de nuestra Cocina Criolla. Son únicos en el mundo !

En Nueva Orleans lo estamos esperando.

Figure 59. **The U.S. Travel Service's advertising appeal to Latin American tourists** is essentially the same as to others—jazz, food, and air-conditioned Huckleberry Finn, all only two hours from home. (Courtesy of the Greater New Orleans Tourist and Convention Commission.)

Figure 60. **The New Orleans Superdome.** Like the building it represents, this 1973 futuristic rendering of the Louisiana Superdome has a Texan inspiration: Houston's Astrodome. The Superdome is also symbolic of the new New Orleans—an attempt to outdo Texas in bigness, shininess, and the size of its color TV screens. Although its cost is Texan, the scale of purported corruption in building it is strictly Louisianian. (Courtesy of the Greater New Orleans Tourist and Convention Commission.)

Figure 61. **A "jazz funeral" beneath the elevated I-10 expressway, c. 1970.** I-10 now occupies the main part of Claiborne Avenue, once a landscaped boulevard which served as the main avenue of a thriving black neighborhood. I-10 was originally planned to run along the Mississippi River in front of Jackson Square and St. Louis Cathedral, but the scheme was effectively fought off by residents of more affluent white areas of the city. Thus, the Quarter was saved, but at the expense of this black neighborhood. (Courtesy of the Greater New Orleans Tourist and Convention Commission.)

Figure 62. **Downtown New Orleans, c. 1973**, as seen at Canal Street and St. Charles, looking toward the Mississippi River and the International Trade Mart Tower. (The big Rivergate convention center projects a half-arch colonnade just in front of the Trade Mart.) Note the flamboyant nineteenth-century commercial buildings, on the left, increasingly in unprestigious uses, alternating with shiny high-rise buildings such as the Marriott Hotel at the left.

Figure 63. **A Mardi Gras Parade on St. Charles Avenue**—a definition of place by civic act. (Courtesy of the Greater New Orleans Tourist and Convention Commission.)

INDEX OF FIGURES

APPENDIX C: CHARTS AND GRAPHS

Chapter 3
THE STAGES OF METROPOLITAN GROWTH

Concerning Geography, History, and Cities

AN OLD APHORISM SAYS that "geography doesn't change." That is plainly untrue, as the changing geography of the Mississippi Delta proves. Still, many geographic patterns are conservative and slow to change, often because they represent a considerable investment of energy, and comparable expenditures are required to change them. To state the proposition differently: more than a few important geographic patterns—human as well as physical—are inherited from past time, and we must look into the past to understand them. Thus, if we are to make sense of the contemporary geography of New Orleans, or any other place for that matter, an efficient way is to turn the clock back and try to reconstruct the geography of the past, blood ancestor of the present. More accurately, we must examine the geographies of the past, for we live with a host of inherited geographies.

For purposes of understanding New Orleans, it is helpful to return to 1718, and the spectacle of Bienville (1680–1768), French governor of Louisiana, confronting the primordial wilderness. First of all, as Freud has taught us, the beginnings of an organism when it is weak and malleable are often more important than its later, lustier days. It is the old story of the bent twig; early episodes often establish patterns and set habits for a lifetime to come. Second, Bienville symbolizes in a rather pure form the kinds of elements that were to make New Orleans the way it is today. On the one hand, Bienville had certain motivations, and these were determined and conditioned not only by his personal quirks and ambitions, but also in a larger sense by the temporal and spatial milieu from which he came—a postfeudal French empire, torn by internal dissensions, but grasping for wealth and glory. On the other hand, Bienville was sharply limited in what he *could* do. The limitations were several, but at a general level are exactly the same that all of us labor under today: the exigencies of physical environment; a technology which enables us to manipulate that environment; a certain level of wealth that lets us put that technology to work; and, not the least, the social institutions, political philosophy, and psychological habits which ultimately guide what we would *think* about doing—or refrain from doing.

The Four Ages of New Orleans

In New Orleans it is helpful to think of several major historic-geographic episodes—each fairly stable, but each begun and ended by brief outbursts of activity which left the city much changed. Each period differed from the ones before and after because each was dominated by different kinds of people, with different attitudes and different tools at their disposal. When each period was done, New Orleans required a new map—actually an old one with erasures, and new sections glued on—the new sections different in location and in pattern from the old ones, often because basic modes of transportation were changing and new land was available to new kinds of technology. The city's population changed, both in numbers and in ethnic composition, partly because new kinds of jobs were becoming available and partly because old ones were disappearing. Most noticeable, if not most important, the city's appearance changed, with different street patterns, different styles of building, and changing uses of land. Above all, each period marks a time when the city was related to the outside world by new kinds of communication that changed the areas with which the city was connected. When the episode was over and the city was ready for a breathing spell, New Orleans had changed in fundamental ways—those who made decisions for the city were different, its economic and social connections with the outside were different, and its internal geography had changed. And, after each upheaval, the city stood in quite a different position in the ranking of American cities, and it faced in new directions.

Four such periods mark the evolution of New Orleans's present-day geography. Although the beginning and ending dates are obviously arbitrary, each period marks a time when the rather fickle city linked its fortunes with different parts of the nation or world.

During the first period, from 1718 to about 1810, New Orleans was a European city, both in physical form and human orientation. The period spans the time of Spanish and French rule, and ended when a flood of American immigrants overwhelmed the city in unprecedented numbers with unprecedented ideas.

During the second period, New Orleans was America's western capital. Instantly wealthy from its economic lordship over the continental interior, the city spread far outside its European walls, meantime taking on new patterns which form the city's geographic skeleton today. The period ended about 1865, less the result of the Civil War than the seizure of New Orleans's old economic hinterland by northern railroads and upstart railroad cities in the North.

During the third period, hardship matured the city, which consciously set about to avert economic disaster by remaking itself physically. Although it fell drastically in national rankings, New Orleans emerged by the mid-twentieth century with a new stability, extensive new territory, and a quite different geographic form—a composite of old and new attitudes and technologies.

The last period, which began about 1945 and continued into the 1970s, saw New Orleans undergoing some of the most sweeping changes in its history, grappling with new competitors, new technologies, and unprecedented social problems. As before, its geography changed once more—as usual, the combination of the city's own efforts and of outside forces largely beyond its control. And, inevitably, its contemporary geography was a pastiche of new forms, laid atop and beside the patterns of the past.

The European City (1718 – c. 1810)

New Orleans did not grow to become a city; it was decreed a city from the moment of its founding—rather as Venus sprang full-born from the sea. And if in its early years New Orleans was somewhat muddier than Venus, the city's founders laid the plans for a capital of a scale and magnificence to suit the territory which it was to rule.

The city's plan was laid out by French engineers in a gridiron pattern—symmetrical, with a central square facing the river. To contemporary Americans, there is nothing strange about this pattern, for it seems much less "European-looking" than, say, the winding streets of old Boston or lower Manhattan. But the gridiron was not merely a convenient way to lay out the land; it represented the New Europe, planted with classical perfection on the barbarian shore. As in

Philadelphia, whose streets were laid out in a gridiron from its very beginning in 1682, the street plan of New Orleans was a declaration of intention. There might not be enough people to fill the grid right away. (New Orleans's grid was not filled until after 1800, and Philadelphia's not until the mid-nineteenth century, but in both places the plan was there before the people, and the settlement was obviously meant to be permanent.) It did not matter particularly if the city's great masonry fortifications turned out in reality to be a rather higgledy-piggledy wooden palisade. The walls were there in the mind. After all, great cities needed great walls, built to the latest standards of military architecture. Indeed, it did not even matter what the land was like, and it was a considerable time before Frenchmen grasped the notion that New Orleans was not built on hills. The plan represented a perfected, purified Europe, ready to be stamped into the soil of the New World wherever Europeans willed it.

From the beginning, image was more important than reality. The Place d'Armes (now Jackson Square) with its new church gained a reputation as the finest thing for hundreds of miles. Never mind that the place was a weedy lot and the church a primitive wooden building. New Orleans had already begun to gain a reputation as a terribly important place, but, to Americans, one that was foreign, papist, and, therefore, dangerous to national aspirations in the Mississippi Valley.

As in Canada, France erred by failing to populate the place adequately. Part of it stemmed from absent-mindedness (France had other things to think about in the eighteenth century), and part of it resulted from deliberate policy. Growing fear of heretics and Englishmen had pushed France into the disastrous policy of screening overseas emigrants to ensure their political reliability. The result of the policy—especially harmful in Canada—meant that only conservative persons were considered suitable as landowners, and most conservative Frenchmen preferred living in France to living in the Mississippi Delta, even with its mythical hills. The populating of New Orleans was extremely slow, therefore, and its governing class was suspicious and xenophobic even by Bourbon standards. As for the rural Acadians who came to people the countryside after the 1750s, they were even more extreme in their views. Hounded from their homes in maritime Canada, they did not look kindly on anyone who was vaguely Protestant or English. Nor did things change much when the Spanish took over in 1767. Spain had even worse domestic troubles than France, and its glittering but rickety Latin American empire gave it even better reason than France to regard New Orleans as a sideshow. Slow migration, moreover, produced a chronic labor shortage, and slaves were imported from the beginning. By the end of the eighteenth century more than half the city's population was black.

Despite neglect, New Orleans continued to grow, largely the result of American settlement in the Ohio River valley which sought trade outlets through the city. Even within the limits of the Vieux Carré,[1] the main direction of growth was upriver, a trend which would never be reversed. Simultaneously, with boats pulled up at the levee—already raised artificially by several feet— the riverfront and the Rue de la levée (now Decatur Street) began to exhibit a line of docks and commercial buildings which would eventually, under American rule, grow so wide and high that one would find it difficult to walk along—or even see—the river.

Clearly the city was reaching out, but it was still relying on water routes. Building roads was just too difficult, the river too accessible. To be sure, a road had been run along Gentilly Ridge (later to be dubbed the "old Spanish Trail" and later U.S. 90), which theoretically led to the Gulf Coast, but it was very troublesome to maintain; the Rigolets and Chef Menteur Pass posed formidable barriers, and it was much easier to go east by boat. And along the river, atop the natural levee, was a River Road about fifty miles long (only eighteen miles of the total lay below the city), but it was of trivial importance compared to the Mississippi itself. New Orleans was literally an island.

The best way to get in or out of the city was still by way of Bayou St. John, and that route had been much improved after Governor Carondolet ordered a canal built to connect the bayou with the backside of the natural levee. Originally laid out as a drainage canal, it was converted so that boats could come up to the rear of the city and unload. (No locks were built to raise canal boats to the level of the Mississippi for fear the levee would be breached and the city flooded.) At the end of the canal, a few blocks behind the cathedral in the never-never-land between backswamp and natural levee, a turning basin was built, giving its name eventually to Basin Street and ultimately determining

---

[1] The Vieux Carré (literally, the "old square" or "old district") was delineated by the palisades on three sides and the Mississippi River on the fourth. Today, the Vieux Carré is officially recognized as a historic district under the Louisiana Constitution, and its official boundaries are Esplanade Avenue, Rampart Street, Canal Street, and Decatur Street. These same boundaries are well-known and recognized by nearly every adult Orleanian.

the location of a thriving commercial waterfront and of accompanying bawdy houses.

Both canal and basin remain as a part of the city's present landscape, although both are considerably transformed. After canal boats were replaced by railroads, the canal was filled and became a branch line of the Southern Railway. The basin, no longer used, was taken over by the city and, after remaining vacant for a long time, became the site for the public auditorium where New Orleans society gathers for the most exclusive of Mardi Gras balls. The red-light district became a public embarrassment and was eventually removed to make room for a suitably sanitary public housing project. The bawdy houses survived next to the railroad station long enough to give New Orleans a lively reputation for night life. Along Basin Street, in the fancy houses, black and white musicians joined to entertain the bordellos' patrons with the blues and ragtime that contributed to the ancestry of jazz. The combination was fortuitous and intriguing—except for natural levees, Spanish governors, railroad barons, and ladies of the night, we might have had no jazz.

Architecture in the old French city is naturally assumed by tourists to be French, but most of it is not. New Orleans was Spanish for the last thirty years of the eighteenth century, and during that time two great fires burned up most of the city, so the rebuilding was naturally in the Spanish mode. Thus, the "French" Quarter looks a good deal more like Castille than the Île de France. A good share of that old Spanish city still stands, a monument to neglect, New Orleans conservatism, and the benevolent ministrations of the Works Progress Administration. Latin American visitors, according to legend, feel more comfortable in New Orleans than in any other big American city. It is not surprising, for the Vieux Carré—with its stucco buildings standing directly next to narrow sidewalks, occasional ornaments of ebullient cast iron, and flashes of tropical gardens in interior courtyards—is decidedly reminiscent of colonial Spain.

The European period came to an end abruptly with the Louisiana Purchase in 1803 and the sale of New Orleans to the United States. Too much is made of the exact date, since official transfer failed to oust Creoles from the seats of power. But neither France nor Spain could have held the city much longer as part of their respective overseas empires. Americans were flooding into the Mississippi River valley at exactly the same time that France was finishing a revolution and sporadically at war with half of Europe. Spain was in worse shape, unable to hold its Latin American colonies even against Indian guerrillas. It was manifestly the destiny of the United States to have New Orleans; there were too few Europeans to hold it against the tide of frontier men and women sweeping into the valley. In all, New Orleans enjoyed too important a location and too flamboyant a reputation to be ignored much longer. The city's geographical chickens had come home to roost.

America's Western Capital (c. 1810–c. 1865)

The United States Census first counted the population of New Orleans in 1810 and, to nobody's surprise, it emerged as the largest city west of the Appalachians. In the whole country it was outranked only by the four East Coast giants—New York City, Philadelphia, Boston, and Baltimore. From an underpopulated French colonial capital, New Orleans had suddenly become a big city and it was shortly to become much bigger.

American migration had mainly done the job (population tripled in the first seven years after the purchase), but the process was circular. New Orleans was primate city of the new West, and that very fact stimulated migration to the city.

THE COMMERCIAL CITY.   Business was booming—then as now a largely commercial business with very little manufacturing. And prospects were excellent, as more and more Americans poured over the Appalachians into the Ohio River valley and into the new lands of the Upper South and Deep South. Europe was building new industry, and so was New England, and both places possessed an insatiable appetite for Midwestern foodstuffs and Southern cotton. Furthermore, these goods were bulky, and, until some kind of dependable land transportation became available, they had to be shipped out by river, no matter where they were eventually headed. That meant steamboats, and a lot of them. Morse's *Gazeteer* of 1823 remarks with a tone of astonishment about New Orleans that "there were 50 steam-boats on the eastern waters connected with the commerce of this city." That was a driblet compared with what was coming. Captain Glazier, the urban chronicler, described the levee in 1883, long after steamboats were obsolete, and even then the scene was remarkable: "Along the riverfront are congregated hundreds of steamers, and thousands of nondescript boats, among them numerous barges and flat-boats; thickly interspersed with ships of the largest size, from whose masts fly the colors of every nation in the civilized world. . . . The throng which comes and goes upon the levee, merchants, clerks, hotel runners, hackmen, stevedores, and river men of all grades, keep up a general motion and excitement, while piled upon the platforms which serve as a connecting link between the watercraft and the shore, are packages of merchandise in every conceivable shape . . ." Altogether, New Orleans had entered a golden age. Between 1810 and 1840, the city's growth rate exceeded that of any other large American city, and if the same rate had continued during the 1840s, New Orleans would shortly have become the country's second largest city.[2]

INTERNAL DIVISIONS. Within New Orleans, conditions were somewhat less golden. As Captain Glazier observed later, "to the French Creoles as a class, who during their long alienation had still at heart been thoroughly French, to become a part of a republic, and that republic English in its origin, was intensely distasteful. This was the deluge indeed, which Providence had not kindly stayed until after their time. They withdraw into a little community of their own, and refused companionship with such as sacrificed their caste by accepting the situation and adapting to it . . ."

Much of it had nothing to do with caste. The old "Quarter" (the Vieux Carré, the Creoles called it) was getting crowded and obviously would not hold the increasing number of newcomers, even if they had been made welcome, which emphatically they were not. As population spilled outward, it established patterns which would be permanently etched into the urban geography of New Orleans.

First of all, it was established in which direction the city would grow, and what the internal character of the new city would be. The natural levée, of course, was the only place to settle, and the city pressed into sugar plantations which had lined the river's banks both upstream and downstream from New Orleans. These additions to the city were called *faubourgs* or, roughly translated, "suburbs." Most of the Americans chose to settle upstream ("Uptown") from the French Quarter, and immediately next to it—rather like a medieval marketplace clustered outside the walls of a fortified European town. The boundary line between established Creoles and newly arrived Americans was what John Chase calls a "nameless no-man's-land," sharply drawn between the two cities. Later on, a navigation canal was planned along the boundary, and a huge right-of-way was reserved. The canal was never built, but Canal Street was named for it—in the best New Orleans tradition, in honor of a myth. Canal Street presently became an enormously wide boulevard, and the median was called

---

[2] Indeed, according to the 1840 census, it almost was. Baltimore and New Orleans had almost exactly the same number of people — 102,313 and 102,193, respectively. Only New York City, with more than 300,000 people, was larger.

"the neutral ground," a geographical recognition of the armed truce between Creoles and Americans. The phrase is now part of standard Orleanian patois, and means the median strip of any boulevard.

Downstream, in the Faubourg of Joseph Marigny, settlement was slower and considerably less affluent. There, population was dominated by Creoles who had spilled out from the overcrowded Vieux Carré and by new immigrants, mainly Irish and German, who formed the city's white lower classes. But to the proper Creole this was foreign territory, too, and the effect was to confine the French Quarter on both its Uptown and Downtown sides. Since the river formed a third side, the only Creole options were to pack more people into the Quarter, which they did; or to mix with the despised foreigners, which they ultimately and gradually did; or to spread beyond the walls toward the back-swamp, which they also did. (Another option—to settle across the river—was not taken up until late in the nineteenth century, and even then not very enthu-siastically.)

Happily for the Creoles, their allotment of backswamp was less ghastly than the Americans'. The sharp bend in the Mississippi where the Vieux Carré is located is accompanied by a lakeward salient of the natural levees. This salient extends far enough northwest to merge with the lower natural levees of Bayou Gentilly and, thus, form a low saddle between the Vieux Carré and the head of Bayou St. John. This saddle came to be known by geologists as Esplanade Ridge, named for the great boulevard which follows its crest. It was Esplanade Ridge which formed the old Bienville portage of 1699, and now, 150 years later, pro-vided the hard-pressed Creoles with a way of expanding their territory inland. The main axis of the ridge is barely above sea level, but it was enough. The Esplanade in time became the great nineteenth-century artery of suburban Creole New Orleans, and it is still a fine street.

Meantime, antagonisms between the several parts of the city ripened to the point where in 1836 the city was formally divided into three self-governing "municipalities"—the First Municipality being the French Quarter, the Second being the new American city in Faubourg St. Mary, and the Third the Downtown Creole-cum-immigrant city. The Third was of little importance to the city's decision-makers and has remained so since. In modern times, its heart is the Ninth Ward, a blue-collar area for whites and blacks which is terra incog-nita to the city's elite, and noticed mainly as the butt of bad jokes.

Although the formal political division proved unworkable and was aban-doned, the antagonisms left tangible marks on the growing city. For example, streets change names as they cross Canal Street (Royal becomes St. Charles, Chartres becomes Camp, and so on). Each city had its own great hotel, although the St. Charles in the commercial American city was naturally larger and more ostentatious than the St. Louis on the French side. (Both hotels went through several architectural reincarnations, but both were eventually demolished.) The American city had its own Lafayette Square, hoping to match the grandeur of Place d'Armes on the French side, though never quite succeeding. Important places such as churches and burial grounds were sharply segregated and usually duplicated. New Orleans, with its two self-sustaining centers, was rather like a double-yolked egg.

Even navigation canals were duplicated, although more for economic than for ethnic reasons. As the American city grew upstream, the Carondelet Canal behind the French Quarter was farther and farther away from the focus of commercial activity, which continued to move Uptown. In 1832, therefore, construction began on a "New Basin Canal" which by 1838 had connected Lake Pontchartrain directly with the back of the American city. It was an exact American counterpart to the Carondelet Canal of the Creoles.

The new canal left its imprint on New Orleans in two important and permanent ways. First, it established another major route into the city from behind—a route which ultimately became the main umbilical cord from the central and western United States. Alongside it were built several railroad lines, the most important of which eventually became the main line of the Illinois Central to Chicago. Still later, when the canal was abandoned, part of its right-of-way was used as the route for Pontchartrain Boulevard, the main approach for the Greater New Orleans-Mississippi River Bridge and Interstate 10, the main route from Baton Rouge, Houston, and the West. Alongside this long-standing routeway there developed a belt of low intensity commercial and warehousing facilities which occupies a wide swath across the "Mid-City" area of New Orleans. Today, as a result, one enters New Orleans from the north or west on an expressway flanked by auto junkyards, lumberyards, warehouses, breweries, and the like. For a city that supposedly breathes romance, it is a strikingly unromantic entrance.

Second, the New Basin Canal profoundly altered the population geography of New Orleans. It was an expensive thing to build, for it had to be hacked by hand through a pudding of muck and buried cypress stumps. To do the job, Irishmen were hired in great numbers, just as they were hired in the North and West to build railroads. New Orleans became the only southern city with any substantial number of new European immigrants. As in so many ways, New Orleans seemed a southern city with northern habits.

Most of the immigrants were settled between the levee and the end of the new canal's turning basin—long since filled and now partly occupied by the New Orleans Transportation Center and the Louisiana Superdome. This strip happened to coincide with the rather seedy outer fringes of the booming business district and seemed a proper place to put the obviously inferior immigrants. The area where the immigrant district abutted the riverfront quickly came to be known as "Irish Channel," a rather tough, low-class area where nice people did not live.

The American elite, meantime, were moving farther uptown, into what is now called the "Garden District," so named because large mansions were set back from the street—in contrast with the old Spanish practice of building one's house on the street and turning inward toward an enclosed court. The use of the word "garden" simply reflects English word usage—the gardens are what most Americans call "front yards." The Garden District is now one of New Orleans's most picturesque and desirable residential neighborhoods, one of the largest and best-preserved antebellum residential area in America. Except for the French Quarter, it attracts more tourists than any other part of the city. Like the French Quarter, the Garden District has acquired status as a "historic district," and, thus, legal means are available to prevent architectural instrusions. The Tourist and Convention Commission says little about the Irish Channel, which has retained its rough, rather seedy character—now half ghetto and half skid row.

THE STREET PATTERN.   The pattern of streets in the new steamboat city was at once curious and portentous, for it was both cause and effect of important things in the city's life. The basic layout goes back to the time before the sugar plantations were gobbled up by the city, when property lines and often field lines extended back from the river, perpendicular to the levee. The pattern was familiar to those experienced with land patterns in certain parts of Europe, where long, narrow landholdings extended back from roads and rivers alike. The purpose was the same in Louisiana: landowners needed access to the road, and there was only one road—the Mississippi. Since the only good land was on the natural levee, with land values dropping to near zero in the backswamp, and since the owners needed access to the river, there was only one solution—to slice the two-mile band of natural levee into narrow strips, "long lots" perpendicular to the river.[3] But since the river was not straight, the strips were not parallel. Behind convex curves of the river, the boundaries fanned out; on concave curves, they were pinched. Where New Orleans was expanding most rapidly in the American city, the meander was convex, so that plantation lot lines formed a fan-shaped pattern—today the most conspicuous feature on any street map of Uptown New Orleans. These lot lines were reinforced in two ways. First, they were obvious places to dig canals, not for navigation, but to drain excess rainwater from the natural levee into the backswamp. (Upriver from New Orleans, similar canals drain contemporary natural levees.) Second, when it came time to build main streets, they were often put along property lines, and thus ran along the canals. In such instances, rights-of-way were often extremely wide. In the early days, these drainage canals were noisome sloughs, the object of bitter complaint, and the canal-side streets were unpleasant places where traffic was heavy, churned to a muddy gruel. (Stories are told of animals mired so deeply that they died in place and were abandoned to decompose.) Later on, the canals were lined with concrete, and eventually covered, to form great wide boulevards. The neutral ground was a fine place to put horsecar tracks, and it was not long before these useful boulevards were bedecked with flowers and lined with great trees. During the nineteenth century, as the city spread Uptown, property line after property line became boulevard after boulevard—Melpomene, Jackson, Louisiana, Napoleon, Jefferson, Broadway, and eventually South Carrollton avenues, to name but the main ones. To glance at the maps, one might suppose that these boulevards diverge from a central focus in Mid-City, and it is easy to conclude that Mid-City is, therefore, a humming beehive of activity. Quite the contrary. The boulevards naturally converge in one place because they are radii of a half-circle whose circumference was already drawn by the Mississippi River. Much of Mid-City is today a derelict wasteland, its character set decades ago when it was the lowest part of an uninhabited swamp.

Cross streets simply followed the river approximately in concentric curves or, more exactly, in a series of straight tangents to the curve, each tangent jogging slightly when it crosses one of the radial boulevards. With straight streets, it was possible to lay out bits and pieces of a grid pattern, but the converging

---

[3] Similar long lots occur wherever seventeenth- and eighteenth-century Frenchmen settled and subdivided rural land in North America: throughout Québec; along the lower Great Lakes (the Detroit River is lined with them); and in spots along the upper Mississippi, the Wabash, the Maumee, and elsewhere.

radial streets force constant adjustments which can be seen everywhere throughout the pre-1900 city.

None of these tangential streets possessed important drainage canals, since they ran parallel to the river and only served as feeders to the arterial canals. There was no natural need for wide rights-of-way, and in the early days none were provided. Close to the levee, in particular, the tangential streets are narrow, utilitarian, and occasionally colorful—such as the unpronounceable Tchoupitoulas (see *Appendix B*), which serves the docks, and Magazine Street, once the main commercial artery of Uptown and today spotted with antique shops and neighborhood stores. But Orleanians had been forced into building wide streets at periodic intervals, and eventually it became a pleasant habit, providing an otherwise crowded city with occasional, great shady boulevards, which today must be put very high on the list of the city's urban amenities.

Thus, despite the high cost of land, it was quite natural to run a great boulevard Uptown, parallel to the river. That boulevard, Nayades Avenue, later to be renamed St. Charles Avenue, was placed along the rear boundary line of the long, narrow, riverfront land grants—the front, of course, being the river itself. Under French law these grants ran back forty *arpents* from the Mississippi.[4] The effect was to locate St. Charles Avenue about halfway between the clatter of the docks and the stench of the backswamp, insulated from both by a decent distance. In effect, the boulevard bisected the habitable part of the natural levee and became the main residential artery of the American city—the counterpart of Esplanade Avenue in Downtown. It, also, was the route of the New Orleans and Carrollton Railroad, which was deliberately built to open the Uptown area to suburban development. Much later on, Claiborne Avenue and Fontainbleau-Broad Avenue were built roughly concentric with St. Charles. Neither of these later streets holds the Orleanians' very special affection as does St. Charles Avenue, the first and grandest of the great unnecessary boulevards. Visitors to New Orleans may dislike certain aspects of the city, but most agree on the charm of St. Charles Avenue. Today, even the most aggressive new-look politicians have been unable to persuade Orleanians to abandon the last of the city's streetcars, which wobble quaintly along the neutral ground of St. Charles Avenue, past wonderful antebellum and Victorian houses, brushing against oleanders and Spanish moss as they make their runs from Canal Street along the whole length of the old American city. Officials of New Orleans Public Service, Inc. (NOPSI), which operates the city's excellent transit system, force a tight-

[4] One *arpent* = 180 feet; hence, forty *arpents* = 7,200 feet, or nearly a mile and a half.

lipped smile when the streetcar is mentioned, for maintenance costs are outrageous and the nominal fare hardly begins to pay for operation. But tourists and Orleanians alike are delighted, and the St. Charles streetcar is now as firmly entrenched in New Orleans as are the cable cars on Nob Hill in San Francisco. It is difficult to prove, but no less obvious, that St. Charles Avenue maintains much of its charm and, therefore, its environmental health partly because of the beloved streetcar.[5]

Curiously, the street pattern of New Orleans profoundly influenced the pattern of white and black population, as both spread out across the growing city. And the racial patterns, like the patterns of streets, are still with us.

RACIAL GEOGRAPHY IN AN OLD PLACE: SUPERBLOCKS AND BACKSWAMP GHETTOS. In early New Orleans, as in most southern towns, social segregation between races did not necessarily imply geographical segregation—except at the most microscopic scale. Slaves, for example, were commonly housed on the quarters of slaveowners, and a racial map of the Vieux Carré would have produced an intricate salt-and-pepper pattern. Even free blacks usually did not live very far from their work—and since many worked as domestics, they necessarily lived in or close to white neighborhoods.

As the city grew beyond the Quarter, however, and spread upriver along the natural levee, geographic segregation began to appear in two quite different forms. First of all, the indispensable domestics (especially after emancipation) commonly were housed in the back streets behind affluent whites, but within walking distance. Similar practices in other southern towns, and even in the North, led to blacks being put in small houses in back alleys with whites in bigger houses on the streets. Whites did not associate socially with the blacks, but they lived close by and often they played together as children.[6]

In New Orleans, the pattern took a characteristically peculiar turn. In the new American city, many of the biggest houses where the richest whites lived

---

[5] In the early 1970s, the federal government joined the growing list of the streetcar's admirers and declared the whole line a National Historic Property—the oldest operating streetcar line in the United States, or so it is said. Since this was written in 1975, all talk of dismantling the St. Charles Avenue streetcar has evaporated. The St. Charles line has become a major tourist attraction, and has served as a model for two more lines: one along the riverfront, mainly for tourists, and the other a restoration of a main line along Canal Street to serve as a serious part of the city's public transit system.

[6] Booth Tarkington's *Penrod* describes the pattern in a fictional Midwestern town at the beginning of the twentieth century.

were located along the great boulevards, and the boulevards, in turn, were commonly separated by five, ten, or fifteen smaller streets. The boulevards, in consequence, circumscribed "superblocks" half a mile or so square, and subdivided into several scores of ordinary city blocks. Inasmuch as blacks lived behind the big houses, often several blocks away, each superblock tended to develop affluent white perimeters with black cores. Thus, St. Charles Avenue was solidly lined with wealthy whites, as were Napoleon and Jefferson avenues, which crossed St. Charles about eight blocks apart. Back from all three streets, however, blacks lived in small, nuclear clusters, and these clusters have survived to this day. Then as now, however, there were poorer whites who could not afford mansions on the great boulevards, and the cores of the superblocks were seldom entirely black.

Such patches of black population by no stretch of the imagination can be called "ghettos" in the contemporary northern sense. Unlike the northern ghetto, these black neighborhoods of New Orleans were quite small and multi-nucleated, with fuzzy boundaries. Internally, they contained a fair amount of open space, and the architecture was not conspicuously different from that in white areas of comparable income. If America had to have racial segregation, the New Orleans pattern was less malevolent than that of most northern cities. Neither whites nor blacks were very far from persons of the other race, and since each group knew their respective neighborhood to be geographically stable, neither felt particularly threatened by the other.

Unfortunately, there was another less benevolent form of racial segregation, and it is the ancestor of some of New Orleans's worst contemporary ghettos. It resulted from the fact that the poorest blacks simply lived where they could. In other cities in later times, such areas were found "down by the tracks." In antebellum New Orleans, it was either along the *battures* or the backswamps. The *batture* is the area on the riverside of the artificial levee, without flood protection and without private ownership. At the foot of Canal Street, the *batture* was used during periods of low water for mooring boats and stacking cargo; ultimately it grew so valuable that warehouses and wharves were built there, its possession was fiercely contested, and new levees were built to protect it against flooding. Thus, the city moved into the river, at the same time building a commercial barrier between the residential city and the Mississippi. Away from the docks, however, the poorest blacks would squat on the *batture* in makeshift shacks, abandoned when the river periodically rose and carried them away. The *batture* ghettos were obviously temporary and of little long-run importance in fixing racial patterns.

Not so the backswamp. With whites occupying the highest and best part of the natural levee in all three municipalities, blacks were pushed into the demiland on the inland margin of the natural levee, where drainage was bad, foundation material precarious, streets atrociously unmaintained, mosquitos endemic, and flooding a recurrent hazard. Along this wretched margin there developed a discontinuous belt of black population, interrupted by the commercial zones along the Carondolet and New Basin canals and by the later building of boulevards which attracted affluent whites. By the mid-twentieth century, however, the backswamp black belt had grown so crowded that the nonblack interstices were filling up, and the old backswamp ghettos were beginning to merge into something that looked like that evil northern phenomenon, the superghetto. Thus, while New Orleans has always had one of the highest proportions of black population of all big American cities, it has—until recently—been one of the least segregated geographically. Recent changes in that condition must be listed as one of the least heartening aspects of New Orleans's contemporary social geography.

REGULARITIES IN AN IRREGULAR CITY.   It is easy to conclude from this catalogue of municipal peculiarities that New Orleans's urban growth before the Civil War obeyed special rules which applied only to it—and nowhere else. It is a tempting conclusion, but untrue. Geographers and sociologists long ago noticed that growing cities in a free economy tend to develop patterns of land use in concentric rings—a central business district, which gradually merges into a ring of warehousing, thence into a wider ring of low income housing, with a ring of higher income residences on the outermost fringes. Such concentric rings have been described in city after city throughout the Western world. Other scholars observed that cities also tend to be sectoral—that is, when a certain kind of land use or a certain kind of people begin to congregate and expand on one side of a city, the expansion will fan outward from the city along major roadways, eventually to form patterns such as the wedges of a pie. Both sectors and concentric rings can be found in New Orleans, too, although the peculiar topography so distorted the regularities that one must hunt hard to find them. Nevertheless, the general principles were struggling to emerge, and if one looks in the right place, they are easy to see.

The sectors are most obvious: the large American sector projecting upstream; the low-income Third Municipality downstream; and the French sector blunted by the backswamp but thrusting a narrow wedge lakeward along Esplanade Ridge. And the concentric rings are there, too, if only in segments, as a slice of a rainbow will appear only in one quarter of the sky where sun and rain occur simultaneously. In New Orleans the concentric rings are clearly formed only where the city was developing without obstacles—and that meant mainly Uptown in the American sector along the natural levee. By the mid-nineteenth century, rings had formed which can still be seen: the civic core along Canal Street, fading into the commercial and warehousing zone upriver, thence into the slum-like Irish Channel, and finally grading into the genteel "suburbs" of the Garden District and ultimately out St. Charles Avenue. A similar but even more compressed series of rings appeared along the Rampart Street fringe of the French Quarter, past the turning basin of the Carondelet Canal, and extending along the stylish Esplanade into the suburbs at the head of Bayou St. John, with a nearby racetrack and jockey club to mark the affluence. All of this emerged in full bloom by the turn of the twentieth century, but the seeds were sown long before. What distorts the general patterns in New Orleans are the peculiar bicultural core of the city, the curious racial geography, and, above all, the stern constraints of local landforms and soil. Modern technology has weakened those constraints, but they were very powerful when the city was forming. Thus, the regularities are there, but one must know how to look for them.

END OF THE GOLDEN AGE. New Orleans's decline from glory also followed a predictable pattern, but even there the observer can be so distracted by local particulars that long-term trends are hard to see. This book is not the place to review Farragut's daring seizure of New Orleans in 1862, the closing of the river, and General Butler's rude behavior to the ladies of New Orleans. But the Civil War was a lurid episode in New Orleans's history, and, according to local legend, it was the war that put a sudden and cruel end to the city's lordly dominance over the Mississippi Valley. Whole Mississippis of tears have been wept over the event, but the tear-dimmed eyes failed to see that the city's decline resulted from nothing more romantic than an upheaval in the technology of transportation. On the horizon to the north was a cloud no larger than a man's hand, issuing from the smokestacks of the new steam locomotives that were hauling goods directly from the Midwest across the mountains to the Atlantic Coast or, more cheaply, to the Great Lakes ports, whence goods were taken east by the Erie and other canals.

The numbers tell the story. When railroads got to Chicago and St. Louis, New Orleans no longer enjoyed a monopoly over the Mississippi Valley's trade, and both cities presently overtook New Orleans in population—St. Louis about 1860, Chicago five years later. The Union Pacific was finished in 1869, and by 1875 the combined population of the Bay Area cities exceeded New Orleans. Before the end of the nineteenth century, six more railroad-industrial cities of the midcontinent had surpassed New Orleans in size—Pittsburgh, Detroit, Cleveland, Cincinnati, Buffalo, and Minneapolis. By the 1890s, New Orleans had dropped to thirteenth place in the nation's metropolitan hierarchy.

But it was no sudden catastrophe that caused New Orleans to be eclipsed. Nor did the city suffer except in relative terms, for population continued to grow in a stately sort of way. It was simply that New Orleans had reached maturity at about the same time that the northern cities were brawling adolescents. The youthful debutante found herself a middle-aged dowager, and her feelings were wounded. Small wonder that the Civil War was used to explain the injury, for the war served New Orleans—as Robert Penn Warren remarks about the South as a whole—as the "great Alibi," excusing all sorts of ills and evils. The war did play a role, but it was not in the usual sense of having destroyed New Orleans; rather, it speeded the industrialization of the North, and most particularly it stimulated the building of northern railroads.

The Maturing City (c. 1865– c. 1945)

If the Civil War shocked New Orleans, it did not numb the city as it did so much of the South. The main reason, perhaps, was that New Orleans retained very considerable economic advantages from before the war; also, while things were very bad afterwards, the city discovered that things were not quite so bad as they seemed. First of all, river traffic had begun to revive in a new form, while simultaneously the city found that it had rather willy-nilly become a railroad center. Second, New Orleans's location at the junction of the Mississippi Valley and the Gulf of Mexico turned out to be marvellously advantageous for plucking the wealth of new commercial agriculture that had begun to flower both in the American South and in Latin America. Finally, it turned out that the city's decision-makers were not the lotus-eating dilettantes of song and story, but realistic, tough-minded people who were willing to make some long-range bets on New Orleans's future and to hedge those bets by rebuilding a substantial part of the city. By the end of the nineteenth century, New Orleans was rather like a patient who has just finished recuperating from major surgery—slimmer and healthier than before the operation, but with a certain caution that dampened the flamboyance and insouciance that preceded the illness.

THE RIVER AND THE RAILROADS. The railroad, it turned out, did not replace the river as a transportation route. What it did was reduce the romance considerably by driving the gorgeous but inefficient general-cargo steamboats out of business.[7] Still, the railroads could not compete with water transportation for hauling bulk cargo in no special rush to reach a destination. Thus, the northern railways carried off the Midwest's general cargo and hurried it eastward, but much of the heavy bulk goods continued to come leisurely through New Orleans—especially grain from the upper Midwest and coal from the newly opened fields of Illinois and western Kentucky. The key to this traffic was the barge—first of shallow draft and hauled individually (originally they were little more than rafts), then, as the river's channel was deepened, of deeper draft and hauled around in great tows that looked like huge moving islands. By the end of the nineteenth century the city had established a near monopoly over bulk cargo from the central and upper Midwest. At the same time, more sophisticated river craft, combined with roads and railroads, had reached out for general cargo as well, and by mid-twentieth century the city had spun a web of trade that extended over a midcontinental region that was larger even than that of antebellum days.

And, contrary to legend, the South did rise again, for Europe and New England wanted more cotton after the war—not less. In the best prewar year, 1859, the South had produced a little over five million bales, but by the late 1890s ten million bales a year was routine. The boom began to deflate after World War I—what with the boll weevil, exhausted soils, and competition from Indian and Egyptian cotton fields—but New Orleans had a good share of the American cotton-marketing facilities at the time when it was most lucrative, and the profits carried the city through what otherwise might have been some very bad times. The cotton boom also helped give New Orleans a more southern flavor than it had ever had before—or was to have again in the future. Correspondingly, the slow decline and eventual disappearance of the Deep South "Cotton Belt" in the twentieth century did more to dilute that flavor than any other single thing.

Resurrection of commerce with the interior did not depend entirely on the river, for while railroads were somewhat delayed in coming to New Orleans (just as they were delayed throughout the South), the 1870s saw the beginning of an integrated rail system in the Deep South, with New Orleans at its hub. The city's advantage was simple: it remained the only genuine big city in the

---

[7] Mark Twain describes that sad process in several brilliant chapters of *Life on the Mississippi*.

South, and, with its long experience in handling cargo, it became a natural magnet for any railway in the region. New Orleans was fortunate, for there were several Gulf ports with better harbors—and better land approaches. All of New Orleans's railroads had to be built on piles and had to cross miles of uninhabited swamps before reaching the city. Any number of other coastal towns—Mobile, for example—would have seemed more reasonable choices, but New Orleans had the head start and shortly became the nation's main rail outlet to the Gulf of Mexico.

This is no place to recount the assemblage of short lines that eventually became New Orleans's railroad system. It took a long time to put it together; indeed, it was the 1950s before the city was able even to condense its five individual railroad stations into a single terminal.[8] When the system was finished, however, New Orleans had extended six major tentacles into the interior of the continent. The backbone of the system was the Illinois Central's north-south line to Chicago, the self-styled "Mainline of Mid-America." The IC reinforced New Orleans's river connections with the Midwest and strengthened the city's already strong trade associations with Illinois—a relationship which it retains to this day. To the west and northwest, the Southern Pacific, the Kansas City Southern, and the Texas and Pacific railways threw New Orleans's trade net over an extremely large area, which included upstate Louisiana, most of eastern Texas, Arkansas, and eventually Oklahoma. Northeastward the Southern Railway and the Louisville and Nashville reached through Alabama and on through central Tennessee to the Ohio River valley, although farther east New Orleans's thrust was blunted by the expanding hinterland of Atlanta, which was rapidly turning itself into the rail capital for the whole eastern South. It was not the last time New Orleans would have trouble with Atlanta.

Despite these successes, railroads were not the city's forte. New Orleans had gotten into the game too late to contest the dominance of Chicago and St. Louis over the midcontinental region, and the coastal South was, until the discovery of oil and gas, one of the poorest parts of the nation's poorest region. Fortunately for New Orleans, the city did not need to rely on the sandy coastal plain for revenue. Appropriately, this half-foreign city found new wealth in overseas trade. New markets were opening in Latin America, and New Orleans was waiting to exploit them.

---

[8] The timing was ironic. No sooner had New Orleans gotten its first genuine union passenger terminal than the American passenger train sickened and fell into a coma. The terminal now serves mainly as a bus station.

THE LATIN CONNECTION.   New Orleans had a special affinity for Latin America from the very beginning, when the city was merely an outpost of Spain's Caribbean and Gulf empire. With the decline of Spanish fortunes and the extension of American hegemony westward and southward, New Orleans saw Latin American independence as an obvious virtue. New nations would surely seek new markets, and, after all, who could foresee the eventual extent of the United States of America's political domain? Looking still farther ahead, what more logical place was there for a new focus of Latin American trade than the great Gulf port at the mouth of the Mississippi?

Disappointingly, the Latin American wars of liberation produced more immediate chaos than trade, and New Orleans became a compulsive dabbler in the Byzantine world of Central and South American politics. (Perhaps the city's experience with Louisiana politics had made that inevitable.) As early as 1822 an expedition had been fitted out in New Orleans to support Bolivar, and during the 1830s and 1840s the city served as a base for Texans in their wars with Mexico. Innumerable filibustering expeditions were launched from New Orleans against hapless Central American states, and when the Caribbean countries were one by one turned into "banana republics" toward the end of the nineteenth century, it was partly a result of collusion between Latin politicians and Orleanian entrepreneurs.

The Latin American linkage proved very profitable. Americans had been drinking prodigious quantities of coffee for a long time, but after the turn of the century their passion for bananas became equally awesome. New Orleans was a prime port of entry for both products, and if the Guatemalan lower classes did not become rich from cutting bananas and picking coffee beans, a good many Orleanians got rich selling them, while in the meantime the city spun another economic web across midcontinental America.

The result of these political and economic connections was to make New Orleans a kind of Latin foothold on the American shore, and the city, in turn, spread its tentacles far beyond the banana coast. Latin commercial offices lined the wharf-front streets, and the city eventually became the home for a consul from every one of the Spanish-speaking Latin republics. Some of the ties were informal, as rich *Latinos* would come to New Orleans on holiday, or send their sons and daughters to learn English at Miss So-and-So's Finishing School or Colonel Somebody's Academy for Young Gentlemen, or to study the Napoleonic Code at Tulane University's famed law school. (A New Orleans's education could be counted on to be genteel and conservative.) Less formal still was the spattering of political refugees who had fled their native land after some abortive coup and who, while plotting the next one, enjoyed the convenient hospitality of New Orleans's growing Latin American community.

In time the Latin American population grew fairly large, although how large depends on who was doing the counting—about 25,000 if one believes the 1970 U.S. Census; 65,000 if one takes the total of Latin American consulates' estimates and adds Puerto Rican and Cuban figures from a local Spanish language radio station; or 80,000 according to the local office of the Social Security Administration. But absolute numbers are less important than the fact that New Orleans never developed a big, conspicuous Spanish-speaking district but instead a number of small *Latino* neighborhoods scattered about the city. One important reason for the absence of a ghetto is that *Latinos* came into New Orleans over a long time and had time to become assimilated. (There was never any deluge, as of Puerto Ricans into New York City or Cubans into Miami.) For another, many of them were affluent and bilingual, so they found no need to huddle together for mutual protection. Above all, there were and are no big homogeneous groups from a single country.[9]

In sum, New Orleans found its Latin connection an agreeable one, both profitable and colorful. And in their turn, it is said, Latin Americans enjoy New Orleans, if for no other reason than the Spanish appearance of the Vieux Carré, which they find familiar and comfortable. At least the Tourist and Convention Commission thinks so, and it has mounted a substantial advertising campaign to lure Latin Americans to the Orleanian vacationland.

THE COTTON EXPOSITION AND ITS LONG-RUN CONSEQUENCES.   In retrospect, New Orleans might possibly have regained its health after the Civil War without artificial stimulation. Perhaps the railroads and barges would have come without enticement, and quite possibly Latin America would have sent its bananas, coffee, and people, too. As matters turned out, however, the city fathers decided to take a hand. They did two things, both of which profoundly affected the city's long-run growth and changed its internal appearance. The first was to stage an exposition. The second was to rebuild the city's port facilities from top to bottom.

[9] The largest national group is Honduran, with substantial numbers from Guatemala and Nicaragua. For a brief time, the Cuban population was fairly large, but by 1973, and the embargo on Cuban refugees, the most noticeable Cuban neighborhoods had seemingly evaporated—their residents evidently gone to other cities or assimilated into the New Orleans population at large.

The exposition of 1884–1885 was, in the best late-nineteenth-century tradition, a glittering extravaganza that would last a year and attract tourists and businessmen from far away. The great 1851 exhibition in London, with Prince Albert and the Crystal Palace, had set the standard for such affairs, and Philadelphia's Centennial Exposition of 1876 had shown what it could do for American cities. In 1884 New Orleans opened "The World's Fair and Cotton Centennial Exposition," which announced to the world that the Civil War was over and New Orleans was open for business again.

It is doubtful whether New Orleans sold any more cotton as a result, and the exposition itself did not break even. But there is no doubt that the city's appearance was considerably changed thereby. On the one hand, the wonders of institutional late-Victorian architecture bloomed as they had never bloomed before, with all the fanciwork and Carpenter Gothic ornaments that so florified the Picturesque-Eclectic mode.[10] New Orleans had always enjoyed its domestic architecture on the flamboyant side, but the Cotton Exposition pulled out all stops. The results were admired and imitated throughout the city, but especially in wealthy areas, which today contain some of the most exuberant Victorian architecture in America.

But to New Orleans in the long run, the important thing about the Cotton Exposition was its site and what happened to that site after the exposition was over. As matters stood in 1884, the location was almost predetermined, for it had to be in the American part of the city, in a place that was big, well-drained, and accessible by public transportation. Only one place met the description—a small rural tract which remained between the advancing edge of Uptown and the recently annexed suburb of Carrollton. The boundaries of the fairgrounds followed old French property lines in a quarter-mile swath completely across the natural levee—a distance of about two miles between the river and the backswamp. St. Charles Avenue and the Carrollton Railway to downtown New Orleans cut squarely across its midriff.

When the exposition was over, New Orleans followed Philadelphia's example and turned its fairgrounds into a great park. On the riverside of St. Charles it remained as Audubon Park, a pleasant, bosky ground with great oaks and little lakes, much beloved of Sunday strollers, golfers, and bicycle riders of

---

[10] Two of the most admired buildings housed, respectively, the Grand Rapids Furniture Pavilion and that of the Republic of Mexico. Despite differences in financial provenience, the two buildings looked wonderfully similar from a distance.

unstrenuous persuasion.[11] Lakeward from St. Charles the land was secured for the city's two biggest universities—Tulane, the self-styled "Harvard of the South," and Loyola, New Orleans's most prestigious Catholic institution. Thus, the Cotton Exposition passed into memory, but the grounds did not. Adjacent areas were changed also, and the margins of Audubon Park and the university campuses became two of the city's most favored locations for the scholarly and affluent. Today, the whole university area remains as one of the city's wealthiest (and whitest) neighborhoods.

THE NEW PORT.   The immediate purpose of the Cotton Exposition was to improve New Orleans's public relations, but no amount of publicity would change the fact that the city's economic foundation—the Port of New Orleans —was in rickety shape. Just as railroad technology was putting steamboats out of business, bigger and faster ships were making old port facilities obsolete. Nor was it merely a matter of building better wharves, although that was involved. The big new ships required deeper navigation channels, efficient means of getting cargo to and from the wharves, and, above all, an integrated administration of the port to ensure that things were to run smoothly and that facilities were to be kept in competitive shape. In New Orleans, however, these conditions plainly had not been met. By 1870, according to Leonard Huber, the state of the port had slipped badly. The fall resulted partly from the Civil War, but not entirely.

Part of the trouble stemmed from silting at the mouth of the river's main distributaries. In the lower river, a fifty-foot draft is commonly maintained by natural processes, but across the sand bars the depths ranged between twelve and twenty feet—and sometimes much less. These depths were awkward but adequate for shallow-draft sailing ships in antebellum days; they were no good at all for new deep-draft steamships, which sometimes had to anchor outside the bars for days, waiting for safe passage. It was a wasteful way to do things, and shipping companies had begun to mutter about going to Mobile or Gulfport to land their cargo. After lengthy and expensive dredging by the Army Corps of Engineers proved futile, New Orleans applied such pressure that Captain Eads was permitted to build his famous South Pass jetties, which, after they were finished in 1879, forced the river into a narrow channel and literally flushed the bars away.

[11] Audubon Park also contains a small artificial hill, built (so the story goes) so that the children of New Orleans could see what a real hill looks like.

Meantime, physical facilities inside the port had been deteriorating badly. Even so, the prospect was less grim than it might have been, for New Orleans had two intangible assets which it retains today. First of all, the city had plenty of time to think about reforms—more time, indeed, than it had any right to. As Donald Patton and other careful students of American ports have noted, a port's customers tend to be extremely conservative. New Orleans had accumulated a large body of customers over the decades, and they would drop away most reluctantly.

The city's second asset was and is institutional—a long tradition of intelligent supervision of the port by the city. Under French and Spanish rule all wharfage had been government property and private use was at public pleasure. This arrangement continued under American rule, although somewhat less formally. Thus, the nineteenth century had seen a rather erratic alternation between state and city administration and between public and private supervision of the port's facilities. After the Civil War, the public had surrendered considerable authority to private lessees, who had proved increasingly sloppy as the years went by. When it became clear that something had to be done, there was ample precedent for public interference.

There is no need to plow through the complex sequence of events whereby New Orleans reorganized its port authority. James P. Baughman has carefully described the labyrinthine process, which extended over many years and involved innumerable political bodies. Suffice it that, when New Orleans perceived the port to be endangered, the city and state took drastic action. In 1896, a landmark law was passed by the Louisiana legislature, establishing the Board of Commissioners for the Port of New Orleans, popularly known as the "Dock Board." This law, together with later amendments, gave the board authority over all water frontage in Orleans Parish and considerable portions of river and canal frontage in adjacent parishes. Within this area, the board had authority to expropriate private property, to demolish and rebuild structures at will, to operate any facility that it chose, and, at its pleasure, to lease portions of any facility to private operators.

In most other American cities, such behavior would have been denounced as rampant socialism—which it certainly was. For a city with New Orleans's supposed conservatism, it would appear unorthodox, to put it mildly. But Orleanians took it calmly. The port was simply too important to be left in the hands of inept or slothful operators.

The Dock Board went to work in 1901, zestfully tearing down decrepit facilities and rebuilding according to the latest standards of design. Within the next ten years, a good share of the port had been totally rebuilt and facilities greatly expanded. In the public's name, the board built cotton warehouses, coal and bulk storage facilities, one of the biggest grain elevators in the world, and a host of other things, big and small. To complement the massive building program, the government also took control of waterfront railroad facilities, heretofore fragmented among various competing private companies. Under the aegis of the Public Belt Railroad Commission, the lines were consolidated, rebuilt, and subsequently operated as a unit under city management. Altogether it was a great improvement, eliminating duplication, speeding the movement of goods by more efficient switching, and considerably reducing port costs.

Ignoring details, one should note three things. First of all, the city was willing to use any means necessary to preserve the health of the port. If the means were arbitrary or even socialistic, so be it. Second, there would be no nice regard for political boundaries. If the port spilled over into adjacent parishes and towns, well, then, the old boundaries would be ignored. (The Port of New York Authority would presently discover the same thing indepently, as would the metropolitan governments of Toronto, Miami, and elsewhere much later.) Third, the new facilities had all been built at about the same time, and, as the city would find to its dismay later on, they would all become obsolete at about the same time. But that was a long time in the future, and meantime the port was booming.

THE CROWDING CITY.   New Orleans was booming, too, and, for the first time in the city's history, space was running out. By southern standards New Orleans had always been a crowded city—partly from European architectural tradition and partly because the city had to be packed onto the finite area of the natural levee. Some of the pressure had been relieved as the city began spilling across the river, the result of excellent ferry service and new jobs in large West Bank railyards where transcontinental trains were marshaled before or after crossing the Mississippi River ferries.[12] But the West Bank towns of Algiers and Gretna were still country villages (even though Algiers had been annexed to New Orleans), and most Orleanians preferred the East Bank, especially as streetcar lines got better and people could live considerable distances from

[12] See *Appendix A* for an explanation of the term "West Bank."

their work. (The streetcars had begun going electric in 1893, and by 1902 all lines were consolidated under one management.)

New foreign immigrants increased the pressures still more. Irish and German immigration had subsided after the Civil War, but presently a new wave surged forward—this time Italians who took up the menial jobs that their predecessors were abandoning as they moved up the social and economic ladder. Eventually these Italians were to constitute the city's largest white-ethnic minority and they continued to set New Orleans apart as the only southern city with a substantial number of unassimilated European migrants. Meantime, they added more people to an already crowded city.

Only three options were open to accommodate more people: to expand the city lakeward from the natural levee; to let settlement crawl father and farther along the levee; or to crowd more people onto the same land. The first option—lakeward expansion—was out of the question for the moment. Although several short railways and "shell roads" had been run out to new resorts and amusement parks on the shore of Lake Pontchartrain, the intervening backswamp was still uninhabitable, and the lakeshore was a dangerous place to live. The lake was shallow, and if a storm from the southeast combined with high tides on the Gulf, Pontchartrain had a nasty habit of backing up and flooding everything in sight. A few shoreline residents, mainly fishermen, had solved the problem in Malay fashion, by building wooden shacks on stilts and hoping for the best. Generally, it worked, but not always.

Expansion along the natural levee was limited, too. On the Uptown side, settlement abruptly stopped at the Orleans-Jefferson parish boundary, which happened to be the boundary of the Orleans Parish Levee District. There, a so-called "protection levee" ran back from the river toward Lake Pontchartrain, and while it kept Orleans Parish dry, the neighboring Jefferson Parish Levee District had to fend for itself—which it did badly. On the Downtown side, in the working-class descendent of the old Third Municipality, growth was even more precarious. There, officers of the Orleans Parish Levee District had been less than energetic in providing flood protection in an area whose income and political influence were small. Periodically, parts of the Downtown area found themselves underwater, and new settlers were not eager to share the experience. Expansion downstream was very slow.

The remaining option was to pack more and more people into the same space. That feat was accomplished as land costs rose and the owners of large suburban lots were persuaded to subdivide their holdings into increasingly narrow slices. It did not have to be that way, of course, for there are other obvious ways of increasing urban densities. Philadelphia, Baltimore, and Boston, for example, had built three-story row houses for decades, and New York City had begun erecting walk-up tenements that were even higher. But New Orleans was suspicious of multistory residential quarters—perhaps because it feared that foundation material was inadequate to support big buildings; perhaps because it was just southern enough to insist on keeping houses separated from each other by some kind of yard, no matter how small. Furthermore, the city never took to apartment living, and even row houses were not much favored— this despite the shortage of land.[13] Given the physical constraints and cultural prejudices, however, there was little option but to build long, narrow houses to fit the long, narrow lots.

The architectural results were striking in the extreme. The most popular low-cost house was known as a "shotgun," allegedly because one could fire a shotgun in the front door and have all the pellets emerge from the rear.[14] The shotgun house simply consisted of a string of rooms lined up one behind the other, usually without benefit of a hallway. The gable of the house ran perpendicular to the street, and the house was rarely more than a story and a half high. In its most elementary form, the shotgun could be very crude, serving as what was euphemistically called "rental housing"—more plainly, the cheapest house on the market. Very often, however, the Orleanian penchant for decoration produced at least a modest efflorescence of finials, brackets, and spindles, which latter-day Orleanians have embraced with unrestrained delight. Commoner even than the shotgun was a so-called "bungalow," or "double tenement," which resulted from putting two houses under one roof—each long and low like the shotgun, but with a common inner wall and central gable. (For some reason, Orleanians would accept two houses under one roof, but no more than two.) Bungalows cost more than shotguns usually, and embellishments were commoner. Then, too, to avoid possible danger from a flood, many of them were elevated on pilings five to ten feet high.[15] The result was a very substantial, two-story double house, with the first main floor well above ground

---

[13] The famous Pontalba buildings on Jackson Square—sixteen individual row houses under a single roof— are much admired by Orleanians, but their form was rarely imitated.

[14] It has never been satisfactorily explained why one would wish to do such a thing.

[15] Although New Orleans's houses seldom have cellars, these understories were often scooped out, walled in, and turned into an informal ground floor, which Orleanians call "basements."

level. Even a simple shotgun could be raised in the same way; such a house is called a "raised bungalow," with a higher roofline than an ordinary shotgun, and with a much higher social status.

The shotgun may be the only house-type in America that originated in Africa. Research by John Vlach strongly suggests that the idea came from the Slave Coast, the shore of the Gulf of Guinea between the Ivory Coast and Nigeria, in which such dwellings are common. Vlach believes that the idea crossed the Atlantic with slaves who were brought to Haiti to work in sugar plantations. During the murderous revolution of 1798, black Haitians sought refuge in New Orleans and brought the shotgun idea with them. There, shotguns were found to fit the city's typically long, narrow lots, and were built by the thousands. Furthermore, when Orleanians finished adding their own favorite embellishments—Carpenter Gothic gimcracks, tiled gables, and louvered French doors in front—they looked like nothing else in the United States. Around World War I, New Orleans's builders gradually began adopting other architectural fads, but by then square miles of the city were covered with shotguns, bungalows, and an astonishing variant known as the "camelback," which begins as a one- or two-family bungalow in front, but rises to two stories in the rear.

The result, as of about 1910, was a city that was aggressively *sui generis* in appearance, a place of great charm for natives and visitors alike. Today, unfortunately, the average tourist in New Orleans is unaware of this highly picturesque half of the city—perhaps because unimaginative tourist agencies see nothing extraordinary about this amazing collection of domestic buildings, but more probably because tour directors are ignorant of workaday New Orleans, since they seldom venture beyond their own "approved" Tours-of-the-French-Quarter, Tours-of the-Garden District, Tours-of-the-Cemeteries, and Special-Two-Hour-Tours-of-the-Harbor-by-Boat. Meantime, however, increasing numbers of Orleanians have begun to "restore" middle-aged shotguns and bungalows, sometimes embellishing them strangely with muted Williamsburg hues and Colonial eagles. While the avant-garde may snigger, the results are often charming—as was much of New Orleans itself at the end of the nineteenth century.

PUMPS, CANALS, AND THE SPREADING CITY.   Then, abruptly, everything changed. New Orleans discovered that it had the capacity to drain the backswamp. For better or for worse, New Orleans would never be the same again. A. Baldwin Wood, a gifted engineer and later the director of the city's Sewerage and Water Board, designed a heavy-duty pump that made it possible to raise huge volumes of debris-laden water a short vertical distance, and to do it fast. It was one of those potent inventions that people in later years would take for granted, but just as high speed elevators changed the geography of New York City by making skyscrapers possible, the Wood pump revolutionized the urban geography of New Orleans by suddenly opening to settlement areas which were thought forever closed.[16]

One might have expected that New Orleans would have exploded geographically, just as dozens of northern cities exploded once electric streetcars had made rural areas available for the building of detached suburbs. (To be sure, a few suburbs were planned at the end of car lines on the north shore of Lake Pontchartrain, but the distance was too great to encourage New Orleans to learn new habits of commuting.) Growth did occur, of course, mostly northward toward Lake Pontchartrain, but it was remarkably slow, considering the pressures of population in the old parts of the city. There were several reasons for delay.

First of all, draining the swamp was a major undertaking, requiring money and time. In addition to the pumps (which were huge and very expensive), an ambitious system of new drainage canals had to be built to carry the swamp water to locations where it could be lifted—either to Bayou Bienvenue and thence into Lake Borgne (the usual dumping place) or, in case of serious flooding, via standby canals to Lake Pontchartrain. New levees also had to be built to protect newly drained land. Furthermore, people were learning that swamp "soils" were not soil at all, but a thin gruel of water and organic material that shrank and settled when the water was removed, and then settled some more. Thus, although the backswamp surface had originally stood at about sea level, pumping caused it to drop considerably below sea level. Flood protection had always been important in New Orleans, but in this new city below sea level it was now literally a matter of life or death. Clearly, the Mississippi River levees had to be raised, a whole new network of dikes built along Lake Pontchartrain to keep out tidal surges, and then a line of inner protection levees raised to connect the levee systems of lake and river. Even inside wealthy Orleans Parish, the work turned out to be very costly, and in the thinly populated Jefferson and St. Bernard levee districts large-scale drainage of backswamps was financially out of the question. Thus, while Orleans Parish passed its original legislation to

---

[16] It also revolutionized the geography of the Netherlands. Dutch engineers came to New Orleans to learn how Wood pumps worked, and fifty years later the Zuyder Zee had been drained.

install its pumping system in 1899, and although much of the middle city had been pumped out within another decade, the neighboring parishes would wait another fifty years—until after World War II—before they could install large-scale pumping and drainage facilities.

But even in Orleans Parish conventional buildings could not be erected in the backswamp simply because surface water was removed. Houses, sidewalks, and streets had a disconcerting habit of sinking—unless sand or other permeable material was brought in to form a foundation pad. For bigger structures, piling had to be driven, often to considerable depths. It was costly business.

Expansion into the backswamp, therefore, occurred neither overnight nor in random locations. Subdivisions of the early 1900s were largely concentrated on the natural levees of the old distributary channels—bayous Metairie and Gentilly—where elevations were five to ten feet above sea level and silty soils helped prevent subsidence of foundations. On the margins of the old distributary levees, real estate dealers contrived ingenious ways to make land and thereby money. In Gentilly Terrace, for example, a middle-income development begun around 1910 on the lakeside of Bayou Gentilly, the developer built lots like polders, by the simple expedient of scooping dirt from the streets and piling it up in pads on either side.

Such building was expensive, however, and it had the effect of restricting the northern part of New Orleans to fairly affluent people with white skins. Part of the reason for this racial segregation had legal roots. The early 1900s, after all, saw an outburst of anti-black propaganda and Jim Crow legislation throughout the South, and it was exactly at that time that the city's population began rolling northward toward the lake. Most real estate dealers in the newly drained northern parts of New Orleans simply would not sell to blacks, but even if they had, few blacks could have afforded to live there. North of Metairie Road and Gentilly Boulevard, therefore, the new areas were almost lily white, and even today few blacks live north of that line. Established black neighborhoods continued to expand, however, mainly toward the newly drained margins of the old nineteenth-century "backswamp ghetto." The Wood pump, as it turned out, was a powerful agent to accelerate racial segregation in New Orleans.

Despite the high cost of land, the city continued to creep northward toward Lake Pontchartrain, and the pace increased with the economic boom of the 1920s. With prosperity came new architectural fashions, now for the first time out of the Golden West. It was the day of the California bungalow, but, as with earlier architectural fads, New Orleans added its own touch—white stucco, red-tiled roofs, and an astonishing efflorescence of concrete sculpture, leaning heavily toward human-sized neoclassic urns and sinister cement wolfhounds arranged symmetrically on either side of the front steps. "Mission style" houses also enjoyed great vogue, as real estate developers loudly invoked the city's Spanish ancestry. Today, large areas of north-central New Orleans have the look of a middle-class Hollywood under the reign of Louis B. Mayer. It is not at all unpleasant.

THE NEW LAKEFRONT.   By the mid-1920s, with population moving inexorably in the direction of Lake Pontchartrain, it was obvious that something had to be done about the lakefront. At the most primitive level, the old lakefront levee was inadequate to protect the growing city against floods from the bad-tempered lake. The lakeshore itself was seedy and disagreeable, lined with fishermen's shanties on stilts, and occasionally spotted by amusement parks which were connected with the city by streetcar lines. Thus, it was almost inevitable when, in 1924, the state legislature commissioned the Board of Commissioners of the Orleans Levee District to design and execute a plan that would modernize the levee, make the lakefront more attractive, and simultaneously concoct a scheme whereby the lakefront improvements would pay for themselves. It was a large order, but the Orleans "Levee Board," as it was more commonly known, was equal to the challenge.

Louisiana's levee boards are considerable creatures, mandated by the state constitution not merely to keep their districts dry, but given all kinds of money and power to accomplish that purpose. Boards can levy taxes, expropriate land inside or outside their districts, run rights-of-way through lands belonging to other public bodies, and even maintain their own police forces. They are rich and powerful institutions, especially in wealthy Orleans Parish, and, since board members are appointed by the governor for terms which run concurrently with his or hers, they are intensely political. They may choose to cooperate with municipal governments, but are under no obligation to do so. In effect, the levee boards are worlds unto themselves.

Thus, everybody expected the board's plans to be ambitious, but when they were unveiled even blasé Orleanians were astonished. For five and a half miles, a stepped, concrete sea wall would be built on the floor of Lake Pontchartrain, 3,000-odd feet out from the existing shore. The area enclosed by the sea wall would then be filled, using material pumped in from the lakebottom outside. Behind the sea wall, the filled area was raised five to ten feet above the lake level—which meant that it would be one of the highest parts of the city. When the job was done, New Orleans would gain not merely a better levee, but an entirely new lakeshore, with about 2,000 acres of prime and pristine land which the Levee Board could do with as it wished.

The public development alone was breathtaking. New Orleans, which had spent 200 years cutting itself off from the Mississippi River with an insulating rind of docks, warehouses, and railroad yards, suddenly discovered that it had a clean, public waterfront lined with beaches, boulevards, and parks, not to mention a new municipal yacht harbor. It is some measure of the project's scale that a municipal airport was added to the Lakefront scheme almost as an afterthought. When the airfield was finished in 1934 (with the enthusiastic encouragement of Huey Long), it was one of the biggest and best in the nation.

The Depression came, leaving the Levee Board in sore financial straits, but it merely stimulated the Lakefront development, for much of the construction was taken over by the Works Progress Administration, which simply picked up where the Levee Board had left off. A public work of this magnitude was meat and drink for the WPA, of New Deal fame.

To an outsider, however, perhaps the most astonishing thing about the Lakefront development was the way in which expensive public land was summarily and casually converted to private ownership. To be sure, the Levee Board had to pay off its bonds. Thus, the rental of land to an amusement park or an airport authority could be explained as prudent acts which provided New Orleans with better public facilities and earned a profit at the same time. Nor could anyone object when considerable land was turned over to Louisiana State University for its New Orleans campus after World War II.[17] But about half of the Lakefront project became private real estate, sold by the Levee Board to help pay off bonds. The new developments were elaborately planned, conspicuously the Lake Vista project, designed in the "garden suburb" tradition of Radburn, New Jersey, with a central common, pedestrian avenues, and dead-end streets to provide "sanctuaries" for children. Altogether, it was very handsome, and because it was laid out with public funds, officials were careful to insist that lots would be equally available to rich and poor alike—what Mayor Maestri happily described as the "poor man's project." It seems doubtful if anyone really believed it, considering the premium location and abundant amenities, and nobody was really surprised when Lakefront became the wealthiest area in the New Orleans metropolitan area—amid public outcries that the law had been persistently violated during the auctioning of land. Nevertheless,

---

[17] Louisiana State University in New Orleans (LSU/NO) was renamed the University of New Orleans (UNO) in 1975.

Lakefront was and is an ornament to the city—one of the very few places where twentieth-century city planning truly improved a large area of an American city. Lakefront is a handsome place, no matter what one thinks of the political means by which it was achieved.

A New and Uncertain City (1945–1975)

As in most other cities, the Depression paralyzed New Orleans's booming growth, and while it lasted there was no significant building except for public works projects. World War II brought a return of prosperity, but the shortage of labor and materials continued the moratorium on building, which lasted for several years after Japan's defeat. By the late 1940s things were moving again, but New Orleans found itself in a new kind of world that operated under different rules than it had known before. The new rules, furthermore, were being made in irritating sorts of places—not the Clevelands and Detroits that had overtaken New Orleans in the late nineteenth century by sheer exercise of industrial muscle, but in shiny new air-conditioned cities of the West and South, whose *nouveau riche* economies rested on aircraft, electronics, and sunbathing. It was bad enough to be overtaken by Houston and Dallas-Fort Worth, but quite insufferable when the 1960 census showed Miami and the vexatious Atlanta to be larger than New Orleans. Worse still, there were unsettling changes afoot in New Orleans itself. It was no consolation at all to know that cities all over the nation were sharing a similar trauma.

Changes took various forms, but at least four were so serious that, in combination, they bid fair to convert the city into a fundamentally different kind of place than it had ever been before. At this writing (1975), New Orleans is grappling with all of them and it will doubtless continue to do so with varying degrees of success.

The first was a change in the technology of shipping, which, in turn, threatened the city's economic foundation, the Port of New Orleans. The second change—an irreversible one—was the sudden suburban explosion of New Orleans out of its old confines, menacing the economic and physical integrity of the old city, and confronting adjacent regions with environmental challenges that they were ill-equipped to meet. Third, with suburban sprawl and the growth of black population came a rapid change in the function of the central business district and the adjacent French Quarter. Finally—and closely associated with the suburban explosion—was an ominous growth of segregation in New Orleans, the alienation of black and white populations, and the decay of inner-city neighborhoods and public services. The combination of problems all arriving simultaneously was profoundly disquieting, especially so to Orleanians who were coming to understand that, while their city was unique in many ways, it was not immune to the various ills that America's urban flesh is heir to. As the perceptive A. J. Liebling remarked in 1961 (as quoted earlier): "I realized that New Orleans might be exotic in some respects but that in others it was exactly like everyplace else."

Revolution in the Port

Of the four problems, the most tractable originated in the Port of New Orleans. The Port's difficulties were rooted in technology and were, therefore, subject to technological remedies. But while the problems were curable, they were no less important or expensive. As Professor James Kenyon has demonstrated, New Orleans depends much more heavily on income from overseas maritime commerce than any other large port in the eastern United States. (In 1967, New Orleans received $3,839 per capita in waterborne foreign trade; its closest rivals were Baltimore with $849 and New York City with $842.) Furthermore, its industrial base is relatively small—fourteen percent of its work force in manufacturing, compared with a national average for cities over 200,000 of about twenty-eight percent. Thus, if the port is sick, New Orleans has very little to fall back on save tourism—an enterprise that is notoriously undependable from season to season. Then, too, the scarcity of manufacturing industry means that the Port of New Orleans derives most of its revenue from transshipment of goods, rather than shipment of goods that originate locally. In consequence, New Orleans has a relatively small captive market of shippers who must use the port's facilities. Most of the customers are at least theoretically free to take their business elsewhere.

Competition between ports has always been lively in the United States, but postwar times brought several changes which inflamed that competition and which endangered New Orleans's second rank position among American ports. On the one hand, land transportation was changing. Trucks (and even airplanes) had begun to challenge the railroads' traditional domination of long-distance freight haulage, and by the 1960s the interstate highway system was making all kinds of unlikely places suddenly accessible to cheap, flexible transportation. Simultaneously, railroad mergers meant that companies which had previously funneled all their custom through one preferred port now had several ports to choose from. (Thus, the Illinois Central, which had sent Midwestern produce routinely through New Orleans, merged with the Gulf, Mobile, and Ohio with its own preferred port of Mobile.) And, with completion of the St. Lawrence Seaway in the late 1950s, Chicago suddenly became a deep-water seaport, threatening New Orleans's long-standing domination over Midwestern ocean-going trade.

But the most disruptive change came from new shipping technology—container vessels to begin with, and then, about 1970, barge-carrying ships. It is easy to understand why containers upset old ways, for they represent the genius of simplicity. They are standard-sized steel boxes that can be transferred quickly from the hold or deck of a ship and put on a truck dolly or special flat-car to be hauled away. Although containers can be carried on conventional freighters, specially designed container ships are much more efficient. The 1970 Bechtel Centroport Study noted that a conventional freighter needs two or three days in port to transfer 1,000 to 2,000 tons of cargo; a modern container ship can transfer 5,000 to 10,000 tons in the same time and with small danger of pilferage or damage by weather. The advantage over conventional modes is so great that by 1970 planners were freely forecasting that more than half of all general cargo would soon be diverted from old-fashioned freighters to the new container ships.

Barge carriers are even more unconventional—even mind-boggling. Variously known by the trade names "LASH" (the Central Gulf Steamship Company's "lighter aboard ship" vessel) or Sea-Bee (the Lykes Company's comparable vessel), these cavernous ships are equipped to lift sealed barges of special dimensions into a specially designed hold, where several dozen barges are stacked in long tiers, rather like trays of pizza in a gigantic oven. In some ways, the barges are even more versatile than containers, since they can carry either bulk cargo or general cargo. (On the other hand, containers can be handled by conventional freighters, whereas barges cannot.) The barge carriers, according to the Bechtel study, can unload their tonnage about twice as fast as a container ship, and about ten times as fast as a conventional general cargo ship.

Barge-carrying vessels are so new that it is still unclear exactly what kind of alongshore facilities will be required to handle their cargo. At the moment, port authorities in New Orleans are inclined to favor barge carriers over container ships, since containers can be offloaded onto planes, trucks, barges, or trains, whereas barges are obviously confined to waterways. Thus, New Orleans, at the intersection of the Intracoastal Waterway and the Mississippi River, is clearly better off with barge carriers than is, say, Mobile, Beaumont, or Houston. Longshoremen, too, prefer barges to containers: the need to load and unload containers quickly makes for intensive but erratic employment, whereas barges can be handled in a more leisurely way, thus providing steadier and more reliable jobs. It will be several years, however, before the technology of handling barges is completely worked out. One can only suppose that it will require major changes in the geography and design of the port.[18]

That has already happened with container ships. The vessels are large and make profits only if they are kept moving constantly. It is particularly important that container ships be loaded and unloaded quickly and that port stops be kept to a minimum. To shippers, the new vessels offer unprecedented economies of scale; to port directors they hold out an ominous future, for if one port is equipped to handle containers quickly and efficiently, other competing ports will be bypassed to wither and slowly die. Furthermore, the situation will grow worse for the second runners, since the big East Coast ports are expecting a majority of their general cargo to be handled in containers within a few years—and the most valuable cargo at that.

For New Orleans, then, the message was clear: if the port was to retain its dominance of a midcontinental hinterland and justify its self-styled title of "Centroport, U.S.A.," it would have to build container facilities, and do it before some other enterprising Gulf port had seized the lead. Nor was it merely other Gulf Coast ports that New Orleans had to worry about. New Orleans's far-flung hinterland had brought the city enormous wealth, but the region's very size made it vulnerable to raiding by competing ports, especially along its margins. Thus, distant ports such as New York City or Chicago (or even Oakland-San Francisco) could damage New Orleans badly, providing they had direct connections to parts of New Orleans's hinterland (which they do), and providing they could handle containers faster and, therefore, more cheaply than New Orleans.

Professor Kenyon notes that New Orleans's port directors are—along with their New York City counterparts—among the canniest and most enterprising in the nation, but the New Orleans Dock Board was curiously unenthusiastic about the container business. Kenyon suggests two possible reasons. First of all, seagoing containers are heavier and costlier than land containers and shippers are reluctant to send them very far inland, especially if they must return to port empty. Because New Orleans's trade area covers an abnormally large territory,

[18] As it turned out, barge carriers were much less successful than had been predicted in the early 1970s. By 2000, container technology had come to dominate Port operations in New Orleans. (See "Transformation of the Port" in Chapter 4.)

containers seemed less attractive than they would to New York City or Baltimore, with their smaller, more compact hinterlands. Second, New Orleans trades heavily with "underdeveloped" areas in Latin America, where modern container facilities are unavailable or poorly understood. Whatever the reason, New Orleans delayed so long that it suddenly found most of its port facilities obsolete. Emergency measures were needed. If nothing else, the sudden discovery that Japan, with its supermodern merchant fleet, had become New Orleans's best customer may have prodded the Dock Board into action.

With the same energy with which the city had rebuilt the port at the turn of the twentieth century, New Orleans began again, in the 1960s, to implement a long-term project that was slated to require three decades for completion. This time, however, it was more than a mere overhaul of existing facilities: most of the existing port facilities would be torn down, and the main functions picked up and moved to the east end of the city. It would be the most drastic change in the economic geography of New Orleans since the city's founding. To justify such efforts, of course, the deficiencies of the old port had to be legion.

They were. About the only things the Mississippi River wharves of the early 1900s had to recommend them were their access to the Public Belt Railroad and the fact that they did not stick out into the river—as did New York City's. But for efficient operation, container docks needed large, alongside assembly areas, big open "stuffing sheds," large rear yards for assembly of trucks or railroad cars, and huge expensive cranes for moving containers quickly between ships and marshaling areas. The riverfront was thought to be impossible. Trucks were forced to use crowded city streets, and the expropriation of enough land to make proper facilities available seemed prohibitively costly. No sensible Dock Board would invest in large-scale refurbishing in an area where payoff would be so small.

The Dock Board's decision was to wipe the slate clean and start afresh. By 2000, twenty-nine existing wharves would be retired, leaving only the Henry Clay, Nashville, and Napoleon Avenue wharves open on the river. The rest would be torn down, and if all went as planned, New Orleans would have a riverfront uncluttered by wharves for the first time since Bienville landed. Indeed, if the city's excellent Parks and Recreation Department (NORD) had its way, the city might expect a waterfront park system the equal of any in the nation.

In place of the old facilities, an entirely new port was under construction in the marshes east of the city. The scale was very large, and there are signs already that the new development was pulling the whole metropolitan area in an eastward direction.

The reasons for locating here went back to the 1920s, when the Dock Board and the city collaborated to build a deep-water canal between the Mississippi River and Lake Pontchartrain. This Inner Harbor Navigation Canal (more commonly called the "Industrial Canal") was only incidentally for lake-to-river shipping, for it was presently attached to the Intracoastal Waterway which led off eastward to Lake Borgne and the Mississippi Gulf Coast, thus leaving Lake Pontchartrain more or less free for recreation. But mainly the Industrial Canal was designed to provide more dock space and, equally important, more room for industrial development that the Dock Board hoped to attract to New Orleans. The canal was finished in 1921 and connected to the river by locks in 1923. By 1934 a long-standing project to improve the West Bank Harvey Lock and Canal was finished, linking the Mississippi with Bayou Barataria, western Louisiana, and the Texas Gulf Coast. Both the Harvey Canal and the Industrial Canal became central links in the newly finished Intracoastal Waterway, which, by federal legislation, eventually led from the Rio Grande to the Florida coast. Traffic grew so heavy by 1945 that the Harvey Lock had to be supplemented with another at Algiers.

The whole system worked beautifully, but not exactly as planned. Instead of heavy industry, the Industrial Canal became lined with facilities to serve the bulk cargo barges that plied the Intracoastal Waterway—storage yards for sand and gravel being fairly typical. The salubrity of New Orleans's atmosphere was thereby preserved, but industrial jobs were not created. Indeed, the city's main success in attracting big industry was through the federal government's acquisition of the Michoud Industrial Facility, some dozen miles east of the city, where NASA eventually began building Saturn rockets.[19] The arrangement has been something less than satisfactory, for the Michoud payroll fluctuated wildly, reflecting the fickle congressional enthusiasm for funding space programs.

When the Dock Board decided to build a new Port of New Orleans, however, the obvious location was the junction of the Industrial Canal with the Intracoastal Waterway. Not only was there plenty of open space available (one hesitates to call it "land"), but transportation facilities were also excellent: two mainline railways, Interstate 10, and "MR-GO" (the Mississippi River-Gulf Outlet Canal) were nearby. The MR-GO headed straight for the Gulf, and thus

[19] The Michoud facility probably resulted less from New Orleans's advantageous location on the Intracoastal Waterway than from the power of Louisiana's congressional delegation.

cut off forty miles from the winding river passage. Although it was promoted as a route for deep-sea shipping, it turned out to be no such thing—since to get from MR-GO (near sea level) to the river, some ten feet above, ships had to pass through the Inner Harbor Lock, a passage which often was so backed-up with ships and barges that delays of several days were common. Most ocean ships still came to New Orleans by river, unwilling to risk the cost of delays at the lock.

Such a project would not work, however, unless deep-draft ships could get from the harbor to the Mississippi quickly—and since the Mississippi continues to flow ten to fifteen feet above the new facilities in the backswamp, large-scale locking is necessary. The old Inner Harbor Lock simply would not do, as it was much too small to accommodate the big, fast container ships. Thus, New Orleans's shiny new port will grow cobwebs unless the lock is either enlarged or relocated. As of the early 1970s, according to the Corps of Engineers, it would cost more than $358 million to expand the existing locks, since they are located in expensive built-up land. By contrast, the Corps estimates less than $200 million to build a brand new lock and connecting canal, which would run from the MR-GO to the river at Violet, a village in St. Bernard Parish about ten miles downstream from the present lock. At the present writing (1975), the Violet project is stalled, opposed by downriver residents who fear that a new canal would cut off their escape routes during hurricanes and might act as a funnel for floodwaters into their neighborhoods. The issue remains unresolved, while the Corps of Engineers looks nervously around for alternative locations. Nobody, it seems, wanted a lock in their back yard.

The Suburban Explosion

It is easy to be hopeful about the future of the port, largely because it is firmly controlled by intelligent, responsible people who not only understand how the port works, but also want to make sure it continues working. It is harder to be optimisic about New Orleans's physical growth, especially since the end of wartime building controls in the late 1940s. From that time to the present (1975), the metropolitan area has simply exploded into the swamps—first toward the East Bank section of Jefferson Parish; more recently into the eastern reaches of Orleans Parish and beyond; and, although the main surge is yet to come, now southward from the West Bank in the direction of Bayou Barataria. Between 1950 and 1975, the built-up area of metropolitan New Orleans about doubled in size, and there is little sign that the expansion is subsiding. Because the new additions have been so sudden—and because they are different in population and appearance from the old city—New Orleans has become two cities in the last twenty-five years or so. Within is the compact, old prewar city; around it in all directions is the new exploded tissue of suburbia.

The results have not been fortunate. As in dozens of other North American cities, New Orleans's suburban landscape is compounded of new cars, new roads, an insatiable appetite for inexpensive houses with open space, deficient land-use controls, unrestrained greed by land sellers and house builders, a studied reluctance of municipalities to cooperate with one another, and an almost pathological desire of local governmental officials to see their particular bailiwicks grow.

In addition, however, New Orleans's suburban sprawl is peculiar in several ways. Most of the newly developed land is built on muck and is sinking at various rates. Much of the land is subject to extremely dangerous flooding. And because New Orleans began spreading out later than most American cities, most suburban growth has been compressed into a very short span of time—mostly from 1960 onward. As a result, the new areas lack the architectural variety of places that grew at different times and in different styles. The contrast between homogeneous new suburbs and the extravagantly varied old prewar city is, to put it mildly, invidious.

Until World War II, New Orleans's patterns of urban growth had differed sharply from those of other big American cities. Outside the protection levees, roads were expensive to build and the swampland was atrociously intractable for buildings. The Wood pumps had changed all that by the 1920s, but no sooner had the suburban expansion begun than depression and war combined to smother it.

EAST BANK JEFFERSON.   New roads were abuilding, however, and they would determine the direction in which metropolitan New Orleans would grow. Before World War II, there were two main highway routes out of the city— Chef Menteur Highway to the east and the braided path of River Road and Jefferson Highway westward to Baton Rouge. These roads, and a few other inconsequential roads, were all tied to natural levees, either of the Mississippi or, like the dead-end roads to Lafitte and Yscloskey, of distributaries of the river. The great break came in the early 1930s, when Governor Huey Long, with customary disregard for tradition and the laws of nature, had his new "Airline Highway" built from Baton Rouge to New Orleans—slashed in great expensive swaths across the quivering swamp.

For twenty years, very little happened along Airline Highway—during the

1930s because nobody had money to speculate in real estate, and after the war because nobody wanted to plunge into the swamps as long as alternative land could be had inside the city. To be sure, a few roadside commercial buildings sprang up, but nobody saw them as a portent of the time when Airline Highway would become the longest and ugliest scar of strip commercial development in Louisiana.

Thus, during the 1930s and 1940s and even into the 1950s, the city's main growth was internal—filling up undeveloped interstices or building immediately adjacent to built-up areas. Even today, behind the Lakefront area, one can find patch after patch of houses that might be described as "Cape Cod Veteran," interspersed with the older, more substantial neo-Spanish villas of the 1920s.

Then suddenly, in the late 1950s, New Orleans acted like a pail that had slowly been filling—and spilled over. It was a different sort of expansion than the city had experienced before. No longer did building advance like a wave from established neighborhoods on the edge of the city, but instead began to be spattered in apparently random distribution beyond the Orleans Parish line, generally following the axis of Airline Highway. Jefferson officials, who suddenly found taxes deliciously rising, promptly dubbed the parish "Progressive Jefferson" and began to build new levees and streets as fast as revenues accumulated. That was very fast indeed, for Jefferson was soon to boast the highest per capita income of any parish in Louisiana.

To attract more people (as if they needed attracting), East Bank officials achieved two great coups: the new multilaned Veterans Memorial Highway, which cut straight across the parish to the St. Charles Parish Protection Levee; and the new Moisant Airfield, shortly to become New Orleans International Airport.[20] Meantime, promoters had succeeded in funding the most ambitious project of all, the Lake Pontchartrain Causeway, a twenty-four-mile span to the "Ozone Belt" of St. Tammany Parish—a bucolic area which had long served as retreat for wealthy Orleanians. The causeway was touted as "the World's Longest Bridge," and indeed it proved too long and too costly for easy commuting. The approach to the causeway, however, obviously dubbed Causeway Boulevard, became the main street of East Bank Jefferson, and sprouted strip commercial development which outdid the most egregious developments along Airline or Veterans highways. By 1973, Veterans Highway had accumulated such extraordinary strip commercial blight that the New Orleans *States-Item* ran a series of features about how ugly it was.

[20] And again renamed the Louis Armstrong International Airport in 2001.

The core of East Bank Jefferson was quintessentially suburban, the huge Lakeside Shopping Center, set in a great desert of asphalt parking lots. Along Causeway Boulevard a crop of boxlike buildings emerged, and the Jefferson promoters promptly dubbed the whole area "Fat City," an elegant phrase which describes what presumably happened to the pocketbooks of those who were clever enough to buy or rent land there.

Just as the neo-Los Angeles landscape of East Bank Jefferson differed from old New Orleans by some light years, the population also differed. The area's high average income did not result from any large influx of the very rich. Rather it was a combination of middle-and upper-middle-income migration of whites, together with the fact that black people and poor people were discouraged from moving to Jefferson by economic and other constraints. A comparison of contemporary racial and income maps of New Orleans shows the results of the process by 1970: the most extensive areas of poverty in East Bank Jefferson correspond to a few patches of black population near Airline Highway and the Illinois Central Gulf Railroad tracks. At the other end of the scale, there is only one area of very rich people, the plush neighborhoods of old Metairie, focused on the Metairie Country Club, cheek by jowl with the Orleans Parish line. In sum, the only important departures from middle and upper income were inherited from prewar times.[21]

By the early 1970s most of the land in East Bank Jefferson had been used up. The completion of I-10 across the parish to center-city New Orleans—the road replete with four gigantic cloverleaf interchanges—simply brought coals to Newcastle, and by 1973 the whole area from Orleans Parish to the St. Charles protection levee resembled one gigantic ill-planned subdivision.[22] And, as typically happens in the last stage of building a subdivision, the last areas are filled up with multifamily buildings, heavily populated by young couples with young children who are using the "garden" apartments of new *new* Jefferson as a camping ground until they acquire enough money to move elsewhere. By 1973,

[21] It is of little comfort to know that the same kind of intraurban migration has occurred within dozens of other American cities since World War II. In nearly all of them, the migration has caused suburbs to be more and more homogeneous, the central cities increasingly alienated from the middle class.

[22] Beyond, in St. Charles Parish, I-10 is built on concrete piles, and for ten miles it cuts through an almost pristine wilderness of marsh grass and cypress. To drive from St. Charles's wild beauty and cross the protection levee into Jefferson's endless suburbia is surely one of the most jarring cultural shocks awaiting a motorist anywhere in America.

however, more than forty percent of the New Orleans metropolitan population lived in Jefferson Parish—a population increasingly distinguished by medium-high income, medium-high educational levels, and a lack of domestic roots. It is easy to find people who are fond of old New Orleans. It is almost impossible to find people who are in love with Jefferson Parish, and it shows in the look of the place.

EASTERN NEW ORLEANS.   Interstate 10 was merely the last in a series of high-ways which "opened up" East Bank Jefferson, but the process was almost fin-ished anyway. In eastern Orleans Parish between the Industrial Canal and the Rigolets, however, I-10 was the open sesame which by the early 1970s was con-verting swamps into a vast new opportunity for suburbanization. And beyond in the piney hills of St. Tammany Parish, of Hancock and Pearl River counties, Mississippi, real estate speculators were beginning to multiply like rabbits.

As of the early 1960s, eastern New Orleans showed signs of duplicating the experience of East Bank Jefferson only ten years later. Already helter-skelter strip-commercial and residential building had begun to spring up along the relocated Chef Menteur Highway, which struck out across the wetlands in a manner reminiscent of Airline Highway. So far there was no interstate highway, and the delay had given land speculators a chance to learn the astronomical profits that could be turned by securing large chunks of land along a proposed interstate corridor and holding onto it. Thus, it was that huge new land devel-opments were neatly arranged along the whole right-of-way of the new I-10 East—with the warm cooperation of the Louisiana Highway Department, which built large interchanges in advance of subdivision building. When I-10 was connected to the mainland by a gigantic causeway-cum-bridge across the east end of Lake Pontchartrain, there remained little doubt about the direction of New Orleans's main growth for the next few years.

By the 1970s suburban construction was already under way and on a grand scale, with several enormous projects contemplated for the future. The largest was called "New Orleans East," fifty square miles (32,000 acres) owned by a single corporation. According to promotional literature, it will be a "totally planned community where 250,000 people will eventually live, work, and play." The advertisement goes on to observe that "it is the largest singly owned parcel of land to lie within the corporate limits of any major city . . . and is equal to one-fourth the total area of New Orleans itself." As of 1973, pieces of

New Orleans East had begun to appear, with billboards at big new freeway interchanges, and bits and pieces of actual development here and there. Much of it seems to portend another East Bank Jefferson, but one must be comforted in the knowledge that it had all been planned in advance.[23]

Still farther out, beyond the Rigolets, other big developments were under construction. One of them, called "Eden Isles," a large area of marsh on the edge of St. Tammany Parish, advertised itself as a "total community," offering "a refuge for Orleanians fleeing the noise and congestion of the city," and promoting its virtues vigorously over local television. Frontage on water was guaranteed for nearly all residential lots by the simple expedient of making land by digging canals, thus making the whole area look like a large marina. According to the promotional literature, "sites are raised to a minimum of 6 1/2 feet above mean sea level," and Everyman had access to Lake Pontchartrain, the Rigolets, and Mississippi Sound merely by getting into his boat and sailing out from the dock in his front yard.

THE MENACE OF HURRICANES AND STORM SURGES. Such developments are raising serious questions about the wisdom, much less the safety, of the new New Orleans. Subsidence is a nagging and expensive problem everywhere. New houses are commonly built on concrete pads, laid on sand, and undergirded by thirty-foot piles sunk into the mush on four-foot centers and held firm by a process delicately known as "skin friction." Such heroic tactics add considerably to the cost of building and they prod developers into selling property as quickly as possible, even though it might be wiser to let it settle for a few years. As a result, a new owner often has the enriching prospect of watching yard, driveways, and sidewalks sink, while his or her house stands firm, sup-

---

[23] Despite planning, New Orleans East was one of many enterprises that went bankrupt with the oil crash of the 1980s. Although the original developers abandoned the huge site, they left behind fragments of completed streets and a few houses. With the passage of time, buyers scooped up fragments of property at bargain-basement prices and, in the absence of effective zoning, built a ragtag-and-bobtail assemblage of cheap houses, apartments, and strip-commercial buildings, a far cry from the original grandiose scheme. For all that, many middle-class blacks in New Orleans's inner-city ghettos saw these ad hoc developments as an opportunity to escape the city's crime and poverty and establish themselves in new quarters. However untidy the new developments looked, by the turn of the Millennium residential quarters in New Orleans East were considerably cleaner and healthier than those in the old ghetto. Thus, while the original developers of New Orleans East aimed their marketing at middle-class and upper-middle-class whites, by the 2000 census most of those whites had decamped, leaving the area as one of the most solidly black areas in the city–and the *only* major middle-class black suburb in the whole metropolitan area.

ported by skin friction. (If the water mains or sewers are sheared away, it becomes even more exciting.) By the time the area is ditched and sprayed against mosquitos, there may be nothing more than a broken driveway to remind the owner that he or she is living in a reclaimed swamp. Memories are short.

Some reminders would be helpful, however, if only for public safety. The main danger in eastern New Orleans is from hurricanes, which frequently and randomly strike the Gulf Coast of the United States with varying degrees of ferocity. Two recent hurricanes—"Betsy" in September of 1965 and "Camille" in August of 1969—have been extensively documented by the U.S. Army Corps of Engineers, and although the Corps is too politic to say so in plain language, the reports make it clear that extensive building in the marshes of eastern Orleans Parish is inviting serious trouble.

The worst threat from hurricanes does not come from high winds, even though wind velocities, which in Camille exceeded 200 miles per hour, can and did shred wooden houses to toothpicks. Rather, the main dangers are "tidal surges," fearful events which occur when high tides are pushed by high winds into constricted channels. On August 17, 1969, in the cold language of the engineers' report on Camille: "at Pass Christian on the Mississippi coast a reliable high-water mark of 22.6 feet was found; less reliable debris marks of 24.6 and 24.2 were also found in the vicinity." Shortly before, the storm had "sideswiped the mouth of the Mississippi River" with "estimated wind velocities of 140 to 160 mph . . . while tide levels up to elevation 16 feet above mean sea level overwhelmed the protective levee system and flowed into the developed areas."

Camille is supposed to have been the worst storm to hit any North American coast in recorded history, and it is easy to believe. Where the storm struck Mississippi's coast, it wiped out large parts of Pass Christian and neighboring towns, killed 137 people, and did more than a half a billion dollars worth of damage in Mississippi and Alabama alone. Barrier islands with significant roads and buildings were simply swept clean. All sign of human occupance was simply erased.

It is worth remembering that Camille missed New Orleans by some fifty miles, but, even so, much of southeastern Louisiana was flooded. It is worth remembering, too, that Betsy, although a milder storm than Camille, approached the city on a disturbingly unpredictable course, caused "massive breaks" in the levee system below the city, and flooded huge areas of eastern

Orleans Parish, then uninhabited, but now slated for "planned residential development."

Real estate developers are reassuring, however. In the Eden Isles subdivision with its sea-level canals and residential lots six and a half feet above sea level, the advertisements read: "Eden Isles . . . for the rest of your life!" To ensure long life, the state of Louisiana has helpfully erected signs along highways, directing people how to get out. During Camille, some 69,400 people were evacuated from flooded areas in southern Louisiana, but, as the report of the Corps of Engineers chillingly comments: "in the heavily developed areas of metropolitan New Orleans with a population of over 1 million, prestorm evacuation in most cases is not feasible." It is, therefore, a relief to know that New Orleans East developers anticipate a population of a mere quarter million, most of whom have not read the engineers' report, which explains why damage estimates may not be very reliable: "Surveyors must use judgment based on available evidence to decide whether waters floated the structure and the winds subsequently demolished it, or whether floating debris driven by wave action in an area of high surges pounded the structure, or if a combination of two or more of these factors constituted the force of major destruction."

Meantime, construction goes on, and Greater New Orleans grows greater by the day. And real estate advertisements wax eloquent about marinas, golf courses, and fun-in-the-sun, but remain strangely quiet about hurricanes.

THE WEST BANK.   Growth on the West Bank, both in Orleans and Jefferson parishes, has been a trifle less hair-raising, having lagged behind the East Bank because it is awkward to get back and forth across the Mississippi. There are two automobile bridges in the metropolitan area—the Huey P. Long Bridge, inconveniently located upstream in Jefferson Parish and built to accommodate the narrow vehicles of the 1930s; and the Greater New Orleans Bridge, which offers a splendid view of the river and business district for drivers waiting in the middle of the bridge for traffic to become unjammed. Frustration has mounted, and new bridges have been proposed at several Uptown locations, midpoint between the older two. Napoleon Avenue was the site of one such proposal, but it was greeted with cries of outrage from Uptown residents, who exhibited selfish prejudices against ripping out oak-lined boulevards to build four-lane, divided, and elevated bridge ramps. Meantime, other promoters had evidently learned the lessons of I-10 and began urging a southerly "bypass" around New Orleans, variously proposed as I-29, or I-410, or the "Dixie Freeway."

Few responsible people really believe that such a road is needed for purposes of bypassing New Orleans. Transcontinental traffic stays north of Lake Pontchartrain and has no reason to come near New Orleans. Intracity traffic that wishes to avoid traffic jams in the downtown area can use I-610, which cuts straight across the city's midriff and misses the central business district by two miles. The proposed project *does* have two purposes, but neither have anything to do with "bypassing." First, the West Bank would get one and possibly two new bridges that would be part of the federal interstate system and, thus, under federal law, transfer ninety percent of the cost from the Baton Rouge highway budget and pass it on to Washington. Second, if the road cut far enough southward, it would "open" all kinds of new territory for suburban development.

Critics of the proposal point out that much of the territory is not merely swampland, but is actually under many feet of water. They also note that the project impinges on a proposed national park south of New Orleans. They charge that the real estate promoters are not looking for a bypass at all, but that they got advance inside information on where the "bypass" would be located, bought up the land, and are simply waiting for the road to be built—thus making enormous profits at public expense. The promoters naturally deny any wrongdoing, and counter by arguing that the road is "needed" because the West Bank's main artery—the West Bank Expressway—is no expressway at all, and is dangerous. While that happens to be true, it is less than persuasive, since the expressway could easily be improved by building an elevated highway down its wide neutral ground. This suggestion is generally ignored, since it is plain that many West Bankers (and speculators with West Bank real estate holdings) simply want new roads and bridges—and without more argument. Possibly it escapes West Bankers that completion of the project might quickly turn the area into a 1980 version of East Bank Jefferson. The promoters obviously know that, and if the public does not, it is merely because they do not keep their eyes open. Perhaps, in view of what has already happened to so much of New Orleans's suburbia, the public feels the issue is lost, and no longer cares.

Changes in the Core

When a city suddenly develops a suburban ring such as the one in New Orleans, the new growth represents more than mere territorial addition. It is a jarring change that sends shock waves through the entire metropolitan area, but nowhere more intensely felt than in the central city. At the root of things are demographic shifts, and a selective migration of people. It has happened over and over again in American cities, large and small. Just as the new suburbanites are overwhelmingly white and generally affluent, the central city is left with a disproportionate number of nonwhites, many of whom are poor and poorly educated. Furthermore, the suburbanites take their wealth with them, not only eroding the tax base of the central city, but eventually causing jobs to move out as well. In 1970 in the New Orleans metropolitan area, for example, only thirty-nine percent of Jefferson Parish's work force commuted to Orleans Parish. Of the Orleanians themselves, some twenty-three percent worked outside the parish. Farther out the figures were even lower, and in St. Tammany—which advertises itself as "close to downtown New Orleans"—only seventeen percent actually worked in New Orleans.

Retail stores move to the suburbs even faster than jobs. Thus, a suburban worker may commute into the city, but he or she does all the shopping in a neighborhood shopping center. The New Orleans City Planning Commission in 1970 reported that the central business district's share of total metropolitan area retail sales dropped steadily—from forty-two percent in 1948, to thirty-four percent in 1954, to twenty-seven percent in 1958, to twenty-four percent in 1963.

New Orleans, however, is better off than the numbers suggest. The city's 24 percent in 1963 compares marvelously with such places as Dallas or Phoenix, whose central business districts retained less than nine percent of metropolitan retail sales. Furthermore, in absolute volume of retail sales, downtown New Orleans is palpably alive—especially at night, when most American cities have barred their windows and abandoned the streets. When Orleanians go out for a night on the town, they still customarily head for the central part of the city.

Most Americans quite properly view decaying downtowns as symptoms of general urban rot—or, even more broadly, of a rotting society. When a city such as New Orleans turns out to be partly immune to a nationwide disease, it is worthwhile inquiring into the cause of immunity. Fortunately, the causes of downtown health are fairly obvious in New Orleans, but, less fortunately, many American cities are incapable of profiting from the New Orleans experience. For them, it is simply too late.

First of all, the processes of downtown decay started fairly recently in New Orleans compared with other cities. The delay was largely a function of delayed suburbanization, which, in turn, resulted from the high cost of draining surrounding swamplands. (Most cities have not had the advantages of location in a morass.) Second, despite suburban sprawl, New Orleans remains a fairly compact place, and from most parts of the metropolitan area downtown is not very far away. Third, as all Orleanians know, and as professors Chai and Juhn of UNO have shown, the city has for a long time been informally governed by a very conservative elite who feel fiercely possessive about their city and who are very slow to make major changes. This conservative group has often been damned by "progressive" elements in the city, but despite the conservatives' alleged sins and wickednesses, they deserve much credit for preventing the orgy of downtown destruction that eviscerated so many American cities in the name of "urban renewal," and that has so obviously speeded the exodus to the suburbs elsewhere. St. Louis, to name but one, discovered its mistake after the destruction was over, and by then the city was almost beyond salvation. In New Orleans, they made the discovery by accident, but possibly just in time.

Salvation of and by the French Quarter

No explanation of the vitality of New Orleans's downtown would make any sense unless there had been a solid physical core of architectural interest and permanent population on which to build. That core is the Vieux Carré—the old "French Quarter"—without which New Orleans's downtown area would probably not be very different from any other old American seaport. The "Quarter," as Orleanians call it, performs several vital functions simultaneously.

Most important, the Quarter serves as the city's chief symbolic totem, and most city residents love it dearly. To be sure, some Orleanians profess to loathe it—because it is "dirty" or "dangerous" or "full of hippies and tourists" or simply because "it isn't the way it used to be." While there is much truth in these complaints, it is also true that most Orleanians feel strongly about the Quarter because it is the real and symbolic core of the city and everybody knows it.

Second, the Vieux Carré attracts large numbers of tourists, who stay out until all hours of the night and spend large sums of money. The best estimates come from a 1965 survey by Hammer, Green, Siler Associates, who found that 1,800,000 people came to New Orleans during the year and spent about $170 million—which makes tourism the second largest moneymaker in the city.[24] The survey found that most tourists, furthermore, were "influenced" by existence of the Quarter in their decision to visit New Orleans—and that tourists who stayed in the Quarter spent more than their counterparts who lived outside. Since the time the survey was made, a good many more hotels have been

[24] By the turn of the twenty-first century, tourism would be number one, and by a wide margin.

built downtown, and these figures probably need to be multiplied by a factor of two or three.

A sizable proportion of tourists, it turns out, come from the Midwest—more even than from Louisiana, Texas, and Mississippi combined. And despite the popular image of Midwestern tourists as clean-cut Disneyland-visiting families with 2.3 children, New Orleans's tourist population includes a considerable number of people who have heard that the Quarter is eccentric and hope for a chance to exhibit a bit of their own eccentricity. It is hard to know exactly how many Bohemians and small-town southern runaways come to the Quarter for that reason, nor is it easy to estimate how many Dr. Jekylls check into French Quarter hotels and emerge half an hour later as Mr. Hydes. There is, of course, a sizable admixture of "ordinary tourists," some of whom come to see the sights, to buy antiques on Royal Street at inflated prices, or merely to watch the year-round carnival that the Uptown end of Bourbon Street has recently become. Whoever the clientele may be, the New Orleans police understand them very well, and all sorts of aberrant behavior is tolerated in the Quarter (especially on Bourbon Street) that would subject perpetrators to instant arrest in other cities, not to mention other parts of New Orleans.

To a good many Orleanians, however, the Quarter's eccentric image is a mixed blessing. A 1969 Gallup Poll caused much anguish when it announced a general public appraisal of American cities. New Orleans, it turned out, stood highest in public esteem for its fine restaurants (only New York City and San Francisco were ranked higher)—no surprise after the Hammer, Green, Siler survey that found a good many people visited New Orleans primarily to eat or be seen eating at elegant places. In addition, New Orleans ranked high (fifth in the nation) for being "interesting and different," and even received "honorable mention" for its "gay night life" and its "beautiful setting"(!). But to the dismay of the Chamber of Commerce, the list of twenty cities perceived as "good places to live" omitted New Orleans entirely. Shortly thereafter the city raised the budget of the Tourist and Convention Commission considerably, and that body began energetically to advertise the city's virtues for homebodies as well as sinners. It has not proved easy. New Orleans has apparently been associated with Bourbon Street too long to acquire a reputation for domestic tranquility overnight.

Irrespective of publicity and hoopla, however, the Vieux Carré's ancient and not-so-ancient buildings provide desirable homes for a very small population of permanent residents. Some of these residents are drifters with marginal incomes; there are still plenty of dilapidated houses in the Quarter. But increasing numbers are affluent folk who pay dearly for the privilege of living in the Quarter and parking their Mercedes-Benz in a Spanish courtyard. In the two Vieux Carré census tracts, for example, the median 1970 value of an "owner-occupied housing unit" came to $44,100 and $37,000 respectively—this against a metropolitan area median figure of $20,000. Most dwellings in the Quarter, however, are neither single houses nor owner-occupied. Rather, most are in multiunit buildings, apartments with smaller and fewer rooms than in other parts of the city. The population that inhabits such places includes many single people and childless couples—well-educated people whose relatively high incomes give them considerable surplus to buy creature comforts. In population, then, the Quarter's permanent population seemingly resembles that of Greenwich Village, but there is a major difference. Manhattan would survive quite nicely without the Village, but without the Vieux Carré center-city New Orleans might very well be an empty shell.

Obviously, the preservation of the Vieux Carré has served New Orleans very well, but unhappily for other cities that might learn from New Orleans's example, preservation until recently was largely accidental. For most of the nineteenth century, the Quarter was ignored by Americans who were too busy pushing their brash new city upriver to pay attention to the crowded old European town. Meantime, many old Creole families stayed in their familiar homes, sheltered against the world outside, but the years were taking their toll. New generations moved out to cleaner and airier quarters, while old buildings crumbled. (Fortunately, the crumbling was slow, since many of the old Spanish buildings were very stoutly built.) By the beginning of the twentieth century, much of the Quarter had suffered severely—not so much from rot, as from attrition by the city along the edges. On the Uptown side, Iberville Street had become a kind of alley to service the rear of Canal Street stores. Rampart Street, of proud name, faced on the abandoned Carondolet turning basin and the Storyville red-light district and had gone to ruin. Along the waterfront, a thick growth of docks and warehouses had cut once-lovely Jackson Square completely off from the river, and Decatur Street was spotted with seamen's bars and flophouses. Toward Esplanade Avenue, skid row was alive and well. In sum, the Vieux Carré was being affected by adjacent areas, but it was doing precious little affecting itself.

It is unclear exactly why New Orleans began to pay attention to the Quarter and to regard it once more as the core of the city. To be sure, the city had always felt sentimental about it, even as it fell apart, and slim volumes of pencil sketches periodically appeared to remind Orleanians that they did not need to visit Tintern Abbey to see genuine ruins. The official pamphlet of the Vieux Carré Commission is typically vague: "With the coming of the 1920's and '30's there was a rebirth of feeling for the Vieux Carré—and New Orleans began at long last to realize that unless something was done to preserve what was left, that soon the whole Quarter would disappear." The remark implies some spontaneous generation of interest, but as John Chase has observed (in *Frenchmen, Desire, Good Children . . .*), it was the WPA that was chiefly responsible for showing Orleanians what they had and how to preserve it.

Perhaps there is a lesson: outsiders sometimes are useful for showing natives the virtues of their home places. However it happened, a state constitutional amendment in 1936 authorized creation of a "Vieux Carré Commission," with power to regulate architecture through control of building permits. Meantime, with WPA money and talent, substantial parts of the Quarter were reconditioned, with primary attention to the area around the French Market and Jackson Square, where five crucial buildings were restored—St. Louis Cathedral, the Cabildo and Presbytère next door, and the two superb Pontalba buildings that flank the square.

As tourists flocked in, it quickly became obvious that rehabilitation was not merely an exercise for aesthetes, but would pay handsomely. It also became clear that the processes of slum-making had been reversed. Land values began to rise, and rehabilitations were increasingly financed by private capital.

It was not done without a fight, of course, and again New Orleans's experience may be applicable elsewhere. The Vieux Carré Commission exercised its authority with vigor, insisting that the Quarter's Mediterranean character be retained. It was, in consequence, routinely denounced as "standing in the way of progress." That it was, if one accepts the usual definition of "progress" as meaning the demolition of distinguished old buildings to make room for new ones of any sort. But the commission's goals were both comprehensive and subtle, and its successes can be credited in large part to its steering a careful and credible path between two insupportable extremes. At the one extreme, the commission did not attempt to freeze the Vieux Carré in the manner of a Colonial Williamsburg; instead, it recognized that, for the Quarter to survive, it had to perform a contemporary function, and that meant change was inevitable. At the other extreme, the commission did not pin its hopes on preserving a handful of "historic" buildings and letting the rest go hang—in the manner of preservationists in too many other American cities and towns where "historic sites" are surrounded by white picket fences and used car lots. Rather, it argued that the Quarter's value stemmed from a quality of total environment—the *"tout ensem-*

ble," they called it—which required that any change, even to modern buildings, had to be in keeping with that environment. Enforcing this viewpoint, of course, put the commission into conflict with innumerable developers and speculators to whom the *"tout ensemble"* was merely an unpronounceable impediment to quick profit. But the Supreme Court of Louisiana endorsed the commission's authority in a landmark 1941 decision that kept the commission in business and saved the integrity of the Quarter.

But the Vieux Carré's defenders won their greatest success in the early 1960s when they beat back federal plans to build an elevated interstate highway along the Mississippi. This "Riverfront Expressway" (I-310) was promoted as an essential part of an "integrated" transportation network for the city, but opponents retorted that the highway would form a Chinese Wall between the Quarter and the river and would ruin Jackson Square and the French Market—the very vitals of the Quarter. The arguments were butressed by a multivolume study of the Vieux Carré—organized by the Bureau of Government Research, but to which all manner of Orleanians and outsiders contributed time and money, and which still remains the definitive study of the Quarter. The expressway fight will be remembered for a long time, for it turned old friends into bitter enemies and shook the city to its roots. But the result was total victory for the preservationists and humiliating defeat for the highwaymen, who took their plans elsewhere. Outside New Orleans, it will be remembered as one of the first times that the federal highway establishment was forced to cancel a major urban highway project for environmental reasons.

The New Orleans victory gave heart to others in San Francisco, Nashville, Washington, D.C., and elsewhere who subsequently fought and defeated the powerful federal highway lobby on similar grounds. There is no monument on the riverfront at Jackson Square to mark this victory, but there should be.

There is no danger any more that interstate highways will be put through the French Quarter. If anything, the Quarter is endangered by too much success, as more and more people compete for the same space. In a free market, there would be little doubt how the issue would be resolved. Hotels, restaurants, and nightclubs would spread rapidly into the Vieux Carré, and a substantial part of the Quarter has already taken on such functions. But without the stern hand of the Vieux Carré Commission, it would be only a matter of time before the whole Quarter would be overrun by tourist facilities, and indeed many Orleanians complain that has already happened. While that is not quite true as yet, the pressure from tourism has already changed the Quarter substantially, and in consequence the Quarter itself is profoundly affecting adjacent areas.

The main pressure is from Canal Street, the traditional commercial center of New Orleans, where new high-rise hotels have been built just outside the jurisdiction of the Vieux Carré Commission. The largest is the forty-two story Marriott Hotel, with nearly a thousand guest rooms and a drive-in "motor lobby," but the Marriott merely portends bigger things to come. It is also a measure of what would have gone inside the Quarter, had not the Commission imposed a ban on high buildings and on new hotels inside the Vieux Carré. Meantime, as commercial tourist facilities press downriver into the Quarter, rents are rising ahead like the swell that precedes a breaking wave. These increased rents have already caused speedy renovation of old houses on the Downtown side of the Quarter, and areas that were only recently slums have suddenly become fashionable. Most of the black population, unable to afford the new high rents, decamped several years ago, and it grows increasingly hard for white people of medium income to keep even modest apartments. Meantime, the city has renovated the old French Market and opened Jackson Square to the river—a decision partly prompted by the Dock Board's abandonment of obsolete docks along the Mississippi.

As these two waves of higher rent roll downstream and lakeward, genuine residential neighborhoods are being squeezed into the northeast corner of the Quarter. Middle-income white people are fleeing across the Esplanade downstream into old Faubourg Marigny, where early Victorian shotgun houses are emerging with newly painted brackets and the "For Sale" signs of fashionable realtors. As might be expected, the ghetto is recoiling under the pressure of higher rents, and Faubourg Marigny is being transformed as the Quarter had been transformed years before.[25] One can applaud the architectural results, but the continued displacement of blacks and compression of already overcrowded ghettos is disquieting, to say the very least.

Texas in Downtown New Orleans: Superdome and Rivergate

The profoundest effect of the refurbished Quarter was felt on its Uptown side toward lower Canal Street, New Orleans's traditional business district. Had New Orleans been an ordinary city, lower Canal Street might have gone the way of lower Woodward Avenue in Detroit, the way of old main streets in innumerable American cities. Indeed, the lower two blocks of Canal had been

---

[25] Exactly the same process, in Washington, D.C., transformed Old Georgetown in the 1930s and is now working along the edges of Capitol Hill.

lined with seedy bars and what were euphemistically called "hotels," and blight was slowly spreading up the street toward Maison Blanche, the city's biggest department store. Several things reversed the process, however, so that today lower Canal Street is taking on a newly scrubbed countenance of shiny prosperity.[26]

The Quarter was the main cause. Lower Canal had served as a kind of osmotic membrane between the Vieux Carré and the central business district, so that when the Quarter began to revive, nourishment seeped across into the business district itself. Then, with the Dock Board's decision to abandon its riverfront wharves, there came a chance to open up Canal Street to the Mississippi and revive the ancient liaison between the city and its river. It all began with the huge new Rivergate project, whose central figure is the thirty-three-story World Trade Center and the Rivergate Exhibition Center just behind it. Unlike so many other big convention centers, which appear to have been dropped into an urban wasteland as if in desperation, the Rivergate Center achieved instant success, though its success is more a result than a cause of what lies nearby. The Trade Center houses many of the city's port-related activities—consulates, shipping lines, and the Dock Board—while convention-eers across the street at the Rivergate find themselves in one of the happiest urban environments in America. To one side is the Mississippi, with its ferry boats and excursion ships; to the other are a dozen excellent hotels, history and doughnuts seven blocks away at Jackson Square, antiques on Royal Street, strip joints on Bourbon Street, and a good many of America's best restaurants scattered between. The Rivergate's promoters advertise persuasively that the facility is within easy walking distance of everything, which is true if "everything" in New Orleans is confined to a few blocks in the southwestern one-fourth of the Vieux Carré. If tourists pay attention to the advertising, that is very nearly all they will see; routinely, many tourists come away from New Orleans having walked up Bourbon Street for four blocks, and returned on Royal. It is a pity, for there is more to New Orleans than one corner of the French Quarter, charming as that corner may be.

The Rivergate was finished in 1968, the Marriott Hotel in 1972. Neither could have succeeded without the Vieux Carré next door. Farther away, however, the business district was in sore straits, and uptown beyond Common Street things went downhill rapidly. The trouble went back to the nineteenth

---

[26] That turnaround was temporary. By the end of the twentieth century, the fortunes of lower Canal Street were very much in question.

century, when the Uptown area was flanked on riverside by docks and rail-roads, on lakeside by the old canal turning basin, railroads, and warehouses. Between these two poles, St. Charles Avenue made its way uptown past Lafayette Square and Lee Circle, once a lovely part of the city, now becoming skid row. Things were bad enough when the railroads and riverside docks were healthy, but after World War II both went into decline, and so did the business district between. The coup de grâce fell with completion of the Greater New Orleans Bridge, whose elevated ramps cut straight across the area to finish the job of neighborhood ruin.

It is something near a miracle that downtown decay was gradually reversed, but the technique turned out to be more expensive and even more controversial than renewal of the Vieux Carré. As the Uptown side of the business district visibly came to pieces, it was plain that the blight would spread unless a barrier were erected against it. That barrier had to stand somewhere between the bridge ramps and the still healthy fringes of the Common Street financial district. The logical line was a compromise along Poydras Street, which runs diagonally between the foot of Canal and City Hall.

The city was obviously incapable of rebuilding Poydras Street, but it could and did build anchors at either end of Poydras, and then actively encouraged new construction along the intervening distance. The Rivergate would furnish one anchor, its strength guaranteed by proximity to the Quarter. The northern end of Poydras posed the real problem, and although activity buzzed around the new civic center with its boxlike city hall, state and city fathers decided that more heroic measures were needed. New Orleans would build a "domed stadium" to house athletic events and large conventions and be a magnet of activity which would complement the Rivergate complex at the other end of Poydras.

There is nothing unusual about civic stadiums, of course. Indeed, New Orleans was overdue for one. The annual Sugar Bowl football extravaganza had outgrown the old Tulane Stadium, and the arrival of the New Orleans Saints had created mild hysteria for the home football team. What was extraordinary about the stadium was the Babylonian scale of the whole thing—more properly it was Texan, both in size and inspiration.

Physically, it would be big enough "to put the Houston Astrodome in the end zone," as one enthusiast prophesied. It would be named the "Louisiana Superdome," with 72,000 permanent seats and room for more on the floor. The dome would rise twenty-seven stories above the old railroad yards and be altogether the most visible thing in New Orleans—perhaps in the whole South. (It is advertised, without conscious comparison to St. Peter's Cathedral, as the "world's largest room unobstructed by posts.") Never mind that it was originally estimated to cost $35 million but turned out to cost almost five times that much.[27] Never mind if skeptics sneered that the Superdome would be filled only half a dozen times a year, and then its departing crowds would create Texas-sized traffic jams. Never mind that its legislative foundation was slippery, and the cost of retiring bonds might hang like an incubus on New Orleans's financial back for generations to come.[28] If Houston had its Astrodome, New Orleans would have its Superdome, bigger and perhaps better. Superdome politics have a familiar Louisiana ring about them—and while the financing is quintessential Huey Long, the whole scale of the thing is ostentatiously un-Orleanian.

For the Superdome is more than just a very large building. It is a symbol of fundamental change in New Orleans's psychology from the old days when the city was run by a handful of old-timers, whose status was confirmed by membership in one of the elite "krewes" —the secret societies that ostensibly organized Mardi Gras parades and balls, but additionally organized New Orleans's formal and informal government. The old, closed, conservative city was open for business, and open with a vengeance, all with a very strong flavor of Texas and Hollywood. Blue bloods watched in horror, as a new Mardi Gras krewe called "Bacchus" was organized—its membership publicly bourgeois. Bacchus's fourth king, for example, was not an old-time Bourbon, but comedian Bob Hope, specially imported from Hollywood to play the role. In olden days, Hope might have been challenged to a duel under the oaks at dawn. In the early 1970s, a million Orleanians and tourists cheered him down Canal Street, as the *hoi polloi* flaunted its new power in the face of the elite.

More than a few old-timers view the changes with dismay, at some variance with Mr. Kohlmeyer, who observed that the Superdome has been "a real shot in the arm for the community." Whether that is so or not, it has certainly proved a shot in the arm for Poydras Street, which is rapidly replacing Canal Street as the main business artery of New Orleans. As of 1973, the catalogue of new buildings is impressive—a twenty-two-story headquarters finished for the

---

[27] Herman Kohlmeyer, one of its original bond brokers, was quoted by Burck in *Fortune* as calling it "the most extravagant thing I've seen in my life," and in Louisiana that is quite a statement.

[28] The weekly *Courier* headlined its August 31, 1973 issue "The Damned Stadium: Blueprint of a Scandal" and devoted a double-page spread to a chart which purported to explain "how the Scandal works," naming in the process many of the city's leading personalities.

Lykes Bros. Steamship Company, a new federal complex under construction at Lafayette Square, and numerous other buildings rising nearby or on the drawing board. Perhaps the most portentous project is "One Shell Square," a gleaming white sixty-story advertisement that Texas oil had settled on Poydras Street to stay. Significantly, it is the highest building in New Orleans, and it fundamentally changed the city's skyline with its huge neo-Seagrams profile. But there will surely be more and, perhaps, higher.

In sum, New Orleans's central business district looks to be in healthy shape—marvellously healthier than most American cities of a million or more people. If the health has a new and radical look, its roots are old and conservative—physically embedded in the eighteenth-century French Quarter and in a municipal elite whose new blood still has a rather blue Bourbon color to it, at least in political philosophy. As broker Kohlmeyer is supposed to have remarked: "The man who built the Taj Mahal didn't ask the permission of the people. Ditto here."

Racial Geography and the Future of New Orleans

It is easy to be optimistic about New Orleans's economic future, as of 1975, at least, but its social future is another matter. As in most other big American cities, New Orleans's main malady is racial.

The facts are devastatingly simple, and in combination they portend no good for the city. In New Orleans, as elsewhere, blacks are relatively poor and ill-housed, and their neighborhoods are poorly attended by municipal services. Educational levels are low, crime rates high. Meanwhile, whites flee and the proportion of blacks continues to increase, as do the isolation and alienation of a population that sees itself abandoned and abused. It is a sorry tale, and no less sorry for being typical of city after city across the United States.

New Orleans's racial experience is especially poignant, for its racial history was less flawed than in many other American cities. In some ways, to be sure, New Orleans was and is a very southern city for blacks. Thus, as Chai has shown, blacks constituted forty-five percent of the city's population, but only 3.6 percent of its "Level I leadership." (In 1973, not one of the city councilmen was black.) Furthermore, to the city's white majority, it was unthinkable that blacks would share equal facilities, and most blacks perhaps did not expect it.

Nevertheless, New Orleans's racial attitudes were consistently less embittered than, say, in Montgomery or even Baton Rouge—and certainly less than in Chicago or Newark. Thus, New Orleans sweated through the hateful summer of 1967 quietly if nervously. Part of the credit for tranquility goes to intelligent mayors, but deeper roots stem from the city's Creole heritage and the rather easygoing attitude of the French toward racial mixing. Part of it stems from nothing more complicated than interracial music-making, for white Orleanians are intensely proud of the ragtime tradition and are not unconscious that blacks were largely responsible for its invention and preservation. Part of it, perhaps, is economic: blacks have worked beside whites for a long time in New Orleans, especially on the docks, and there were no periodic economic catastrophes to provoke the recurring large-scale unemployment of blacks that so poisoned race relations in Detroit's auto factories or in the boll weevil belt of the rural South. But a major reason for New Orleans's history of good race relations—or at least the absence of overt violence—was the traditional geographical fragmentation of black neighborhoods in the city.[29]

Professor John Adams of the University of Minnesota has observed that two conditions commonly presage racial violence: the expectation of a better life that is routinely frustrated, and ghettos so big that blacks see only blacks, where resentment feeds incessantly upon itself. New Orleans satisfied neither of these conditions. The New Orleans Bourbon elite never dreamed of holding out to blacks the expectation of better living conditions, and if the streets fell into disrepair in black areas, that was the way things had always been. Then, too, if a black felt especially aggrieved, he or she could do what millions of other southern blacks had done—get on a train and go north, more often than not to Chicago at the other end of the Illinois Central Railroad. It is unprovable but quite likely that New Orleans's bitterest racial dissatisfactions were shipped off with unhappy migrants to Chicago, relieving pressures in New Orleans, but with explosive results in Chicago—a kind of differential migration of hatred. And later on, California apparently received some of New Orleans's exported racial troubles. Huey Newton, the Black Panther, first gained a violent reputation in Oakland, but his hometown was New Orleans. And as long as New Orleans's ghettos remained small and fragmented, there was little chance for resentment to reach critical mass, particularly if the ghetto was not too

[29] It is important to recall that New Orleans has been racially tranquil only in fairly recent times. The Reconstruction and post-Reconstruction periods saw episodes of savage violence–perpetrated by whites against blacks, from the 1870s through the end of the nineteenth century. The violence was prompted, it seems, by white reaction against "uppity" blacks who had exercised real power during Reconstruction, and it was designed to "put Negroes back in their place." It was a strategy of terror, and it worked. There was no serious black presence in New Orleans government until the election of "Dutch" Morial as the city's mayor in the late 1970s.

crowded. Quite accidentally, New Orleans's distaste for high-rise buildings and its southern predilection for open space probably helped to relieve tensions that incited violence in the crowded streets of Harlem and South Chicago.

It is disquieting to note that nearly all of these things are changing—mainly in the direction of probable future trouble. At the base of it, the city has grown more segregated in recent years. Most obviously, New Orleans's multinuclear ghettos have been growing together, especially in the old backswamp areas where the poorest blacks always lived. Significantly, the location of ghettos had not changed much. Back in 1940, for example (the earliest census date for which we have detailed racial data at a large scale), the black neighborhood cores were located in the same places they had been for more than a century, but individual black neighborhoods were smaller and separated from one another. Since 1940, black population had grown and spread, but there has been very little leapfrogging into new parts of the city, especially not into affluent neighborhoods. One major exception is the Pontchartrain Park development where blacks were allegedly given their own golf course to avoid pressure to integrate white golf links during the 1950s. Not surprisingly, Pontchartrain Park was ninety-nine percent black by count of the 1970 census, and the subdivision is cut off from the outside by canals and railroad tracks so securely that it takes an expert to find the entrances. In no sense is Pontchartrain Park an integral or integrated part of the city.

The same is true of New Orleans's ten big public housing projects, which are now almost 100 percent black and mostly isolated from the mainstream of city life. By standards in other cities, New Orleans's public housing is reasonably good—fairly well-built, with moderate population densities and considerable open space. The first projects were completed in 1938, when segregation was still legal, and four were reserved for whites—Iberville, Florida, St. Thomas, and Fischer. Desegregation did not bring integration to any of these projects, however, since each served mainly as places of refuge for blacks displaced from private housing in nearby neighborhoods. Iberville, considered one of the best because it was especially well-built and located close to the French Quarter, took in black refugees from the Vieux Carré who could not afford to pay skyrocketing rents. St. Thomas has served exactly the same function for the lower Garden District, where private renewal is displacing blacks from old elegant houses, and Florida apparently took in people from the enormous infamous "Desire" Project, generally regarded as the worst in the city.[30] Thus, while the

[30] Three out of four families who live in Desire have incomes which fall below the census's definition of poverty.

projects sometimes provided better housing from a physical standpoint, the rapid switchover from white to black population has merely replaced one kind of segregation with another.

To make things worse, black neighborhoods have endured increasing pressure from whites bent on "improving" the city. One form of pressure has come from freeway building, and while there is no direct evidence that highways were deliberately located in black neighborhoods, a comparison of racial maps with highway maps makes that conclusion inevitable. Experience in other American cities suggests that urban highways are often located where political opposition is weakest—presumably the reason why the Highway Department abandoned its Vieux Carré schemes, but found no difficulty running I-10 along North Claiborne Avenue, thus converting the main street of New Orleans's biggest African-American neighborhood from a broad, landscaped boulevard into a dingy, concrete cavern. While the short-run costs of road building doubtless were relatively low on North Claiborne, one must wonder what it will cost in the long run to repair the social damage wrought by the expressway, or if it can be repaired at all.

The other form of pressure is equally strong, and emerges when whites "discover" the architectural virtues of an old black neighborhood. As of the early 1970s, three such areas were being "reclaimed": Faubourg Marigny, already mentioned; the lower Garden District around Coliseum Square; and "old Algiers," just a five-minute free ferry ride from the foot of Canal Street. All three are areas of fine, flamboyant Victorian houses which had been abandoned by upwardly mobile whites, and it was quite natural when poor blacks moved into them. All three are well worth preserving, and if something is not done, their wooden buildings will surely disintegrate from neglect, moisture, heat, and termites. Thus, on architectural grounds, one must applaud the restoration. But the blacks have fled, unable to pay the new high rents. Some whites may be comforted that the blacks are out-of-sight and out-of-mind, but such processes cannot help but make New Orleans more and more segregated, alienated, and prone to violence.

By contrast with other big cities, New Orleans has a good record for housing its black population—if one counts units and does not look too closely at individual structures. According to the Taeubers, between 1940 and 1960 the city built about as many housing units for blacks as it did for whites—half again better than either Memphis or Birmingham, a fact which may help explain the difference in the three cities' histories of racial violence. But at the same time, the "index of residential segregation" crept up and up. New Orleans's 81.0 was already high for a southern city in 1940, but it was up to 84.9 in 1950 and 86.3 in 1960. Since the Taeubers define the index as meaning "the minimum percentage of non-whites who would have to change the block on which they live in order to produce an unsegregated distribution," it would require that 86.3 percent of New Orleans's nonwhites move for integration to be achieved. It is small consolation to know that most other American cities are neither much better nor much worse than New Orleans in this respect, but it is even less comforting to review the record of racial violence in cities with similar indexes.

Typically, racial tensions have seriously damaged the public school system. Southern states were never noted for extravagant support of public schools, and when money had to be split between two separate racial systems, the results were truly miserable—especially on the nonwhite side. Public schools in southern Louisiana were particularly rickety since many Catholics sent their children to parochial schools and disliked paying school taxes from which they derived no immediate benefit. Affluent Protestants often emulated the Catholics, and New Orleans gradually developed a system of private schools—some fair, some excellent—which served not merely to educate, but to function as gatekeepers for admission into the city's ruling elite.

Brown v. Board of Education's order to integrate schools, therefore, was a severe blow to an already sickly public system. Affluent whites in Orleans Parish avoided sending children to integrated schools by enrolling them in private and parochial schools or by moving to whiter parishes outside. Many white families who could not afford to take those steps did so anyway. St. Bernard and Plaquemines parishes, under the semifeudal rule of Leander Perez, never bothered to conceal their hostility to black immigrants, and the black population is consequently small. Jefferson Parish, with only one black school child out of five, as of 1970, has developed a large-scale busing system that keeps the white-black ratio as homogeneously high as possible. As a result, during the 1960s whites abandoned public schools in Orleans Parish at precisely the same time as the black school population has been increasing rapidly. As this chapter is written (1975), the departure of middle-income white families with school-age children from Orleans Parish resembles a stampede, and school administrators grow more apprehensive by the day. The fear that integration would ruin New Orleans's public schools apparently is turning into a self-fulfilling prophesy. Meantime, the hope that the school system can serve to ease racial tensions is doomed in Orleans Parish unless present circumstances literally reverse themselves. The prospect is bleak.

It is always hazardous to predict the future course of human affairs. In matters of race, however—which have too often decided whether American central cities live or die—too many signs in New Orleans point in ominous directions. Although several recent mayors have tried with some success to increase the number of black city employees, the progress is painfully slow, and while segregation increases, blacks grow increasingly restive. So far there has been no outbreak of major violence, but there is no guarantee against it. White Orleanians know it, and within the city they huddle together in white enclaves—or flee to the suburbs, where one can go for miles without seeing a black face. Neither tactic bodes much good for the city's future.

Epilogue to Book One
YET STILL A FINE CITY?

U NLIKE NEW YORKERS AND BOSTONIANS, most old-time Orleanians cour-
teously refrain from giving unsolicited advice about how other people
should run their cities. Quite naturally, Orleanians do not take kindly to advice
from outsiders on how to run their own. New Orleans is different, we seem to
have agreed—so different that Orleanians have little to learn from other
places, and so different that they have little to teach them.

Perhaps we need to reform such habits of thought and consider that the rest
of America may have a good deal to learn from New Orleans and vice versa.
The lessons may not be immediately obvious, and they may be easier for an
outsider to recognize than the ordinary Orleanian—many of whom rarely
move very far beyond the precincts of their beloved city.[1]

One ventures to suggest that the great failures of urban America have been
general failures which stem from common origins: the overcrowding of workers' quarters in the nineteenth century; the failure to keep air and water clean;
the destruction of neighborhoods by railroad tracks, auto expressways, and air-
ports; the cruel pressure on blacks to live within the confines of an "inner city";
the decay of central business districts; and so on through the dismal, familiar
litany. To the degree that these failures are epidemic, it is because most

---

[1] A very unofficial and unscientific survey of several freshman classes at the University of New
Orleans in the summer and autumn of 1973 revealed a surprising number of young Orleanians
who seldom traveled outside New Orleans and showed little desire to do so.

American cities are tied to a national model of behavior. One city does something, and presently all are doing it. Our impatience is our undoing. By the time we discover Los Angeles's mistakes, every other city has made the same mistake itself. American cities are like lemmings.

By contrast, the great successes of urban America have been highly particular . . . cities that have danced to a different drum. San Francisco's successes are San Franciscan—not somebody else's. Boston is successful to the degree it is Bostonian—not because it has conformed to some standard national model. And the same is true of New Orleans—successful to the extent that the city has preserved its individual identity. It is significant, perhaps, that San Francisco, Boston, and New Orleans have all failed most miserably in precisely those areas they share with the rest of the country: sprawling suburbs, faceless and interchangable downtown buildings, expressways that murder neighborhoods, slum clearance programs that wreck whole sections of the city and expel the people who lived there. In the United States, at least, urban success requires aberrant behavior.

One can push the argument too far, to be sure. Cities should not encourage freakiness—that way leads to Disneyland. Nor should cities resist innovations just because they are innovative; no sensible person denounces chlorination of New Orleans's water simply because God put no chlorine in the Mississippi River. But we should not be afraid to talk—as Albert Bush-Brown talks—of our "right to a fine city," and to recognize that fine cities are made from the delicate interweaving of tangibles and intangibles which take time to weave, and which are not easily mended once they are torn.

Thus, New Orleans. Bourbon Street does not make the city a wonderful place, nor the French Quarter, nor superb food, nor Mardi Gras, nor even the humane urbanity that makes so many ordinary Orleanians so extraordinary—but the *tout ensemble* that speaks of special people, rooted for a long time in a special place. If this is true or even partly true, then other American cities might look to New Orleans for guidance, and should look to their own special qualities for their own special salvation. (New Orleans, meantime, might consider declaring such things as nationally franchised restaurants to be crimes against the city.)

Conversely, the two most potent forces that threaten to destroy the special qualities that make New Orleans a fine city are not particular to New Orleans, but are parts of a national epidemic. One is suburban sprawl. The other is increasing racial segregation. Both are obviously related, both produce alienation and hostility, and both may have gone so far that they may be irreversible.

But it is plain to a reader of New Orleans's history and geography that the city began to lose its special qualities at about the time that Mr. Wood's swamp pumps made it possible for affluent whites to flee the city in their automobiles, leaving behind the fine old city to become a great black ghetto with white enclaves. As the city becomes blacker, poorer, and more segregated, as the suburbs become whiter and more sprawling, it becomes harder and harder to put the urban Humpty Dumpty back together again. New Orleans becomes more and more like the rest of the nation.

There are no obvious antidotes to suburban sprawl and racial segregation in New Orleans. Indeed, in the context of urban America in this last third of the twentieth century, there may be no solution except to abandon our cities and start afresh. Some northerners seem quite ready to do that, but the new urban models usually look better on the drawing board than they do outdoors in the cold light of day. Levittown is Levittown everywhere, and it is still unclear whether Reston really works. But New Orleans clearly did work—and it may yet, if Orleanians resist the temptation to act like everybody else. And if they abandon efforts to keep their fine city, their sin will not be easy to pardon.

Yet New Orleans retains two special advantages which may still hold out some hope. First of all, it does remain a fine city, despite recent depredations. Second, it has always been a laggard, and laggards have a special advantage over those at the forefront of progress. They can—to paraphrase Lincoln Steffens — look over into the future to see if it works. From New Orleans's vantage, its racial future is writ large in Detroit—its suburban future projected in the deserts around Phoenix—the future of Poydras Street on display in Houston's anonymous parody of a downtown.

New Orleans, of course, may choose to go that way—and failure to act will guarantee it. But if the city is to choose another course, time is running out. For most of its history, New Orleans was an island, protected against national fads by the insulating swamps, by Creole aloofness, by poverty, by a host of natural and artificial devices which kept the world at arm's length. Over that long time, New Orleans has had the leisure to plant and nurture the special qualities that made it a fine city. But the barriers are down, and the world is crowding in.

The city fathers have recently been saying rather stridently that "Pride Builds New Orleans." And so it has. But pride alone is not enough. New Orleans will remain a fine city only so long as it remains a special place, and contemporary America is intolerant of special places. New Orleans will remain a special place only if the city takes special measures to define the qualities that made it that way, and to defend them with all the power at its disposal. Failing that, New Orleans will go the way of Houston and Phoenix. After that, pride will scarcely make any difference.

Coda

Again and again we read that the nucleated city is a lost institution in the Western world—an antique relic whose time is past. It may be so, especially in the United States, which started city building late in humankind's urban career, and whose automotive technology has already destroyed more cities than Atilla ever dreamed of. But the Great City, for all its warts and flaws and corruptions, is surely one of the wonderful accomplishments of humankind. It is too soon, perhaps, to know whether we can build suburbs to rival the center of Paris or shopping centers to rank with the markets of Florence or Peking, but one may be pardoned for doubting it. What we do know is that genuine cities already exist—urbane, cosmopolitan, and self-conscious centers of civil affairs.

There are not many places like that left in the United States, but pre-1950 New Orleans was surely one of them. Just as surely, it is threatened by the same forces which have already destroyed less lusty cities all across the New World and are even now assaulting the gates of the Old World's finest cities. If Americans really mean it when they say that the creation and preservation of humane environments are worthy national goals, then the protection of New Orleans's civic integrity is clearly a matter of high national priority. Clearly, too, the matter cannot be left to the tender mercies of the free market, much less the obsolete medications prescribed by schools of urban planning.

Plainly, there is no simple way to turn back the host of enemies which already besiege New Orleans—be they racial hostility, suburban sprawl, or nothing more sinister than the rising tide of mediocrity that threatens to flood the city with tourist gimmicks and Houston plastic. Indeed, there may be no solution at all: perhaps democratic automotive society is simply incapable of creating and preserving delicate physical environments—those treasured spots such as New Orleans which can never be recreated, but which are so easily and readily plundered. But if this nation cannot find methods to protect a New Orleans from despoilation, and if it cannot find ways to employ those methods, the failure will cast serious doubt on America's ability to protect any valued part of its national environment.

BOOK TWO

The City Transformed,

1975–2002

Chapter 4
Rediscovering the River

IF ONE CAN IMAGINE a snapshot taken of New Orleans as it entered the last quarter of the twentieth century, embracing the whole city and freezing the moment in time, it would have made a pleasing picture. To casual visitors and connoisseurs alike, the city looked wonderful—or at least large parts of it did. New Orleans had miraculously managed to preserve and maintain a stunning array of distinguished old buildings, matched by few other big American cities. It was a sybaritic city—wallowing happily in some of America's best indigenous food and music, and periodically celebrating its *joie de vivre* by throwing civic parties that were famous nationwide. Mardi Gras was merely the biggest of those festivities, but hardly a season went by when Orleanians were not parading through the streets in bizarre costumes, celebrating something or other—whether real or imagined made little difference.

In 1975 there was plenty to celebrate. Above all, the economy was jumping. The oil and gas industry was enjoying a wild economic boom, thanks to recent action of the Organization of Petroleum Exporting Countries (OPEC). Only two years before, OPEC had clamped an embargo on exports of its oil and forced the price of crude to unprecedented levels. When the dust from the Middle East finally settled, the wellhead price of crude oil had tripled. Louisiana, along with Texas and Oklahoma, sitting on some of the biggest oil and gas fields in North America, was suddenly rich beyond the dreams of Huey

Long. Fortunes were made and made again, as amazed spectators stood by and watched. Everybody who wanted a job could get one, it seemed, and the jobs paid better than they had in living memory. A. J. Liebling, that inspired chronicler of Louisiana's political shenanigans, had remarked that the state was "slithering in oil." And New Orleans, as Louisiana's largest city and financial capital, slithered with the best of them. Wages and tax revenues had risen to delicious new levels, and the Shell Oil Company had just finished building the city's highest skyscraper that rivaled the biggest and shiniest of those in Houston.

Then, too, if one did not look too closely, the city's residents seemed to be getting on well together—or at least better than anyone had reason to expect. Idiosyncratic as always, New Orleans had escaped the riots that had riven big cities elsewhere in the nation. In 1975, if one believed the data, the city was truly biracial; according to the census, blacks and whites were almost exactly equal in numbers. To be sure, the city was far from integrated, and there was no doubt that the old white Establishment still ran the city. But at least Orleanians were not committing racial mayhem as the inhabitants of a good many northern cities had done only a few years before. New Orleans seemed to live in a different and happier league than Detroit or Washington, D.C.

On the surface, at least, things looked good. New Orleans was "the Big Easy," the "city that care forgot." *Laissez les bon temps rouler*, the Cajuns like to say, but the good times seemed to be rolling in New Orleans as well.

The World's Fair of 1984

In the city's best tradition, it was a time for celebration, and a big one had already been scheduled. Several years earlier, New Orleans had acquired the license to hold a World's Fair, planned for 1984 and timed to observe the centennial of the city's famous World's Fair and Cotton Exposition of 1884. That earlier fair had signaled the city's emergence from the bad times of the Civil War and Reconstruction, and pointed the way to a new and better epoch. The 1984 fair would do much the same thing, serving notice to the world that times were good, that the city was open for business and ready to welcome and entertain as many visitors as wanted to come. As it turned out, both fairs were also alike in their pecuniary misfortunes. The 1884 fair had lost money, but the losses of the 1984 fair were so large that it became the first world's fair in history to declare bankruptcy.

As in 1884, however, the fair's financial travails were much less important than its long-run impact on the city's geography. The Cotton Exposition had carved out the grounds which would become Audubon Park, and had helped reinforce Uptown New Orleans as a place of upscale gentility. The 1984 fair had a similar effect on the city's central riverfront. Its long-run effect was to help convert a considerable swath of decaying wharves, warehouses, and slums into some of the city's most attractive and vibrant territory—in sum, to give New Orleans a wonderful new riverfront.

Unlike the 1884 exposition, which had been located on the generous grounds of an old sugar plantation beyond the city's edge, the 1984 fair was built on a discontinuous site of eighty-five acres, strung out over almost a mile of riverfront between the foot of Poydras Street to the footings of the Greater New Orleans Bridge, and, except for its river frontage, the fairgrounds were totally surrounded by densely built-up urban tissue.[1] But the demolition that made room for the fair caused few tears to be shed: as a member of the City Planning Commission observed at the time, the site was "an area of the City that had been virtually forgotten."

And after it closed, the fair was forgotten, too. To be sure, it had all the things that a twentieth-century World's Fair was supposed to have: a theme (which nobody could remember), a monorail, a cable car that stretched across the Mississippi River, and a Great Hall. But its impact had just begun. When the celebration was over, the Great Hall was converted into "Phase I" of a new "Ernest N. Morial Convention Center," which would eventually become one of the largest municipal convention halls in the United States.[2] The Morial Center was clearly built to attract large numbers of out-of-town conventioneers, and constituted visible assurance by the city that the neighborhood around it would be cleaned up and vigorously policed.

It was very encouraging. Across the street, lakeside of the 1984 fair site, private developers had been working to upgrade a rather ratty district of obsolete warehouses, vacant lots, half-abandoned commercial properties, seedy bars, and run-down housing.[3] This area, wedged between the Convention Center

[1] The Greater New Orleans Bridge is officially known as the "Crescent City Connection." The pretentious new title has not taken hold among the citizenry, who have clung to the old usage– often calling it simply "GNO" or, more generically, "the bridge." I have gone along with the custom and employed the traditional name.

[2] Ernest N. Morial, a Creole, was elected in 1977 as the first nonwhite mayor of New Orleans since the end of Reconstruction in 1876. His election ended a century of white rule in New Orleans.

[3] For the special meaning of "Lakeside," "Riverside," "Uptown," and "Downtown" in New Orleans, see *Appendix A*.

and the abutments of the Greater New Orleans Bridge, was dubbed "The Warehouse District"—slated to become a downtown home to artists, antique shops, museums, coffee houses, funky restaurants, and a number of up-market apartments and offices carved out of the newly reconditioned warehouses and commercial buildings—a kind of New Orleans version of New York City's SoHo and the East Village. Between 1984 and 2000, as the Convention Center grew larger and larger, the Warehouse District took on a momentum of its own, rolling inland and uptown like some large tropical snowball. Before the century was out, the Warehouse District had become one of the most successful real estate ventures in the city, and was becoming a destination in its own right, spattered with hotels and smaller lodgings, and a magnet both for tourists and residents of the city. It succeeded far beyond what most observers would have expected—an unintended consequence of the 1984 fair, but a very welcome one.

It was not the only such consequence, however. The fair and the convention center that followed it served as a vigorous incentive for a much more ambitious enterprise which had begun some years before: to open for public access a great stretch of frontage along the Mississippi River.[4]

The New Riverfront

It is a truism that New Orleans's success is uniquely a consequence of the city's location on the Mississippi River. But New Orleans was, from the beginning, an essentially commercial city, and it was taken for granted that the riverfront would be used for commerce. Claims for other uses—parks or public promenades, for example—were rarely entertained; the riverfront had too much commercial value to waste on idle fripperies. Over the course of time, the river that had created the city was cut off from the city's people by a thick rind of wharves, warehouses, railroad tracks, and, of course, the growing bulk of the levee. It was next to impossible for an ordinary citizen to walk from Jackson Square to the Mississippi River—and, indeed, the Mississippi River was not even visible from Jackson Square.

Nobody apologized for this state of affairs. After all, most other U.S. ports had done similar things to their waterfronts and for similar reasons. New York

---

[4] It is a considerable irony that the Convention Center itself has now grown so large that it has become, in Coleman Warner's words, "something like the Great Wall that . . . has blocked visual and physical access to the river for pedestrians" (personal communication, January, 2002).

City, Philadelphia, and Seattle and other lesser places had sealed themselves off from the waterfronts that nourished them; in those cities and many others, ordinary citizens could live their lives without ever seeing the water, much less taking pleasure from it.

Paradoxically, the only people who lived next to the Mississippi were homeless people who squatted in temporary shacks on the *batture*, a sand bar that accumulated during times of slack water on the insides of the river's meanders. Those sand bars were long, crescent-shaped strips on the riverside of the levee, and had no protection against flood. Thus, when the river rose, as it did every spring, residents of the *batture* decamped until the water fell again. And because this waterfront space was used for landing cargo, no matter how temporary the "land" might be, the indigent residents of the *batture* necessarily coexisted with piles of cargo and the comings and goings of stevedores, not to mention the noisome detritus left stranded by the murky polluted river. However disagreeable the *batture* normally was, it formed a significant swatch of real estate during times of low water; the East Bank's riverfront was all located on the inside of a large meander—hence the sobriquet, "Crescent City." Because riverfront real estate was so valuable, the levees were eventually advanced riverward to annex the *batture*, and with it the poor black population that lived there more or less permanently. That strip along the river is still home to a sizable number of poor blacks, not descendants of the original *batture* residents, but living in the area for the same reason. People of means—white people, that is—then and now avoided living near smelly, noisy, unsavory wharves, warehouses, and railroads. But land use along the river has gradually changed, and so have prices for residential real estate. The crescent-shaped neighborhood of poor blacks is increasingly pressed by affluent whites who are aggressively seeking to gentrify the Uptown riverfront.

But the traditional aesthetic disdain for the riverfront had led to the proposal in 1946 (now infamous) to build a high-speed, limited-access "Riverfront Expressway" along much of New Orleans's Mississippi River shoreline.[5] As we have seen already, the proposal dragged along for years, but was eventually rejected, amid loud cheers from the city's preservationist community, and

---

[5] The scheme had been contrived with the help of Robert Moses, the "power broker" who had used his role as chief of New York City's Triborough Bridge Authority to tear down and rebuild about one-sixth of the New York metropolitan area. In the process, Moses had built the East Side and West Side highways, which had sealed Manhattanites off from both the Hudson and East rivers.

especially from aficionados of the French Quarter—which the Expressway would have cut off completely from the Mississippi. The rejection of the expressway was an event that was farther-reaching than even its most ardent opponents might have guessed.[6] As long as the dispute lasted, with the expressway always a looming possibility, little was done to improve or even maintain the waterfront's docks, warehouses, and railroad tracks that lay between the Quarter and the Mississippi. In any event, many of these docks were obsolete and ripe for demolition. Thus, in 1969 when the Expressway scheme was finally cancelled by U.S. Secretary of Transportation John Volpe, the city set about to demolish the old docks in front of the French Quarter, and turned the area into a riverside park-cum-promenade. It was named the "Moonwalk," after the city's well-liked mayor, Moon Landrieu, and was opened in 1972. It was an epochal event, the first step toward reclaiming the Mississippi River as "the people's river."[7]

The Moonwalk was only a harbinger of better times for the riverfront and adjacent neighborhoods. In 1980–81, at the height of the oil boom, an upscale shopping center, "Canal Place," was built at the foot of Canal Street and very near the riverbank. Thus, the process of opening the riverfront to the public was well underway when the World's Fair arrived on the scene to give the process a shot of municipal steroids. When the fair closed in 1984, the process of riverfront improvement continued. In 1986, just as the Convention Center was being started, James Rouse was engaged to build a "festival market" along the river. Rouse arrived in New Orleans, trailing clouds of commercial glory from his successes in restoring Boston's ancient Quincy Market and reclaiming Baltimore's old waterfront—where he built a festival market that he called Harbor Place. Rouse had created both of those markets in run-down parts of their respective cities, adapting old buildings to tourist-oriented commercial uses, a formula which turned out to be wildly successful in drawing great crowds of visitors and residents to enjoy a new "festive" environment on or near the waterfront. By so doing, Rouse had gained a national reputation as a kind of architectural Midas who knew the secret of turning urban debris into acres of gold. New Orleans's version of Quincy Market was the "Riverwalk," stretching upriver from the foot of Canal Street to the edge of the new

[6] For a fine, detailed account of the whole Expressway affair and what it did to New Orleans, see Baumbach and Borah's *The Second Battle of New Orleans*. The book is a cliff-hanging page-turner, and is obligatory reading for any serious student of the city.

[7] I am indebted to Mark Tullis for this felicitous turn of phrase.

Convention Center, much of it actually built on old docks. Thus, the Riverwalk opened still more of the Mississippi riverfront to the public, who could either shop in the Riverwalk or stroll along an elevated balcony to look out at the river.

Spurred by these successes, other improvements were inevitable. Diagonally across Decatur Street from Jackson Square, the Jax Brewery—a fine, old, red-brick pile from 1895—had outlived its usefulness as a beer-maker, and was converted into a multistoried mall that sold sundry trinkets to tourists in an atmosphere of *fin de siècle* industrial charm. In 1990, another big new section of riverfront was opened to pedestrians with the creation of Woldenberg Riverfront Park, extending from the Moonwalk upriver nearly to Canal Street. At the end of the park, where Canal Street met the river, a splendid new "Aquarium of the Americas" was built, forming a highly visible punctuation mark where the city's two main thoroughfares—Canal Street and the Mississippi River—intersected.

To cap the enterprise and to serve as both tangible and symbolic declaration that New Orleans genuinely had a *new* riverfront, a new streetcar line was created in 1987–88, complete with bright-red antique trolley cars, to connect the Convention Center upriver to the downriver end of the Quarter—a distance of about two miles. Along its way, the streetcar offered passengers (mainly tourists) convenient access to the Big Easy's most delectable tourist attractions: from the newly boutiqued French Market, along the Moonwalk to coffee and *beignets* at the Café du Monde, past Jackson Square with its cathedral, fortune-tellers, sidewalk artists, and wandering musicians, past the Jax Brewery to Woldenberg Park and its open vistas to the river, on to the Aquarium and the Algiers Ferry terminal at the foot of Canal Street, past the Riverwalk and Julia Street Cruise Ship terminals, finally arriving at the Convention Center itself. The new streetcar line was like the monorail at a permanent world's fair, only much better. The riverfront streetcar was more than just a gimmick; it was a genuine civic improvement. Citizens and tourists alike were charmed.

Then in 1999, after years of haggling and political legerdemain, Harrah's of Las Vegas opened a large, glitzy, and newly legal land-based casino on the uptown side of lower Canal Street.[8] This is not the place to recount the adventures, misadventures, and threatened bankruptcies that attended Harrah's final arrival on Canal Street, in a thick miasma of Louisiana politics and rumored

---

[8] The Louisiana legislature had legalized casino gambling in 1992 to compete with Mississippi's highly lucrative gambling establishments. Harrah's had come to town two years later, taking temporary residence in New Orleans's Municipal Auditorium while awaiting completion of the Canal Street building.

skullduggery. But when it arrived, it was one more sign that the riverfront, between the Convention Center and the French Quarter, was *the* place to be in New Orleans—and certainly *the* place for tourists to go.

When the dust from demolition and rebuilding had settled, New Orleans had gained for itself an altogether new riverfront. To those who had not visited the city in a long time, most of the Mississippi River shoreline from the French Quarter to the footings of the Greater New Orleans Bridge was unrecognizable—albeit charmingly so. But much more important, for the first time in almost two centuries the people of New Orleans possessed a genuine permanent connection with the Mississippi. It was not a minor matter, given the river's central role in making the city what it was, and is.

Missing, of course, and largely unmourned were the work-worn old warehouses and docks that had made the city a successful port. Most of what replaced it was designed to attract tourists and extract money from them. That change, it turned out, would portend a larger change in the way the whole city operated. To many residents, it was not entirely a cheerful prospect. Meantime, however, it all looked wonderful, and largely was.

Upriver, in a quite different context, there were other changes of a more down-to-earth kind. The Port of New Orleans, for so long the city's economic mainstay, was undergoing a major reformation, which would presently transform and greatly improve another large swath of the city's riverfront.

Transformation of the Port

The Port of New Orleans had traditionally played a uniquely important role in the life of the city. From the beginning, it was the city's *raison d'être*, and for almost two centuries it had dominated the city's economic life. Toward the end of the twentieth century it had ceased to play the same dominant role as in the past, but it remained a vital part of the city's life. According to the latest available figures published by the Dock Board in 1994, port activities generated more than 23,000 direct and related jobs in the city, and yielded $216 million in state and local taxes. As one student of New Orleans's economics remarked, "More than any other industry, the port's industry has the ability to create more high paying jobs across a broader spectrum of the workforce than any industry I've studied."[9]

[9] Timothy Ryan, dean of the College of Business Administration at the University of New Orleans and a frequent commentator on New Orleans's economics, as quoted in *The Port Record*, a publication of the Board of Commissioners for the Port of New Orleans, July-August, 1999.

During the 1970s and 1980s, however, not much had been done to modernize the port's facilities, and, in the words of Keith Darcé, business writer for *The Times-Picayune*, the port had drifted into "a state of decline . . ." The decline was more relative than absolute, but no less real for that. New railroads and interstate highways were capable of carrying container cargo at high speeds, so that seemingly insignificant ports now posed threats to New Orleans's long-standing domination of maritime trade in the Gulf of Mexico. The Port of Houston was already a major competitor, and had been building new facilities at a rapid and menacing rate. And ports to the east — Biloxi, Mobile, Pascagoula, and Tampa — were doing similar things on a smaller scale.

Equally challenging was a rapid and revolutionary change in shipping technology. Containers, long a staple of maritime trade, were increasing both in numbers and in size, providing economies of scale that were destined to undercut ports that failed to provide new and bigger container facilities. By the year 2000, the biggest container ships were four times larger than they had been only a decade before — behemoths 1,200 feet long and 150 feet wide, whose size resembled the giant ore freighters of the upper Great Lakes. These big new carriers achieved economies that promised to make their operators a great deal of money. But at the same time, they required correspondingly huge new docking and loading facilities, not to mention deeper and wider navigation channels to serve them. Ports that failed to enlarge to accommodate these monsters were clearly destined for maritime limbo.

The Port of New Orleans was plainly falling behind. Facilities that had been heralded as waves of the future in the 1960s and 1970s were now seriously out of date — especially the city's main container port along France Road and the Inner Harbor Navigation Canal, a.k.a. the Industrial Canal.

The Inner Harbor's problem was wretched access. There were two ways that ocean-going ships could get in: ships could enter from the Mississippi River by way of the Inner Harbor Lock, or from the Gulf of Mexico by way of the Mississippi River Gulf Outlet Canal (MR-GO). Both routes were fatally flawed. The Inner Harbor Lock had been opened in 1921 to handle the smaller ships of that time, but it was utterly incapable of accommodating the huge new container ships that were already beginning to ply the Gulf. The Army Corps of Engineers had given up its repeated attempts to build a big new lock at the town of Violet, downriver from the present one, and had returned to an older plan to enlarge the existing lock to about triple its 1921 size. But study after study and hearing after hearing had met with outraged and noisy protests from environmentalists and nearby residents alike. The environmentalists charged that any serious dredging of the Industrial Canal would exhume a witches' brew of noxious chemicals and heavy metals which had accumulated over the decades in the mud of the canal's bed.[10] The residents simply wanted the lock to go somewhere far, far away. Even if the Corps could win public approval of the project—a highly doubtful proposition—it would take at least a decade to finish and cost at least half a billion dollars, and possibly quite a lot more.[11] Even if Congress could be persuaded to spend that kind of money for a navigation lock—and that was very unlikely—the passage of ten years would put the Port of New Orleans hopelessly out of the running with other up-and-coming Gulf ports.[12] As with earlier proposals, the Industrial Canal Lock project seemed to be stuck in deep and toxic mud.

MR-GO, the other way of getting into the Inner Harbor, had its own lethal defects. Lacking reinforced banks for most of its course, MR-GO required constant and expensive dredging just to keep it open. Part of the canal had been gouged through sea-level wetlands, but the rest was merely a submarine trench dug into the muddy ooze on the shallow bottom of Breton Sound. Both sections, especially in the sound, had banks the consistency of warm Jello, and were given to slumping even in calm weather. In times of storm, slumps were

[10] According to a study commissioned by the Lake Pontchartrain Foundation, these include lead, mercury, and arsenic, not to mention "high concentrations of naphthalene, which becomes volatile when exposed to air." Dredging would remove three million cubic yards of sediments, but release chemicals into the nearby waters of Lake Pontchartrain. The lake, thanks to protean efforts by civic groups, had gotten almost clean enough to swim in, and Lakeside residents were outraged by the prospect of poison by dredging.

[11] The proposed lock accounted for only a fraction of the total project cost. A good share of the money was slated for building two or more big new bridges with enormous approach ramps to carry automobile and truck traffic high over the expanded canal—ostensibly to provide emergency evacuation routes in case of hurricanes. Many local residents were not entranced by the prospect of their neighborhoods being invaded by bridge ramps that would rank in size with some of the lesser Egyptian pyramids.

[12] Congress was gun-shy of major expenditures by the Corps on navigation projects, especially in the South. Congressional critics were fond of pointing to the porcine Tennessee-Tombigbee Canal Project as a horrible example of how not to spend public money. The Ten-Tom Project (as it was called) was designed to connect the two rivers, and was intended to make it possible to barge coal from east Tennessee and Kentucky fields more or less directly to the Gulf of Mexico via northeastern Mississippi and southwestern Alabama. As it turned out, the Corps's cost-benefit analysis had forecast that Ten-Tom would attract five times as much traffic as it did in fact, and the project's total cost set a standard for profligacy which broke every record in living memory. An expensive new canal project in New Orleans was automatically suspect, particularly in view of Louisiana's reputation for free-spending ways. This view, of course, was shared by neither Louisiana's state officials nor its congressional delegation. Officials both in New Orleans and in Baton Rouge saw the canal project as essential to commerce.

inevitable and often massive, sometimes blocking the canal completely until dredges could be brought in to remove the gelatinous obstacle. In 1998, Hurricane Georges had produced such mass slumping that MR-GO was closed for several months, leaving the France Road container docks totally cut off from the outside and forcing container ships bound for New Orleans to seek docks elsewhere.

To make it even worse, MR-GO's thirty-six-foot draft was too shallow for the big new container ships, which drew up to fifty feet of water—a prodigious depth compared to what had gone before. Dredging to that depth would have required not just deepening the canal by fourteen feet, but widening it, perhaps by dozens or hundreds of feet—otherwise the banks would cave in and block the canal. Thus, whatever was done, dredging would have to go on eternally, a nagging drain on the budget of the Corps's New Orleans District.

Environmentalists had been warning for a long time that *any* canal promoted erosion of coastal marshes and encouraged saltwater intrusions into freshwater wetlands, poisoning biota and ultimately destroying entire ecosystems. A canal fifty feet deep would need to be enormously wide; furthermore, it would provide a funnel for salt water in such volumes that it risked causing a first-order ecological calamity. Vast areas of marsh might be destroyed.

As was its long-standing custom, the Port of New Orleans took action, and just in the nick of time. (It was like an episode from *The Perils of Pauline*.) In 1986, J. Ronald Brinson was appointed to head up the Board of Commissioners for the Port of New Orleans—the "Dock Board," for short. Brinson had been the youthful head of the National Association of Port Authorities, and was nationally known for his knowledge, energy, and entrepreneurship. Brinson, along with a good many other observers, had concluded that there was no feasible way to provide suitable access to the Inner Harbor facilities. The best thing to do, he and others proposed, was to forget about the Inner Harbor container facilities, and forget about MR-GO as well. Instead, the Dock Board would help create an entirely new container port, this time *on* the Mississippi. Brinson concluded that there were two ways to do that. Each, in its own way, was revolutionary.

The first proposal, which had been bandied about for some time, was to ignore the entire Port of New Orleans and build a new "Millennium Port" not only close to the entrance of the Mississippi and convenient to Gulf shipping, but also designed to accommodate any imaginable kind and volume of traffic. It was estimated that the Millennium Port would cost upwards of a *billion* dollars, and nobody was willing to predict how long it would take to complete.

Until the millennial day arrived, Brinson suggested a back-up plan: the Dock Board would demolish and rebuild the existing Uptown port facilities at Nashville, Napoleon, and Louisiana avenues, and turn them into a new state-of-the-art container port — designed to replace the inaccessible France Road facilities on the Industrial Canal. The latter could still serve as a stopover point for barge traffic on the Intercoastal Waterway, and could still handle low-value bulk cargo such as sand and gravel. But serious shipping — and that meant containers — would go to the new Uptown riverside port.

This is not the place to go into the intricate political shoving matches that the Millennium Port proposal set off. The most irksome problem was that nobody could agree exactly *where* Millennium Port should be built. (Perhaps half a dozen locations were in the running, and each had its own special pleaders.) As long as the port's location was up in the air, the Louisiana legislature was in no hurry to appropriate money to help build it. There were weeks of delay, which became months, and promised to become many years. Meantime, Brinson concluded, there was no time to be lost in upgrading the Port of New Orleans. Houston's new port was already under construction.

Brinson's pragmatic response was to undertake "medium-scale" improvement to the port's Uptown riverfront facilities.[13] What Brinson wanted was nothing less than a wholesale rebuilding and modernization of New Orleans's Mississippi riverfront wharves. Until the Millennium Port arrived (and who knew how long that would be?), these new riverfront wharves would serve as the ultramodern containerized keystone of the port.

Paradoxically, improvement of Uptown river frontage had previously been thought impossible.[14] There was not enough room between the residential city and the riverfront to erect a big, sophisticated loading facility, not to mention yards to stack containers and stuffing sheds to load them. And city streets were too narrow and crowded to accommodate the trucks that had to carry cargo to and from the Interstate Highway System at the Greater New Orleans Bridge — some three miles downriver. Brinson's Dock Board had ingenious answers to both difficulties.

---

[13] It is worth nothing that the Uptown project was "medium-scale" only when compared to the gargantuan scale of the proposed Millenium Port. *Any* port project under Brinson's direction was likely to be ambitious, and this one was no exception.

[14] By people, including me. See pages 71–75 of this book. It was a bad call in 1975 that did not reckon with people such as J. Ronald Brinson. *Mea culpa.*

The space problem would be addressed by building two gigantic gantry cranes at the Nashville Avenue wharves, capable of loading and unloading containers at the unheard of rate of one per minute, and sometimes even faster than that. The new high-speed gantries permitted very rapid turnaround, so that a given ship needed to use precious dock space for only a short time—to be replaced by yet another ship.[15] In short, the new gantries would achieve savings in space by achieving savings in time. The Dock Board liked the new arrangement, since fewer docks were needed to handle the same number of ships. And shipowners liked it, because their vessels needed to be at the wharf for only a very short time.

But fast gantries were no good unless there were means to get containers off the docks in a hurry, to make room for more containers. Big new stacking yards were built for short-time storage of containers, and big new warehouses were created to provide shelter for break-bulk cargo until it could be transshipped. But trucks, like ships, needed to move on and off the premises in a hurry. New Orleans's crowded Uptown streets were no place for fast-moving trucks, but the Dock Board had an answer for that problem, too. A special road would be built for trucks only, the two-lane, high-speed "Clarence Henry Truckway" parallel to the levee, and enclosed by formidable chain-link fencing. Trucks are driven at expressway speeds between the wharves and the bridge, and thence via interstate highway, wherever in North America there were roads.[16]

Brinson's design for the new Mississippi River port facilities succeeded beyond the most optimistic hopes. The Nashville Avenue wharves and gantry cranes were completed in 2000, and the new wharves at Napoleon and Louisiana avenues would be finished shortly thereafter. In Brinson's words, the complex would be "a multipurpose marine facility capable of handling any kind of ship: general cargo, break-bulk cargo, or container cargo . . ." Even without

[15] These cranes were finished (in Brazil!) in the year 2000, and shortly afterward installed at the Nashville Avenue site. To watch them unload a ship's containers and to lower them onto waiting eighteen-wheeled trucks is to behold a level of speed and efficiency that puts the lie to the myth of southern lassitude.

[16] At the present writing (late 2002), the Truckway is finished except for a few blocks. It is expected to be completed shortly, and, when it is, the streets of Uptown New Orleans will be free of dock-bound eighteen-wheelers for the first time in a very long time. It is one of the few projects in recent years that seems to have pleased almost everybody. The shippers love it, the truckers love it, and many Uptown residents are ecstatic. In all fairness, however, completion of the Truckway was delayed by a furious neighborhood dispute over exactly *where* its last few blocks would be located.

Louisiana Avenue, the Nashville and Napoleon avenue terminals could handle 500,000 standard-sized containers a year, a fifty percent increase in only three years.

In addition to the much-admired containers, however, New Orleans is served annually by about 400,000 quite unromantic barges, which carry immense volumes of cargo up and down the Mississippi and its tributaries. Modern barges are not the hulking rafts of former times; nowadays, they are efficient and specialized vessels, capable of carrying almost any imaginable cargo. The list of those cargoes resembles those brain-numbing lists of "principal products" that used to appear in elementary school geography texts. The lists may seem boring until one realizes that their variety directly reflects the productivity and wealth of the Mississippi River valley, America's heartland. Viewed in those terms, one stands in awe at the size, complexity, and sophistication of those barges that can handle such an array of goods with so little fuss. In the language of the Dock Board's annual report: "There are traditional open-hopper barges that carry bulk cargo like gravel and coal; general cargo barges that carry more valuable things like steel, plywood, timber, or cotton; tank barges for fuel oil, molasses, chemicals, edible oils, or even liquefied gas; covered hopper barges that carry cargo that needs to be kept dry, like grain and paper; and deck barges for heavy equipment, appliances, and vehicles."[17] In a phrase made trite by country auctioneers, the barges can and do carry items too numerous to mention.

All of this volume and variety, however, tends to conceal the disquieting fact that very little of these cargos is consumed locally. Unlike Houston, a port which serves the enormous Texas market for consumer goods and industrial raw materials, New Orleans is relatively unimportant as a terminal. Rather, the city is what is called a "through-port," which means that it specializes in the transfer of cargo from one carrier to another, and then ships it on. This elementary fact reflects the near absence of manufacturing industry in metropolitan New Orleans. In effect, the port *transfers* a great deal of cargo, but it doesn't *do* much to it. One of the few products that undergoes major processing in the city is coffee, which is roasted and ground in a wonderfully aromatic facility alongside the river. It is a fine thing to smell, but it is not so fine when one remembers that coffee-roasting is not exactly heavy industry. In New Orleans, both industry and industrial jobs are in short supply.

[17] As quoted in "Barge Lines," *2000–2001 Port of New Orleans Annual Directory.* New Orleans: Board of Commissioners for the Port of New Orleans, 2001, p. 34.

Chapter 5
END OF THE BOOM: THE OIL BUST OF THE 1980s
AND THE DISASTERS THAT FOLLOWED IT

∾

*A*ND THEN the roof fell in.

In the mid-1980s, the price of oil collapsed, and with it the economic boom in New Orleans—and, indeed, most of Louisiana. Old-timers who could remember the 1930s compared the catastrophe of the 1980s in New Orleans with the worst times of the Great Depression. To be sure, nobody was selling apples on the streets, but life for many Orleanians was very bad indeed.

Like so many other unpredicted calamities, the collapse of oil prices originated in a far-off place, little-known to most Orleanians. It all began in the Middle East, which sits on about half of the world's known oil reserves.

In 1960, a group of Middle Eastern states formed the nucleus of what would become OPEC—the Organization of Petroleum Exporting Countries. OPEC's avowed aim was to help oil-producing countries throw off foreign domination, seize control of their own oil fields, and fix prices at whatever level they pleased, without interference from their former colonial masters. During the 1960s and early 70s, they had achieved little success, and the prices of oil had remained low and varied only slightly.

All that changed in 1973 with the outbreak of the Yom Kippur War between Israel, on the one hand, and Syria and Egypt, on the other. Many Western countries supported Israel, and to punish them the Arab members of OPEC imposed an embargo on oil exports. The result was a 400 percent increase in price in a period of six months.[1] Although an accommodation was ultimately worked out between Third World oil-producing countries and First World oil-importing countries, OPEC had tasted blood and kept the price of crude artificially high through self-imposed caps on wellhead production. Oil money poured into the coffers of OPEC countries, but oil-producing places outside of OPEC—such as Louisiana—were also showered with unearned and unexpected windfall profits.

But prices had only begun to rise. The Iranian Revolution began in 1979, followed by outbreak of war between Iran and Iraq in 1980. Prices went up and up again and finally spiked at nearly $50 per barrel the following year. Prices then dropped slightly, but remained at levels that still seem astronomic.

New Orleans benefited hugely—or, at least, a good many Orleanians did. With money pouring in, major oil companies spent money with lavish unconcern. In the city, the most conspicuous monument to oil money was the Shell Oil Company's "One Shell Square," finished in 1972, the highest building in the city, a gleaming white structure that might have been plucked bodily from the Houston skyline. Meantime, the unaccustomed profits helped hire well-paid executives and managers to staff oil company offices in New Orleans.

Oil prices continued to ride high through the mid-1980s. By then, however, the hard-line OPEC alliance showed signs of unraveling. OPEC members who had promised to keep production down (and, thus, prices high) were caught releasing more oil onto the world market than they had agreed to. The OPEC countries that were already rich (among them the Saudis) viewed their colleagues' behavior as cheating them of their rightful profits. In 1985, the Saudis lost their patience and took action which reverberated around the world. To punish their errant colleagues and to reclaim what they perceived as their fair share of the loot, the Saudis let oil prices float, pegged to the spot market—that is, determined by immediate supply and demand, and substantially lower than the artificially high OPEC price. The next year the Saudis dropped the second shoe, and more than doubled production from Arabian wells.

With that, OPEC price caps vanished, and the bottom simply dropped out of the oil market. As late as 1985, the price of oil at the wellhead had been $35 per barrel. By 1986, it had plunged to $10.

---

[1] These, and other data relating to the world oil market, are from "Oil Price History and Analysis," *Energy Economics Newsletter*, 1999, Web site: http://www.strg.com/prices.htm, p. 3.

The effect on Louisiana in general—and on New Orleans, in particular—was shattering. The drop in prices meant a shrinkage of corporate offices and presently a general "retrenching." In plain English, that meant that offices were closed in New Orleans and consolidated in Houston, the oil capital of the United States. As one oil executive is supposed to have said: "We *had* to be in Houston. We didn't have to be in New Orleans."

Other disasters followed quickly. In the absence of manufacturing jobs which might have taken up some of the slack, New Orleans saw a dismaying exodus of men and women who had held well-paid posts with oil companies. In 2000, Coleman Warner of *The Times-Picayune* quoted the pastor of a suburban church as saying: "I'm sure we had a hundred families in the church who were working for one of the major oil companies twenty years ago, and we've probably got ten now." In Warner's words, "Confidence vanished. . ."

A few émigrés tried to buck the tide. Poignant stories were told of families who had left New Orleans to find jobs elsewhere, but had returned because they loved the city—only to be forced out again when they could not find jobs that paid decent wages.

The loss of oil revenue telegraphed itself through New Orleans's economy and society. Few people were left untouched. Companies went broke, or fled New Orleans for greener pastures elsewhere. Tax revenues plummeted, pinching the budgets of public service agencies at exactly the time they were needed most. Unemployment increased, and the pain was most palpable in segments of the population that lacked money, education, and job skills; consequently they were unable to leave New Orleans to seek work elsewhere. By 1990, unemployment among black males had risen to eleven percent (more than double the rate for whites), and many blacks who managed to keep jobs were often very poorly paid.

The story of New Orleans's agony was documented in a grim report by Julius Kimbrough in 1997. Almost a third of the city was in poverty, Kimbrough noted, the highest rate to be found among twenty-five cities of similar size in the nation. Forty-two percent of black families lived in poverty—again the highest rate among cities in the study. Nearly half of New Orleans's children lived in poverty.[2] And among single black women living with children, almost two out of three lived below the poverty line. The grimmest statistic of

---

[2] The oil bust did not *create* black poverty, which was already endemic in New Orleans, but it exacerbated the poverty that already existed.

all, perhaps, revealed that the majority of the poor population—fifty-eight per-cent—had incomes less than half of the federal poverty level. As Kimbrough summed it up: "Images of poverty abound wherever one looks in New Orleans."[3]

The Great Population Shift in Numbers and Race

No matter how bad the economic times, there was reassurance in the knowl-edge that New Orleans had survived such traumas in the past, and had recov-ered to tell the story. But the bleak economic conditions tended to obscure a demographic shift that seemed to portend permanent and irreversible change. That population shift had begun more than fifty years before, and its causes went back much farther. Like so much else in New Orleans, they were deeply rooted in the past, and deeply rooted in matters of race.

At the end of the Civil War, the population of Orleans Parish had taken on a pattern that would hold steady for nearly a century.[4] The city's total population grew at a steady and dignified pace of about 5,000 people per year. And the racial composition also held fairly steady, at a ratio of whites to blacks of between two and three to one. Ever since the end of Reconstruction in 1876, New Orleans was a city dominated by whites—in wealth, power, and absolute numbers.

Then, in the 1950s, things began to change. Jefferson Parish, whose territory contained a good share of undrained backswamp, suddenly found enough money in the post-war prosperity to build levees and pump water out of its East Bank backswamps. The newly drained "land" was promptly converted to instant sub-urbs—in much the same way that New Orleans had thrust new housing north toward Lake Pontchartrain fifty years before.

Starting in the 1950s, the population of Jefferson Parish embarked on a forty-year binge of uninhibited growth. The new immigrants were mostly middle-class and blue-collar whites, and most of them came from the city of New Orleans.

---

[3] The 2000 census emphatically reconfirmed Kimbrough's findings. When the numbers of poor people were tallied for all fifty states, Louisiana emerged dead last, with the worst poverty rate of any state in the Union. And in New Orleans, the poverty rate was even worse than the state's. As the ultimate ignominy, a survey of family income in 216 counties and parishes across the nation ranked Orleans Parish as 213th. The only counties to rank lower were two hapless counties in the Rio Grande Valley, and the sorrowful Borough of the Bronx in New York City.

[4] The City of New Orleans is coterminous with Orleans Parish, and has been for a long time.

Although Jefferson Parish possessed several nodes of black population in older settlements such as Harahan, it was clear that black people were unwelcome in the new suburban areas. Even in 2000, most of the populated territory in East Bank Jefferson Parish contained very few blacks.

Population in Orleans Parish continued to grow during the 1950s, but for the first time the growth was caused almost entirely by an increase in black population. White population growth had ceased, and the emigration to Jefferson Parish's (and elsewhere) had caused the white population to decline—for the first time in a century. It was the first inkling of significant white flight—an event that had been afflicting racially mixed cities all over the nation.

Between 1960 and 1970 the census recorded the first absolute decline in Orleans Parish's population since the first U.S. census in 1810—and that decline continued through the 1970s and 80s. The decline slackened somewhat in the 1990s, but the total population continued to fall nonetheless. From a high of 628,000 in 1960, the city's population dropped to 485,000 in 2000—a loss of almost a quarter of the total population. The city's population was smaller than it had been since 1940.

The loss in total population resulted entirely from the decline in the number of whites. Indeed, black population continued to grow at a steady pace (except for a slight dip in the 1980s, probably attributable to the oil bust). But in the half-century between 1950 and 2000, the City of New Orleans lost almost two-thirds of its white population. This was white flight with a vengeance, and there was little comfort that similar things were happening in most big American cities with a high proportion of black population. Indeed, it wasn't supposed to happen in New Orleans at all. Hadn't all the authorities explained how race relations in New Orleans were traditionally more benevolent and pacific than in rowdier cities to the North and West? Wasn't New Orleans exempt from racial strife and distrust?

The answer was an emphatic no. Whites had run the city and had exploited the nonwhite population in ways that now seem unforgivable. Black resentment was palpable, but a good many whites still retained racial attitudes that evoked images of South Africa during the times of apartheid. To those whites, they were members of a superior race, and the idea of living next to blacks as equals was unthinkable—much less the idea that New Orleans might actually be governed by blacks. In fact, that day was not long in coming. The city's majority went from white to black about 1974, and in the election of 1977 Ernest N. ("Dutch") Morial was elected as the first nonwhite mayor since

Reconstruction. To be sure, Morial was a Creole of very light-colored skin, and a good many whites voted for him.[5]

So there were racial tensions; everybody knew that. But whites and blacks had been living close to one another for a long time in New Orleans. What precipitated the sudden bolting of so large a number of whites? As is so often the case in large-scale migrations, the causes were multiple and complex. Nevertheless, one can recognize forces that were *pushing* whites to leave the city. Simultaneously there were forces *pulling* whites to the new suburbs.

The "push" forces were triggered by a series of disreputable events that arose largely within the city's large, blue-collar white population. In 1954, in the epochal case of *Brown v. (Topeka) Board of Education,* the U.S. Supreme Court ruled segregated public schools to be unconstitutional, and ordered them integrated "with all deliberate speed." The speed in New Orleans was more deliberate than speedy, and it was not until late in the decade that a federal court ordered the New Orleans school system to quit stalling and get about the task of integration. The order to integrate was met with passionate and profane denunciations from a number of blue-collar whites, and it culminated in a shameful spectacle that was heavily covered by national TV and radio. Diminutive black girls, well-scrubbed and wearing their best white frocks, were escorted to the school doors by burly dignified U.S. marshals. Then, while movie and TV cameras rolled, a group of white women stood in conspicuous locations, shrieking obscenities at the children, while a mob of admirers egged them on with cries of encouragement. It was a scene that was watched by a sickened John Steinbeck, who was passing through New Orleans at the time and recorded the events in the vivid last chapter in his best-selling book, *Travels with Charley.* The antics of New Orleans's lady hooligans caused revulsion across the nation, and shredded the city's long-standing reputation for relatively calm race relations.[6] Whites, who were opposed to their children attending integrated public schools and who were beginning to express fear of Orleans Parish's rising crime rate, decided to get out. Large numbers moved across the

[5] That is, they voted for him the first time he ran. Once elected, Morial turned out to be a classic bare-knuckle pol, who built a formidable machine, based largely on black support. Many of his white supporters abandoned him in the next election, but it did them little good. The black proportion of the electorate had continued to grow, and Morial was re-elected to a second four-year term by a thumping majority. After that, a white candidate for mayor simply had no chance at all.

[6] Calm for the last century or so — if calm means a lack of race riots. There had been shocking outbursts of racial violence at the end of Reconstruction, and riots had broken out several times between then and 1900, when another violent outbreak occurred.

boundary into Jefferson Parish—at the time, in the 1960s, the only large-scale suburban development available outside of the Orleans Parish Public School District.

That flight was exacerbated by several unfortunate attributes of New Orleans's public school system. As we have already seen, the cards were stacked against black schools anywhere in the segregated South, but the stacking was doubly egregious in New Orleans, owing to the city's large Catholic population and a large parochial school system. Catholics who could afford the tuition sent their children to Catholic schools and they showed little enthusiasm for paying any more public school taxes than they absolutely had to.

Blue-collar and middle-class white families, unable to afford private school tuition for their children, were panicked by the prospect of their children having to share facilities with blacks. As they saw it, the only option was to move out of New Orleans into a school district which was still all (or nearly all) white. From the early 1960s to the late 80s that meant, *faute de mieux*, moving to Jefferson Parish—which they did in droves.

But for those blue-collar and middle-class white families, there was pull as well as push, which impelled them to move. Jefferson Parish offered spanking new suburbs, just like the ones seen on television, with newly built houses full of modern conveniences. And unlike the crowded streets and old houses of old New Orleans, the Jefferson suburbs offered new houses with big picture windows and air conditioning, yards with green grass, and wide streets and big new shopping centers, just like suburbs all over America. All this—and little threat of blacks moving into the schools or the neighborhood. It was no accident that George Corley Wallace, of Alabama, the loudly racist candidate for president, carried Jefferson Parish by a sizable margin in the election of 1968.

Meantime, back in New Orleans, as white numbers declined, black population continued to increase, both as a proportion of the whole and in absolute numbers as well.[7] Whereas in 1950, whites had enjoyed a two-to-one majority, in 2000 the ratio had more than reversed itself: blacks outnumbered whites by nearly three to one. In Orleans Parish, there were fewer whites than at any time since 1850. Racially, New Orleans was a different kind of city than it had ever been before.

Racial geography was different, too. The fragmented black ghettos of old-time New Orleans were getting bigger and beginning to merge into "superghettos," unlike anything that the city had seen before. With the racial

---

[7] The absolute growth of black population was mainly the result of natural increase. Hardly anybody, black or white, was moving into the city during the depression after the oil crash.

switchover, it was whites who now found themselves set apart from the majority of the city's population. One could hardly describe white districts as ghettos in the traditional usage of the word; golden ghettos would be more accurate. White neighborhoods, by and large, were financially comfortable, if not affluent, and contained much of New Orleans's distinguished and stately old domestic architecture—conspicuously in the Garden District, the St. Charles Street corridor, the French Quarter, and Faubourg Marigny. A second area of white territory was much more recently built, and stretched back from the Lake Pontchartrain lakeshore between City Park and the Jefferson Parish boundary. All in all, New Orleans was more segregated than it had ever been, and the inequities between rich and poor were as extreme as at any time since the legal end of slavery. In the meantime, a good share of New Orleans's middle-class population had decamped.

It is no news that poverty breeds crime, and it did so with terrible effect in New Orleans during the late 1980s and early 90s. For a time, New Orleans was the murder capital of the U.S., and it was little comfort to know that the majority of murders were committed by young black males against other young black males. The killings were often associated with disputes over drugs or gang turf, and many, if not most, were exacerbated by alcohol. Muggings and robberies were commonplace, and many citizens were terror-stricken, especially affluent whites who lived near the boundaries of poor black neighborhoods. Across the city, and not just in affluent areas, razor-wire appeared atop household walls, and throughout the city heavy padlocked chains were wrapped around the ornate iron gates that barred entrance to private dwellings. And in a city that was looking to tourism to rescue its economy, there were too many muggings of affluent tourists to escape the notice of the national media. Fearing for a major loss in tourist revenues, the city roused itself and reorganized the police department, simultaneously beefing up the police presence in sensitive areas—in heavily used tourist destinations, and in the vicinity of public housing projects, entirely inhabited by poor blacks.[8] With a high police visibility and with heavy-duty private security measures much in evidence, sizable parts of

[8] The St. Louis Cemetery No. 1 on the lakeside fringe of the French Quarter, is a famous tourist destination. But the Iberville Public Housing Project lies just across the street with a population that is all black and all poor. Muggings in the cemetery have become so common that the police routinely warn tourists not to visit the cemeteries without escorts—and at night not to visit them at all.

New Orleans had the look of a Third World city. And, at the same time, the city's educational system had taken on a similar look.

The Catastrophe of Public Schools

It is generally acknowledged that the New Orleans Public School system is an academic and social calamity. The case is not hard to document; the evidence is unfortunately obvious. Both public officials and the media are outspoken in their dismay. In early 2001, *The New York Times* described what it called "a steadily deteriorating school system" in Orleans Parish. The *Times* then went on to quote Marc Morial, then mayor of New Orleans, as saying: "We shouldn't be afraid to say it. The schools are in crisis. It's the defining battle of the 21st Century in this city."

Student test scores bear out the charges. In 2001, for the first time, the state of Louisiana undertook to grade the quality of its schools on the basis of student performance on standardized tests. In its report on the New Orleans high schools, the state's Board of Education graded eight of the city's nineteen secondary schools as "academically unacceptable," and another six were ranked below the state average in academic achievement. Ironically, two of the worst, near the bottom of the state's scale, were the nobly named Booker T. Washington and the George Washington Carver high schools.[9]

While few deny that the school system is catastrophically off the rails, explanations vary. Most people agreed that the schools need more money—a lot more money. It was generally agreed, however, that there were two other proximate causes, and both went back a long way. The first was white abandonment of responsibility for the Orleans Parish public schools, and the second was the scarcity of a tradition of educational aspirations in the poorest segments of the black community. Both of those phenomena are closely linked, and they are deeply rooted in New Orleans's past.

Under slavery, it was illegal to teach blacks to read or write—lest literacy would make slaves "uppity" and become troublemakers through reading seditious literature. And after emancipation, the white establishment continued to

---

[9] Just as ironically, students with high test scores and academic aspirations could attend Benjamin Franklin Senior High, a magnet school in the Lakeview district, "known for its rigorous academic climate." The state school board ranked Franklin as "the best high school in the state." Nearly all of Franklin's seniors go on to college, whereas only twenty-three percent of Booker T. Washington's 1997 freshman class even made it to high school graduation. Franklin's students are largely white.

oppose schooling for blacks.[10] Since whites ran the political establishment, their opposition was dreadfully effective, and remained so until recent time. As one scholar remarked: "It was not until the 1960s that an African-American generation in the South had access to universal secondary education."[11] Many in the white establishment were opposed even to the most meager support for black education. One scholar cited an episode in the early 1930s when a private charity offered to pay the entire cost of a new public vocational high school which would be open to blacks. The offer was refused on grounds that such a school "would result in all the Negroes in the entire state coming to New Orleans."[12]

Up through the 1950s, public schools were rigidly segregated, and black schools were purposefully neglected. The result, of course, was generations of blacks who were systematically maleducated, or deprived of formal education altogether. (A sizeable number of New Orleans black citizens remains functionally illiterate—although estimates vary on the exact number.) As a further result of this destructive policy, there developed no tradition of "schooling experience" within many black families—and no knowledge of how to create one.[13]

So it was that, after *Brown* and the mass exodus of white students from the public schools, the New Orleans public school system was abandoned to an academically dispossessed black population. Thus, in a cruel irony, the white reaction to *Brown* in New Orleans created a new and equally pernicious version

[10] President Abraham Lincoln on 1 January 1863 issued the Emancipation Proclamation freeing the slaves in those states and territories still in rebellion against the Union. During Reconstruction (1865–1876), while New Orleans was occupied by federal troops, schools had been integrated, and children of both races attended public schools side by side —without evident harm to either group. For many years this chapter of Louisiana's educational history was systematically suppressed, and the "official" historical version of Reconstruction was that of noble whites suffering bravely under the brutal heel of military government, in collusion with corrupt and ignorant blacks. That was the version of Reconstruction history as told in standard Louisiana history books for the white grade schools. See, for example, Harriet Magruder's *A History of Louisiana*, published in Boston, New York City, and Philadelphia in 1909 by D. C. Heath and Co. See, especially, Chapter LIV, "After the War," and Chapter LV, "The Ku Klux Klan." "Negroes would not work," the history asserts, "and became impudent and dangerous. They became a source of great peril" (p. 327). The chapter goes on to recount the brave and honorable deeds of the Klan, helping to save Louisiana from black and Yankee oppression. A similar version of Reconstruction was also told in the government sponsored WPA guide to New Orleans, published in 1938 for a national audience, and still a standard reference work for the city.

[11] James Anderson, "a historian who directs educational policy studies at the University of Illinois," quoted in an article by Coleman Warner in *The Times-Picayune* of November 9, 2001.

[12] The citation is from James Anderson in the Coleman Warner article cited in footnote 11.

[13] Again, these ideas were attributed to James Anderson, in the same article by Coleman Warner.

of school segregation, the very condition which *Brown* had been designed to eliminate. The newly segregated school system continued to see a very high drop-out rate at the high school level; a 1990 survey showed that almost half of all black Orleanians possessed neither a high school diploma nor its equivalent, while the figure among whites was only about one in five.

The worst consequence of the wretched public school system is, of course, the educational impoverishment of black children, which, in turn, closes off a host of opportunities to those children as they grow older, not the least of which are hopes of decent jobs. It remains to be seen what the state's new testing program will do to improve New Orleans's public school system, but at least the problem is beginning to get the attention it deserves. But the maladies of the schools are deep-seated and self-perpetuating. As *The Times-Picayune* editorialized in April of 2001: "It will take years of sustained improvement before the (Orleans Parish) schools deserve to be called good."

The New Orleans schools are notorious, far beyond the limits of the parish. According to many observers, that reputation has played a major role in repelling potential migrants to New Orleans. That is especially true of middle- and upper-middle income families with quite ordinary educational ambitions for their children. In addition, it is widely believed that out-of-town businesses, which might otherwise have considered the city as a place to situate themselves, have simply dismissed New Orleans out-of-hand as a plausible location for their offices. It is a classic Catch-22: bad schools repel middle- and upper-income immigrants, and the absence of such immigrants deprives the schools of the moral and financial support they need in order to improve.

It is some consolation to know that the Catholic Diocese of New Orleans has opened small elementary schools which poor children can attend tuition-free. Such external intervention may be the only educational hope for poor black children, but at the present writing (late 2002) the efforts are operating at too small a scale to make much difference to the city at large. Meantime, the prospects for most of New Orleans's black children remain bleak.[14]

---

[14] The flight of white population to the suburbs obviously had profound effects on the racial composition of suburban school systems. The charts and graphs in *Appendix C* show that impact vividly, and they also reflect the flight of middle-class Orleanians, not to mention the increasing tendency of Jefferson Parish parents to put their children into private schools. In Jefferson, where the total population is overwhelmingly white, black children outnumber white in the public schools, the result of white children being transferred to private and parochial schools. As of the 1999–2000 school year, the same tendency was just beginning to appear in the outer suburbs of St. Tammany Parish—although the black population of St. Tammany is much smaller than either Orleans or Jefferson. In a few years, however, it would not be surprising to discover St. Tammany beginning to emulate Jefferson's example, while Jefferson slowly comes to be more and more similiar to New Orleans itself.

Housing for the Poor in a Poor City

Disasters seldom occur in isolation. As the end of the twentieth century approached, it was becoming obvious that New Orleans faced not just a crisis in schooling, but a crisis in housing as well. There simply was insufficient decent housing to shelter the city's poor people. And because the city's population of poor people was huge, the housing problem was correspondingly huge.

The main problem lay with public housing, run by the Housing Authority of New Orleans (HANO). In 2000, according to HANO's figures, the agency owned and operated 11,235 dwelling units, more than ninety percent of which were in ten "major public housing developments"—what the public at large generally called "The Projects."

The original motivation to build free, or nearly free, housing for needy people was a noble enterprise. It had begun during the Depression of the 1930s, when all kinds of ordinary people had lost their jobs and found themselves driven into the street. It was a desperate situation, to which the federal government responded, by helping states and municipalities to build subsidized housing for those in need. It was an unprecedented act of high-mindedness. At the time, nobody had the remotest idea that such a generous enterprise could possibly go wrong. But, then, nobody in the 1930s could have foreseen the changes in the racial geography of the U.S. that occurred in the last half of the twentieth century, nor did they dream that public housing would become one of America's worst urban nightmares.

New Orleans was among the first American cities to build large-scale public housing for low-income people. The first major "project" was the Iberville complex, completed in 1941, just lakeside of the French Quarter, on the site of the notorious Storyville red-light district near the turning basin of the abandoned and filled-in Carondolet Canal.[15] It was classic New Deal "slum clearance,"

[15] Storyville is an essential part of New Orleans's legend, and innumerable tales have been told about it. A city alderman, named Sidney Story, had decided that prostitution could not be banned, but ought to be limited geographically. The city council, in its wisdom, decided to confine it to a commercial district next to the turning basin of the Carondolet Canal, a gathering place for vagrant sailors in search of on-shore amusement. Because Storyville was off the beaten track of respectable citizens, sailors, prostitutes, barkeepers, and even drug-dealers could go about their business without attracting undue public attention. Storyville became well-known, to put it mildly, and there was even an official *Blue Book* which served as a guide and directory to the district's sundry delights. Storyville met its nemesis in 1917, when Woodrow Wilson's Secretary of the Navy was Josephus Daniels, an unyielding foe of liquor and other forms of vice. On the demand of Daniels's Navy Department, Storyville was shut down as a "war measure" for the protection of sailors, but when the war ended, it "never regained its former status." (The elegant wording is from the WPA's *New Orleans City Guide*.) By the 1930s it had become a half-abandoned slum. Storyville's demolition to make room for public housing was a shining metaphor for New Deal reform programs. With Storyville gone, alabaster cities could indeed gleam, undimmed by human vice, and burnished by high hopes of creating a new Zion. For a sanitized account of Storyville's rise and fall, see the Federal Writers' Project of the WPA, *New Orleans City Guide*, 1938, pp. 217–219.

where undesirable neighborhoods were demolished and replaced by buildings where people in need could find orderly, sanitary, and agreeable places to live. In many instances it was assumed that public housing would serve an urgent but temporary need; thus, when the bad times eventually ended, families could regain their financial footing and find more spacious and elaborate dwellings elsewhere. Meantime, there was Iberville: about 850 units, in well-built brick units, three stories high, with spacious, grassy courtyards shaded by spreading oaks. It was an uncrowded, highly domestic atmosphere, and a very pleasant one.

As was typically the case in those days, each housing project was racially segregated, and the original occupants of the Iberville Project were all white—many of them economic refugees from the French Quarter across the street. By the 1960s, when the courts ordered public housing to be desegregated, New Orleans had built almost a dozen major projects, which by the century's end housed more than 30,000 residents.

It is uncertain exactly when the realization finally sank in, but by the 1990s it was generally agreed that the projects had gone seriously off the rails. The courts had ordered an end to segregation in the 1960s, and, in a cheerless parallel with the schools after desegregation, the projects saw white families depart and blacks move in. By the 1970s, the projects were almost totally black, and, as time went on, the projects became places that concentrated the poorest of the poor—ill-educated and often unemployed. And like similar projects in northern cities, New Orleans's projects housed a disproportionate number of single mothers with dependent children—and in many of the projects females outnumbered males by a ratio of two to one. The projects had become nuclei for the city's most desperate and hopeless poverty, and fertile grounds for social disintegration. Police statistics revealed that the projects were centers for some of New Orleans's highest rates of violent crime.

Bad as the projects were, most of the city's residents tried (successfully) to avoid them. It was possible for most Orleanians to go about their daily business without going near a project. That was particularly true in the case of a project such as Desire, generally acknowledged to be the city's worst. The Desire project was located in such an isolated part of the city that it could safely be ignored and neglected by the city's movers and shakers—not to mention most of the city's residents who had never laid eyes on Desire except at a great distance.

But there were other ways of ignoring the projects. Detailed maps of the downtown area inevitably showed such features as the ancient St. Louis Cemeteries No. 1 and No. 2, but the Iberville Project, literally across the street and occupying a much larger area than the cemeteries, was simply not shown on most maps. (In this book Figures 4 and 5 are exceptions.) The projects were expunged from public knowledge in much the same way that Stalin had ordered all mention of Trotsky expunged from the Great Soviet Encyclopedia. Iberville was not shown on the map, so Iberville did not exist. But Iberville could not be totally overlooked. It had degenerated to the point where tourists were warned against visiting the adjacent cemeteries without escorts, lest they be assaulted and robbed, presumably by miscreants who lived across the street in Iberville. It was said to be dangerous for a visibly affluent person to venture close to a project.

All that changed abruptly in the late 1990s when HANO was declared to be so badly run that it was placed under federal supervision. Meantime, national policy-makers had agreed that large-scale public housing in the United States had failed, partly for architectural reasons, but largely because it had led to the exclusion of poor, powerless people from the mainstreams of urban life. Under a federal program called "Project HOPE," the worst of the old projects would be demolished, and the cleared areas used to build new "mixed-income" housing. Part of this new housing would be for poor people, subsidized as before, but the bulk would be made available at "market rates" for people of higher income. And the new housing would be designed as if it were created for people of means; no longer would public housing be designed to look cheap. "The idea," as *The Times-Picayune* put it, "was to avoid the isolated concentration of poor people that often became breeding grounds for crime, drug abuse, and despair." Poor people would live cheek by jowl with middle-class and even affluent people, as they rarely did in American cities.

It was in that spirit that HANO, under federal supervision, ordered the demolition and redevelopment of the infamous Desire Project. Few tears were shed; hardly anybody except a few displaced residents had kind words to say about Desire. But it was a different matter when HANO decided to demolish and redevelop the St. Thomas Project, in the Uptown part of the city, close to the Mississippi River.

St. Thomas had been built in 1941 to help accommodate the sizable number of poor and near-poor people who lived in the nearby Irish Channel and neighboring areas. Since it was completed, however, two things had happened to seal the project's fate. The first was the same kind of social degeneration that had afflicted the other large public housing projects—not just in New Orleans, but all over the nation. The second, however, was peculiar to New Orleans Close by St. Thomas were some of the city's most affluent neighborhoods, conspicuously in the Garden District. And just downriver from St. Thomas, the combined successes of the Convention Center and the booming Warehouse District were drawing increased investment from real estate developers and redevelopers, who correctly viewed the real estate which St. Thomas occupied—and the district around it—as a potential, serious money-maker. A poor and run-down public housing project was clearly a festering sore in what otherwise might become an up-market and profitable residential and commercial district.

So HANO, in its wisdom, decided to demolish the St. Thomas Project, with about 1,500 units, and replace it with federally funded mixed-income housing. The whole redevelopment project was slated to create 1,142 new units, "ranging from luxury condos to a continuing-care retirement community." Of the total, 337 units would be subsidized and earmarked for low-income people. Commercial development would be part of the new project, including a very large Wal-Mart with an equally large parking lot, to be erected in the place of some old but architecturally distinguished buildings that stood empty, or semi-empty, along adjacent arterial streets. Wal-Mart and its backers argued (correctly) that there was no large cut-rate store in the near-Uptown area, and that the residents would benefit from having one.

The resulting uproar had a predictably Orleanian tone about it. The displaced black residents at St. Thomas complained bitterly that the new project would eject them from their homes to make room for affluent whites. That charge did not seem unfounded, since there were nowhere nearly enough dwelling units to house the displaced residents. But HANO—and the developers—assured them that there was plenty of room for them in subsidized housing elsewhere in the city. The ex-residents of the demolished project denounced the developers as schemers, liars, profiteers, and racists. Law suits were brought to stop the proceedings, but they failed to slow the demolition of St. Thomas.

Meantime, throngs of residents (mainly white) denounced the Wal-Mart scheme on environmental grounds. Preservationists decried the demolition of existing antique buildings, and denounced Wal-Mart's plans for big-box architecture and oceans of asphalt parking lot, as grossly out-of-scale for a fine-grained old Orleanian neighborhood. Residential neighbors echoed the preservationists, calling the development a suburban-style insult to the milieu of a richly textured old city—and the destruction of a neighborhood which could never be replaced. Local merchants whose shops lined Magazine and Tchoupitoulas streets predicted that Wal-Mart would pull the economic rug out from under their small enterprises, and drive them out of business—leaving Wal-Mart as the sole retailer for a once-lively commercial district. Other residents, mainly blacks, supported Wal-Mart, on grounds that the superstore would provide them with consumer goods that were otherwise unavailable in Uptown New Orleans, and at modest prices which would help low-income people balance their family budgets—something that the funky little shops of Magazine Street could and would not do. Anti-Wal-Mart preservationists—mainly affluent whites—were promptly denounced as racists, who had begun by stealing the houses of poor blacks, and were now in the process of denying them access to affordable food and clothing. All in all it was a messy and bitter fight, but it seemed likely (as this was written) that the black establishment in City Hall would endorse Wal-Mart's plans, albeit with some restrictions on the size of the parking lot, and some refinements to the company's big-box architecture. Meanwhile, few responsible observers will predict whether mixed-income housing will really work, nor will they forecast the effect of the nation's biggest retailer opening its doors in an old, traditional New Orleans neighborhood. It is safe to predict that the results will be mixed, and that nobody will be totally satisfied—except a few real estate developers who stand to make a great deal of money from the transformations.

Aside from the difficulties with large-scale public housing, New Orleans also has a serious problem with the decay and abandonment of private housing for low-income people—mainly black. In the poorer parts of black New Orleans, there is a very low rate of homeownership; rental properties are the rule. It is possible to travel the streets of low-income black neighborhoods and see one dilapidated house after another; plainly neither owners nor tenants have been much motivated to maintain the property. It is hardly surprising that, as houses deteriorate, tenants and owners often abandon them completely, leaving the mostly wooden houses to the tender mercies of wood rot, Formosan termites, or street gangs and drug dealers who move into vacant dwellings to conduct their operations. There may be cities in the United States where one can abandon a house without serious consequences, but New Orleans is not among them. As Coleman Warner wrote in a *Times-Picayune* article entitled "A Blight on the City": ". . . abandoned blighted houses number in the thousands in New Orleans, making up a sizeable share of the 37,000 vacant housing units (in the city). New Orleans easily ranks among the most troubled cities in the nation on this issue . . . Abandoned houses easily rank as the No. 2 (city problem) in the minds of many Orleanians—just behind crime."

Although New Orleans's population of middle-class blacks is small, a scattering of black families who could afford it have been moving into "eastern New Orleans," an inclusive name for a belt of former swampland south of Lake

Pontchartrain and east of the Industrial Canal. The area was one of the last, large undeveloped areas within the bounds of Orleans Parish, and, before the oil crash, grandiose plans had been laid out to develop it into suburban housing for upwardly-mobile whites. A partial network of drainage canals had been built, along with a patchwork of streets and utilities—and in several small areas, a few houses as well. A goodly number of whites had actually moved in, seeing eastern New Orleans as their last chance of in-town suburban living. Despite heavy advertising, affluent buyers were not to be found, and the ambitious developments were abandoned or went bankrupt—among them "New Orleans East," the biggest and most elaborate of the schemes. In the following years, various builders bought up parcels of semi-drained "land" on an ad hoc basis, and a patchwork of low-cost houses and apartments was built. These were gradually occupied by blue-collar and middle-class blacks, whereupon the area's small white population decamped. Eastern New Orleans is now one of the few examples of middle-class black suburbia in the metropolitan area.

Chapter 6
A New Population Geography

Suburbs were slower to develop in the New Orleans metropolitan area than in most other large American cities. The reason was simple: there was very little well-drained land outside the city. As we have seen, however, suburban pressures after World War II had inspired developers to drain the east bank of Jefferson Parish, and had converted it into instant suburbs. By 1980, Jefferson had become the second most populous parish in Louisiana, with almost as many people as New Orleans itself.

The migration to East Bank Jefferson Parish was highly selective. Most of the new suburbanites were middle-class and blue-collar whites, and their migration to Jefferson Parish goes a long way toward explaining the near absence of a white middle-class in New Orleans City. But East Bank Jefferson Parish clearly welcomed neither poor people nor black people. Although few public officials will admit that parish residents practiced systematic racial bias as East Bank Jefferson filled up, detailed maps of black people and of white people strongly suggest otherwise. Except for a few black ghettos, most of East Bank Jefferson Parish's territory remained white.

Jefferson's population explosion occurred mainly between 1940 and 1980. But then, abruptly, the migration stream stopped, as if a spigot had suddenly been turned off. Since 1980 the population remained essentially flat—in numbers, if not in composition.[1] East Bank Jefferson Parish was full—an ocean of tract-style houses, shopping centers of all sizes, and untidy strip-commercial building along most of the arterial roads. Would-be suburbanites, who still lived in Orleans Parish, were beginning to look elsewhere, and so were some disenchanted folk who had moved to Jefferson, only to find it falling short of Nirvana. A good many evidently were not enthralled by the prospect of living in a poorly drained version of post-World War II Los Angeles.

Meantime, a sizable number of Orleanians had looked longingly to the prospect of suburban living on the north shore of Lake Pontchartrain in St. Tammany Parish. Indeed, for a long time, a few city-dwellers had spent the hot summers in cottages on the lake's north shore in what came to be called "The Ozone Belt"—realtors' language to describe a place that was marginally cooler than New Orleans in summer and with marginally fresher air. But St. Tammany was too far away from the city for reasonable commuting around the edge of the Lake, and, until the 1960s, roads were narrow and traffic exasperatingly slow.

Then, in 1959, things began to jump. A twenty-two mile causeway—advertising itself as "The Longest Bridge in the World!"—was completed across Lake Pontchartrain, from East Bank Jefferson Parish to Mandeville in St. Tammany. Commuters from New Orleans immediately began to take up new suburban residence in and around Mandeville and Covington, and more joined them when a second causeway span was built a few years later, effectively turning it into a high-speed, four-lane highway. While the causeway helped to start a wave of suburbanization into St. Tammany, the migration was far from being a tidal wave—perhaps because tolls on the causeway discouraged people of modest means, perhaps because of the bridge's frequent traffic jams.

But the demographic tsunami was not long in coming. With the completion of Interstate 10 in the late 1960s, with its colossal bridges and causeways across the east end of Lake Pontchartrain, the drive from New Orleans to Slidell in eastern St. Tammany Parish dropped to a fraction of its former time. A whole new world of potential suburbia was open to the huddled masses of greater New Orleans, and they came in droves.

It is worth recalling that the country north of Lake Pontchartrain differs enormously from that to the south. The lake itself and everything to the south

[1] The demographic makeup of the Parish was already changing before 1980, and it changed substantially after that, largely through aging of the existing population and the decline in numbers of school-age children.

of it—New Orleans included—is part of the Mississippi River's deltaic wet-lands. To the north, faulting has uplifted the surface to elevations that are slight, but high enough to be free of most serious flooding. Subsequent erosion by run-ning water had carved the poorly cemented bedrock into low, infertile hills of yellow sand or red clay that evoke images from one of Erskine Caldwell's gothic novels. As long as St. Tammany was isolated from the outside world, it offered few opportunities to make a living—save for a bit of fishing and cutting spindly pines for use as wood pulp or lumber. The land really was not good for much—except for building houses, and that was a notable exception. And those houses began to appear as soon as Orleanians found that they could drive I-10 from New Orleans to Slidell at speeds in excess of seventy miles per hour. During the 1990s, St. Tammany's population grew faster than any parish in Louisiana, and the air was redolent with the scent of diesel fumes, newly excavated earth, and newly printed money.

To the native inhabitants of St. Tammany, zoning had always been anathe-matic, an un-American (and certainly un-southern) concept which would infringe on landowners' rights to do whatever they wanted with their property rights that are viewed as absolute and inviolable by many rural people in Louisiana.[2] Over time, zoning did come, but it was too fragmentary and too paltry to prevent the usual excesses that accompany the too-rapid development of rural areas. To be sure, St. Tammany did not look quite as bad as Jefferson, partly because most of it was newer and there was more elbow room. Meantime, its landscape had taken on a rather eccentric two-layered charac-ter—highly visible to a motorist who drives U.S. 190 from Slidell to Mandeville.[3]

The lower and older layer of the landscape is fairly typical of the upcountry South, and the ingredients are unmistakable to anyone who has driven across the rural South, carefully avoiding cities and main roads: weathered wooden houses of indeterminate age, gray from lack of paint, their sagging verandahs opening onto packed sand yards, strewn with pine litter—the same yards deco-rated with elderly pickup trucks in various states of disrepair, bearing license

[2] This kind of semianarchic libertarianism is neither limited to Louisiana nor the South. But the South has more than its share, and it is not confined to rural areas. It is no coincidence that the largest city in the South and the fourth largest in the U.S., Houston, is without zoning.

[3] Most people drive I-12, the new alternative to U.S. 190, but the latter is a much better way to see St. Tammany's landscape in convulsive transition.

plates (if any) from times long past, cablights for spotting deer, and bumper stickers exhorting viewers to support Second Amendment rights and the speedy impeachment of Bill Clinton; cinderblock churches, painted white in some earlier incarnation, and often embellished with crosses made of glass bricks, embedded in the cinderblocks, and occasionally illuminated from behind with vivid blue or red neon; small ramshackle barns, with sagging roofs, and faded advertisements for Mail Pouch Tobacco or Dr. Pierce's Golden Medical Discovery; roadside signs bearing apocalyptic messages, admonishing passersby to repent their sins, or to purchase remedies for constipation, dyspepsia, or sour stomachs—other signs on a more positive note;[4] exhortations to try The Dixie Cafe's fried catfish, or Jimmy-Joe's Boiled Peanuts "2 mi. ahead on R," or instructions on how to tune your car radio to inspirational gospel messages; unpainted wooden gas stations, with unpaved driveways and two pumps in front and a third alongside the building for kerosene, clouded windows glowing with neon beer signs, and offering cut-rate gas, cut-rate alcohol, live bait, and boats for rent by day or hour; and rutted tracks leading off into the piney woods toward unknown destinations—houses? a trailer park? a rural church?—where there is no livestock save for occasional lost chickens, only the sagging remnants of a few old fences, long abandoned, where somebody once tried to farm the paltry earth but gave up long ago. This bottom layer of the cultural landscape is an antique, and belongs to another day and place. In any event, nobody is making any more of it in St. Tammany Parish, and it is slowly fading away.

Atop this old landscape, and separated from it by a yawning cultural and temporal discontinuity, is a much newer layer of landscape, an unfinished mosaic of twenty-first-century exurban artifacts, some so new that the machines that made them are still at work: bulldozers, backhoes, and utility company ditch-diggers to bury utility lines and cables, lest they offend the sensitive eye. The scale of this new landscape is huge and coarse-grained, and, compared to the older landscape, consumes land with a lupine appetite: enormous new shopping centers, clustered around the interchanges of I-12, just to the north, with parking lots sensitively landscaped with mature magnolias and crêpe myrtle, and anchored by upscale department stores with home offices in Dallas; stores in the malls selling Gucci handbags or North Face hiking gear;

---

[4] James Dickey in his novel *Deliverance* first called attention to this roadside evidence of rural southerners' curious preoccupation with their gastric disorders.

along the road, branches of New Orleans banks, done in reassuring neo-Williamsburg styles, complete with manicured lawns, 24-7 cash machines, and imitation hitching posts to discourage motorists from driving on the grass; walled subdivisions with wrought-iron gates and uniformed guards ready to bar one's entry or hand out colored brochures from real estate agencies in Slidell and Baton Rouge; inside the gates, postmodern McMansions in vaguely neo-Queen Anne style and thousands of square feet of living space, three or four attached garages with basketball hoops and at least one ocean-going vessel parked amphibiously on a trailer in the curving driveway; along the road, signs with subdued gilded lettering, announcing animal clinics that cater not to farmers with cattle and hogs, but to nearby residents whose miniature poodles need to be barbered, shampooed, or manicured; discreet auto agencies with vast glass-fronted showrooms, where one can buy a needed Jaguar convertible or Mercedes SUV, mostly new but a few "pre-owned"; and roads turning south toward Lake Pontchartrain with directions to marinas—"Yacht moorings, spaces available." And everywhere along the road, signs for more: COMMERCIAL ACREAGE FOR SALE, WILL BUILD TO SUIT, HOME SITES ALL UTILITIES, SHOPPING CENTER COMING SOON, BAPTIST CHURCH WILL BE ERECTED ON THIS SITE ALL WELCOME . . .

Age is a relative thing when it comes to suburbs, and it is clear that suburban growth comes in stages. By Orleanian standards, Jefferson Parish is an "old" suburb, even though most of its buildings are less than fifty years old. But its population is not increasing, and the 2000 census reveals that there is the beginning of net outmigration from the parish. Some of those outmigrants are removing to St. Tammany, metro New Orleans's "new" suburb. David Rusk, the well-known analyst of modern American cities, issued a report on the condition of greater New Orleans in 1999, and in it he compared booming St. Tammany Parish with the sagging fortunes of Jefferson. "Today's winners become tomorrow's losers," he said. "That's the Iron Law of Urban Sprawl."

Iron law or not, it is clear that Jefferson Parish has seen its day while, at the turn of the twenty-first century, St. Tammany's had just begun. If one is asked to forecast St. Tammany's future, the signs along the sides of U.S. 190 provide an unequivocal answer: we should expect more of the same. It remains to be seen whether St. Tammany's government can pull itself together and create a working plan to prevent the parish from becoming "tomorrow's loser." If experience in Louisiana's suburbs is any guide, however, one can be pardoned for doubting it.

Meantime, Back in the City:
The Expansion of White Territory

Although a good share of Orleans Parish's white population had bolted for the suburbs during the last four decades of the twentieth century, a small but significant number remained behind, and they inhabit some of New Orleans's most distinctive and handsome districts. The largest numbers are geographically concentrated in two upscale East Bank neighborhoods, which contain some of the city's priciest and best-maintained housing stock.

The older district, where much of the white establishment had long ago rooted itself, is a long swath parallel to the Mississippi River, stretching from the old suburb of Carrollton and the adjacent Tulane/Loyola/Audubon Park neighborhoods on the upriver side, downriver along St. Charles Avenue, through the Garden District as far as the Warehouse District, then hopping the central business district into the French Quarter and Faubourg Marigny. The newer of the two white districts lies between the upriver (western) edge of City Park and the Jefferson Parish boundary—an area loosely called the "Lakefront Neighborhoods," but actually extending about three miles inland from the actual shore of Lake Pontchartrain. The white population of both districts is largely affluent and deeply entrenched, and it seems unlikely that either area will change very much in racial composition.

Many of the whites who stayed in the city have one thing in common that distinguishes them from those who fled: they are mostly died-in-the-wool urbanophiles who enjoy the amenities of urban life and are not amused by visions of green lawns and backyard barbecues. And to hear some of them talk, they are vociferous Orleanophiles; whether natives or not, they love the city in spite of its numerous defects—which most of them know only too well. Some are bound by ties of nostalgia: they have grown up in the city and are used to it; they proclaim loudly that they cannot imagine living anywhere else.

Among the whites who stayed, there is constant pressure to find more housing, even though population density in white districts is generally much lower than that in the crowded precincts of black New Orleans. Thus, in more than a few instances, old established white districts have gradually expanded, and the directions of expansion are not random.

Much of the white expansion takes the form of 'gentrification'—the reoccupation and restoration of run-down or abandoned housing by upwardly-mobile people, mainly white. Gentrification has occurred most commonly in areas of good-quality but neglected houses, often of considerable age and architectural distinction, which over the years had been allowed to degenerate, either through ill-chosen modifications or simply through neglect. In the typical scenario of gentrification, those run-down old houses are bought up by architectural sophisticates at bargain-basement prices, the residents are ejected, and the new owners (the so-called gentry) then restore the houses to their former grandeur.[5] Many of the gentrifiers are not gentry at all—certainly not in the British sense of the word—but commonly are young couples without much money who are willing to expend their own sweat-equity in fixing up an old house—doing most of the painting, reroofing, and repairing of the plumbing and wiring themselves—until the place becomes livable and even gracious.

Gentrification often occurs in waves, commonly because the initial rehabilitation of a run-down neighborhood by middle-class or affluent whites is risky—both financially and physically—and white would-be gentrifiers feel safer if they are members of good-sized group, all engaged in the same enterprise at the same time. Gentrification in New Orleans has followed that pattern over the last several decades, and several well-known districts were rather suddenly turned from slums (or semi-slums) into upscale and often expensive neighborhoods. For those who were lucky and got in on the process early, there was a great deal of money to be made, as prices for restored houses in up-and-coming neighborhoods suddenly began to rise—partly because of physical reconstruction, partly because a given neighborhood was suddenly viewed as a desirable place to live.

Virtually all of the gentrification occurred in the old city, on or near the Mississippi River and along Esplanade Ridge. And that gentrification occurred in two well-defined areas.[6] The first occurred on the Uptown side of the central business district, and was largely impelled by the expansion of commercial activity, first from Canal Street toward Poydras Street in the 1970s and 80s, and then,

[5] Gentrification is a cause for much resentment among African-Americans and others, who charge that gentrification's common effect is to turn poor black people out of their homes for the convenience and enrichment of up-market whites. While it is true that gentrification has been a force for architectural preservation in many cities and towns, its social consequences have often been very destructive.

[6] There was little or no occasion for gentrification in the affluent Lakefront neighborhoods; most of them had been built up after World War II and there were no antique treasures nearby to attract the attentions of rehabilitationists. Algiers Point, on the West Bank, with a sizeable number of old semi-dilapidated houses, on the other hand, has been a major target for gentrifiers.

with the creation of the Morial Convention Center, mainly in the 1990s, still farther uptown into areas that had only recently been neglected—to put it politely. A good deal of that territory had been decidedly slummy.

As we have already seen, the Convention Center had encouraged the restoration of commercial buildings, most conspicuously in the Warehouse District, where a number were converted into medium-scale and upscale apartments and condos. Then, too, there appeared a "Museum District," between the Warehouse District and Lee Circle, the district anchored by the fine Romanesque pile of the Confederate Museum's Memorial Hall, the Contemporary Arts Center (redesigned in the early 1990s to much critical acclaim), and the creation in 2000 of the National D-Day Museum. Other museums and galleries are and will be scattered around the neighborhood, adding to it a certain air of dignity and stability, not to mention drawing tourists and with them a considerable police presence. And with the demolition of the St. Thomas Public Housing Project and its site built up with newly respectable housing, gentrification spread rapidly throughout the large but ill-defined zone between the Greater New Orleans Bridge, the Garden District, and the Mississippi River.

Within that zone, several famous old areas were targets for upgrading, conspicuously the Irish Channel, and a much neglected area which suddenly lost its anonymity when it was dubbed "The Lower Garden District" and abruptly began to gentrify. The initial stages of that gentrification had been provoked by the publication of a splendid five-volume series of books about New Orleans's architecture, sponsored by the Friends of the Cabildo. The first of the series, published in 1971, dealt with the Lower Garden District. While these architectural books were not the first of their genre, they were handsome, authoritative, and widely distributed among the city's movers and shakers. And because they were published during a period when the city was prosperous and when preservationists had begun to achieve widespread success, the books made an unusual impact by focusing attention on areas which had formerly been neglected by the city's architectural gurus.

Then, as gentrification spread and became increasingly profitable, it was further encouraged by cheerleaders in the land development business, who used the real estate section of *The Times-Picayune* to depict these areas as hot properties for those who wanted fine old housing at rock-bottom prices. As prices rose, those houses presently ceased to be bargains, especially after the newspaper and various realtors began to hawk the merits of vernacular house-types that had heretofore gone unnoticed by many promoters. Lavishly illustrated articles appeared, introducing architectural tyros to the architectural virtues of workaday houses such as shotguns, bungalows, Creole cottages, and even camelbacks—none of which had been particularly fashionable until they received the official imprimatur of mass media. When that happened, public opinion promptly followed.

In addition to this upriver surge of gentrification, there was a second surge that originated in the French Quarter and was propelled in a downriver direction. It was prodded not only by demand for more gentrifiable antique housing, but also by major changes in the Quarter itself.

As we have seen, the French Quarter had taken on an aura of antique elegance, only after strenuous private and public efforts to rescue and burnish it, mainly in the first four decades of the twentieth century. By mid-century, however, the Quarter had become a cherished icon for Orleanians, and a major destination for the city's increasing throngs of tourists.

The Quarter was also home to a good many permanent residents—some of whom, such as Tennessee Williams, were famous for their artistic achievements and others simply because it was interestingly eccentric place to live. For would-be Bohemians, living in the Quarter was a domestic version of living in a 1920s Parisian garret.

Meanwhile, the Quarter received a good deal of admiring publicity from out-of-town and resident literati alike, depicting it as charmingly unlike anything else in the United States, and a laid-back refuge for folk of cosmopolitan taste and eccentric life-styles. More and more people came to the Quarter, curious to see what the publicity was all about, and what had become a pleasantly funky old neighborhood in time turned into something quite different. With more and more people came more and more traffic, more noise, and more drunken partying both inside and outdoors. To that was added a rising tide of commercial tackiness, and, as that happened, old-time residents began to move elsewhere. The Vieux Carré Commission had met with success in preventing demolition of the Quarter's antique buildings, and had persuaded the city to ban the erection of new hotels. In spite of that, a good many family residences were illegally converted into tourist accommodations—thus adding to the general commotion and reducing the number of private residences. And there were stories of rich Texans coming to the Quarter and buying a fine old house for use as a *pied à terre* for Mardi Gras and occasional weekend parties, but leaving it vacant for the rest of the year.

For these reasons and doubtless others, the number of permanent residents in the Vieux Carré began to drain away. In 1940, slightly more than 11,000 people lived in the Quarter; by the end of the century, the number had declined to fewer than 4,000. Although there were signs that the hemorrhage was slackening, there was little sign that the Quarter would regain its old-time residential character.

It required no feats of imagination to discover where the Quarter's residents had gone. A good many apparently had simply moved downriver a few blocks across Esplanade Avenue, settling down into Faubourg Marigny, one of New Orleans's earliest suburbs and the locus of a good variety of fine nineteenth-century houses. Here was opportunity for gentrification on a grand scale, and before long Marigny was converted into a place that resembled the French Quarter in the early twentieth century—a district of distinguished but decayed houses, almost as old as those in the Quarter, and now being restored by new immigrants. And, inevitably, gentrification was rolling still farther downriver into the neighborhood of Bywater and more slowly into Tremé .

Out of the Closet: The Gay Landscape of New Orleans

A significant proportion of the new generation of gentrifiers moving into Faubourg Marigny were gay men. Although some had been former residents of the Quarter, a goodly number had come from outside the city, seeking refuge in New Orleans, traditionally the most tolerant and easy-going city in the South.

New Orleans had long been the seat of a significant but largely clandestine gay community, predating the epochal Stonewall riots of 1969 in New York City.[7] The term "significant" cannot be translated into exact numbers; the census does not enumerate population in terms of sexual preferences. Nevertheless, the census *does* tally the number of households where living quarters are shared by two members of the same sex, and the census tracts which contain the French Quarter and Faubourg Marigny show up as having some of the highest numbers

---

[7] The riots occurred on 28 June 1969, when the New York City police raided the Stonewall Inn in Greenwich Village, a well-known gay hangout. The police had a long-standing practice of raiding gay bars and arresting gay men for various offenses, real or imaginary. At Stonewall, however, resentful gays resisted the police and fought back. Riots followed and continued sporadically for several days, amid publicity that spread nationwide. When the police finally backed down, there was national jubilation among gays, who still celebrate the anniversary of Stonewall as a day of gay liberation, and a turning point in social attitudes toward gays and gay attitudes toward themselves. After Stonewall, little by little, the condition of gays in the United States grew markedly less oppressive.

of same-sex male households, not just in the city, but of any in the entire nation.[8] A good deal of the information about gay New Orleans is unavoidably anecdotal, although that does not necessarily detract from its accuracy.

Long before Stonewall, when nearly all American homosexuals were closeted (that is, they kept their sexual orientation secret), there were clandestine grapevines within and between American communities of gay men that stretched all across the nation. Certain places and areas were known to be homophobic (anti-gay), while others were reputed to be islands of tolerance. Most of rural and small town America had a reputation for homophobia, a reputation well-deserved in the conservative and fundamentalist Upland South, including much of Louisiana outside New Orleans. By contrast, tolerance was to be found especially in big "sophisticated" cities, where eccentric behavior of all kinds was common and unremarkable. And unlike small towns, big cities were places where gays could lose themselves in the mass of population, and where small gay communities could take form without much public notice or opprobrium. Seaports such as San Francisco, New York City, Boston, Chicago, and New Orleans, with large itinerant populations, were fertile grounds for the development of such communities, which were well-known to those who were plugged into the national underground network.

New Orleans possessed all the properties necessary to encourage the early growth of a major gay community. Homophobia was virulent in the southern Bible Belt, which extends to the very margins of metropolitan New Orleans. Even in easygoing Cajun Louisiana, an openly gay male was unlikely to have an easy time. New Orleans, on the other hand, had a long-standing reputation as a place that was tolerant of aberrant behavior, including sexual orientation—a place where elaborately dressed drag queens, for example, had long been a

[8] Nobody claims that these particular census data are very precise, but they seem to be useful in making comparisons between census tracts. Informal postcensus interviews revealed that many gay couples were not counted in the 2000 enumeration of same-sex households, and knowledgeable observers, gay and straight alike, admit that the 2000 data undercounted the actual number of gay couples—but by how much, nobody really knows. The same questions, however, were asked in the 1990 census, and the 2000 data are more than six times as large as those in 1990. Although fundamentalists and others professed to be dismayed at this "increase" in the gay population, most see the astronomic increase as simply indicating that more and more gays are not afraid to be identified and tallied. Rather than an increase in gay population, the numbers apparently reveal a more relaxed attitude toward homosexuality in some parts of the United States.

deliberately outrageous part of Mardi Gras celebrations.[9] Exotic behavior was conspicuously acceptable in the French Quarter, providing only that the behavior was not *too* exotic and did not spill out publicly into the city's more staid neighborhoods. Thus, if a young gay man from the rural South sought a place to live among others of like inclination, the French Quarter was an obvious and convenient place to go. There, a young gay man could be assured of admission to the city's homosexual community, where there were networks within networks which could help him find new friends and get a new job—perhaps quite a good job. Even before Stonewall, as more and more of New Orleans's gays emerged from the closet, there had developed a gay Establishment, which operated gay newspapers, bars, hotels, rooming houses, and business directories—making it clear that gays were welcome, either as permanent residents or as tourists.[10] The French Quarter of New Orleans was a world away from the worlds of Natchitoches and Napoleonville.

So gays came to New Orleans, and they continue to come. Estimates of their numbers vary wildly, but the most conservative set the figure at two-and-one-half percent of the city's total population—although gay publications naturally think the number is a good deal higher. No matter what statistic one accepts, it cannot begin to reflect the powerful influence of the city's gay population on the economic and social geography of New Orleans. That influence has taken several very conspicuous forms.

In the first place, gays played (and continue to play) a formidable role in neighborhood gentrification. The city's traditional gay community was centered in the residential northern corner of the French Quarter (that is, Lakeside and Downriver); there, a number of gay bars set up business, serving the combined functions of watering holes and places for gossip and liaison. Those bars also functioned as unofficial entry ports for gays who had newly arrived in the city, or simply for gay tourists who came to visit and mingle with the indigenous gay population.

---

[9] "Drag" in homosexual argot means "women's dress." Drag queens are homosexual men who adopt outrageously female dress, makeup, and hair-style—and who affect defiantly feminine behavior as well.

[10] More recently, bars and lodging places, hospitable to gays, are openly advertised on New Orleans's Web sites. The internet has proved a powerful tool to distribute information to a highly dispersed national population of gay men and women.

But the rising rents and increased commotion, which had driven straights (heterosexuals) from residences in the Vieux Carré, did the same thing to gays, who were among the earliest refugees from the Quarter to move into Faubourg Marigny, eventually converting it from a semi-slum into one of the more picturesque and prosperous neighborhoods in New Orleans. White gay males, many of whom enjoyed a fair amount of disposable income, functioned as the spearhead of up-market restoration, settling in Marigny at a time when most New Orleans's whites would have shunned the district as seedy and dangerous.

New Orleans was not the only city—or even the first—where gays played a major role in neighborhood restoration. In San Francisco, gay white males had done similar things some years earlier. There, gay men in search of stylish but inexpensive housing had spotted the Castro district, just off upper Market Street, as a place of great architectural elegance, but where racial conflict between blacks and Hispanics had made the place too violent and dangerous for most San Franciscans' tastes. In consequence, fine old houses were renting or selling for abnormally low prices. In effect, gays got the chance to buy distinguished old Victorian houses at panic prices because they were willing not only to invest "sweat equity" to restore those houses themselves, but also to put up with a certain level of personal peril—at least temporarily. The first gays to settle in the Castro were subject to the very real threat of "gay-bashing" by homophobic black and Hispanic males. But, after all, gay-bashing in San Francisco was not unique to the Castro, and it was viewed by local gays as one cost of building their own community.

But the long-term results in Faubourg Marigny were similar to those in San Francisco's Castro. As more and more white gays moved into the neighborhood, nonwhites withdrew—not just because they found gays distasteful, but because the area's increased elegance was beginning to force real estate prices up beyond the means of low-income residents. Eventually, both the Castro and Marigny were converted into picturesque and attractive residential neighborhoods—largely white and heavily populated by gays.[11]

Meantime, the bars that had signaled the traditional gay presence in the Vieux Carré began to appear in Faubourg Marigny as well. As of 2001, a New Orleans gay Web site listed seventeen gay bars in the Quarter and seven in

[11] Gays had played a similar role in colonizing and gentrifying neighborhoods along the near North Side of Chicago, along South Street in Philadelphia, and elsewhere, of course. It is worth noting that the Castro is much more homogeneous in its gayness than is Marigny—where the population is a heterogeneous combination of straight and gay people.

Marigny. Marigny is now thoroughly gentrified, and real estate prices have risen to a point where middle-class gays often find them difficult to afford. It is hardly surprising, then, that gays have begun moving across Franklin Avenue still farther downriver and, as of this writing, are beginning to colonize Bywater.

The gay presence in New Orleans is also felt in more flamboyant ways. In 1972, a small number of gays had thrown a costume party which was used to poke fun at what they called "Southern Decadence," and suggested that those in attendance dress up as a "decadent Southerner." The celebration was held on the Sunday before Labor Day (to give the attendees the Monday holiday in order to recover). The choice of Labor Day was no accident. Early September had a nasty reputation as the hottest, stickiest, and most unbearable time of the New Orleans summer. Technically, that may not be absolutely true, but it seemed so to anyone who had already been forced to endure a long hot New Orleans summer. More important to the organizers, it was a season when residents had the city to themselves. Residents who could afford it left town for cooler climes, and the rest went indoors and stood in front of their air-conditioning vents. Visitors stayed away in droves, and hotel rooms went begging.

That first celebration was a great success, and, as Keith Darcé described it (in a personal communication): "the organizers decided to make the party an annual event, and the following year the group gathered at their favorite bar in the French Quarter in costume, and paraded back to the house." Over time, the parade was institutionalized with the name "Southern Decadence," and turned it into a prolonged bar hop—the celebrants walking (then lurching) from gay bar to gay bar in the Quarter until few were competent to celebrate further. As time went by, more friends were invited, and friends of friends—and the Labor Day celebration gradually became famous among the city's gays as a time when New Orleans (or at least the Quarter) was theirs for the weekend. Meantime, celebrants' costumes became increasingly extravagant, designed to spoof drag queens and any other gay stereotype they could think of. As the celebration grew still larger, it began to attract out-of-town visitors—mainly gays from the Lower South—who drove into New Orleans for the Labor Day weekend to join the festivities.

Southern Decadence remained largely a New Orleans affair, but by the early 1990s the attendance had grown to several thousand, and the spontaneous bar hop had grown into a bibulous rout that expanded into two full days and surged off the parade route into adjacent streets and alleys. Still, the event retained a kind of down-home informality—this according to sources in the gay community. Then, in 1996, *Ambush* magazine, a local gay tabloid, used its national Web site to promote Southern Decadence as a genuine "occasion," inviting all and sundry to visit New Orleans and join the revels. The response was so large as to dumbfound the local tourist establishment. Management of the Bourbon-Orleans Hotel, one of the largest in the Quarter, discovered that the hotel was booked solid three months in advance — something that usually happened only for Mardi Gras. Meantime, a good many hoteliers confessed they had never heard of Southern Decadence. As an official of the city's tourist bureau remarked, the event had been "flying under our radar."

But no more. In 2000, two years after the first national publicity, *Ambush* estimated that Southern Decadence drew 100,000 visitors to the city, and had a financial impact in the neighborhood of eighty million dollars. Hotels, which used to rent rooms on Labor Day for rock-bottom prices, had begun to charge premium rates and demand a several-day stay, as they had done for a long time with Mardi Gras. By that time, the event could no longer pretend to be a low-key informal event. Serious organization was required: a "grand marshal" and an official parade route were designated, the police closed streets and diverted traffic, and stern warnings were issued, cautioning revelers that "inappropriate behavior" could land them in jail.[12] In a sense, extra-high hotel rates constitute a kind of informal badge of the celebration's sucess, but in case any doubt remained, the mayor himself wrote an official letter of welcome to the 2001 attendees of Southern Decadence. His Honor enthused: "We (the city) are honored to have this exciting event." And indeed it was exciting, for it was the XXXth anniversary of Southern Decadence.[13]

It is clear, then, that gays have arrived in New Orleans — or at least in part of New Orleans — not just socially and economically, but politically as well. After long debate and much political pressure, the New Orleans City Council passed two ordinances that had long been demanded by gays. One extended the same legal protection to gays as had long existed for women, blacks, and the handicapped in matters of housing and employment. The second extended spousal health care benefits to domestic partners of city employees. Gay political clout is limited, however: to date (late 2002), no openly gay person has been elected to public office in the city of New Orleans.

---

[12] Southern Decadence officials specifically warned against "overt sexual behavior, nudity, and public urination."

[13] In New Orleans — as elsewhere — the use of Roman numerals clearly denotes events which are not only Official, but also Serious and Traditional.

But it is less than clear that *all* gays have arrived. The gay presence in the city is overwhelmingly white and male. As for lesbians, the census suggests a small concentration in the Bayou St. John neighborhood, riverside from City Park—and another in Algiers Point. Lesbian concentrations, however, are much less dense than those of gay men—and it is also evident that the two groups do not live in close geographic proximity.

Gay blacks are another matter. In a city wherein the total population of blacks outnumbers whites by more than two to one, it is reasonable to suppose that there are perhaps twice as many gay blacks as there are gay whites. For whatever reason, however, "black men are far underrepresented in the visible gay community," according to Keith Darcé. No one explanation seems wholly satisfactory to account for the apparent discrepancy, but it is worth noting that New Orleans's blacks lean strongly toward religious denominations that are Protestant and fundamentalist in doctrine. Such groups tend to be aggressively homophobic—hardly a hospitable environment for a hometown boy to make his gayness publicly known. One suspects, too, that, for similar reasons, black lesbians might be less inclined than whites to declare their sexual preferences in public.

Chapter 7
TOURISM IN NEW ORLEANS

SINCE 1975, THE TOURIST INDUSTRY has come to play a dominant role in the economic life of New Orleans. It was not always so.

From the early nineteenth century onward, the city had acquired a national reputation as a beautiful and gracious place—and the nearest thing to a foreign city that Americans were likely to see within their national borders. Institutions such as Mardi Gras and jazz festivals made New Orleans seem especially attractive, and visitors came in a steady stream—although the stream was steadier in spring and autumn than during the long hot summer. But tourists were something that natives took for granted: "We are New Orleans," they seemed to say. "Of *course* people will come to see the wonders of our city."

As late as the first half of the twentieth century tourism remained as a kind of urban sideline, and it was seldom viewed as very important. In fact, among many Orleanians, it was fashionable to complain about tourists as a sort of chronic nuisance that well-bred Orleanians had learned to tolerate, if only barely. Business people such as hoteliers and restaurateurs earned money from the tourist trade, of course, but that trade was not highly esteemed. People of real substance in New Orleans—the ones who appeared at fashionable clubs, or visited their downtown offices in white linen suits—made their fortunes in commerce or from languorous trading in traditional commodities such as cotton and sugar.[1] Early in the twentieth century, when oil was discovered at Spindletop in East Texas and then in Louisiana, respectable fortunes could be made in the oil and gas industry. But tourism was easily ignored. Aside from an occasional obligatory grumble, most Orleanians paid little attention to the tourist industry. That indifference was easy to explain. New Orleans's main tourist destinations were highly concentrated—focused mainly on the French Quarter's combination of rich food, live jazz, and antique architecture—or the stately homes of the Garden District. A few tourists occasionally found their ways to the St. Charles Avenue streetcar, often by accident, or ventured out to Lakefront for a seafood dinner. But tourists rarely visited most of New Orleans, and they almost never ventured beyond the confines of white New Orleans. Few of them saw the ordinary streets and houses where most Orleanians lived, and the reverse was true as well: most Orleanians rarely encountered tourists in the course of their daily lives. Tourism was something that most people in the city took for granted, or simply ignored.

The collapse of oil prices in the mid-1980s changed all that and left large numbers of people without jobs. Furthermore, the city had virtually no manufacturing industry to provide fallback employment. And the Port of New Orleans, once a place that hired large numbers of stevedores, had mechanized most of its operations; thus, while more and more cargo passed through the port, fewer and fewer workers were needed to move it.

For many Orleanians, there were simply no jobs to be had. Many of the jobless left town, often permanently. But for those who remained, jobs *had* to be found. Lacking any alternative, they were found in tourism. There simply was no other sector of the economy that was prepared to employ any large number of people.

Even before the crash, the city had been promoting tourism as a serious economic venture. The first effects were visible in the 1960s and 70s with the building of several large hotels—the Marriott on lower Canal Street being, perhaps, the most conspicuous. But the effort shifted into high gear as the new Morial Convention Center took form, and as lower Canal Street and the riverfront in front of the CBD (Central Business District) and French Quarter were handsomely refurbished and opened to the Mississippi River.

But it was not enough to attract tourists as individuals or small groups. Efficiency demanded that they be enticed in organized groups, and preferably

---

[1] Degas's famous painting, *The New Orleans Cotton Exchange*, depicts a scene of linen-clad cotton merchants, relaxing in their city offices.

very large groups. And that meant that New Orleans had to promote the convention business, and do so on a large scale. Conventions had been coming to New Orleans for as long as tourists had been coming, but the oil crash stimulated a new and vigorous effort to bring more and bigger conventions than ever before. The city's tourist bureau received a new name, "The New Orleans Metropolitan Convention and Visitors Bureau" (NOMCVB); it was equipped with shiny new downtown offices, new welcome centers, and a hefty budget increase. In the words of its chairman, Michael Reiss, the Bureau would become a "well-oiled sales machine." An equally pressing goal was to make the city's residents recognize that tourism was not only important, but also respectable. As Reiss remarked: "The overall goal is making tourism first in the minds of the community." New Orleans could no longer afford the luxury of regarding tourism as an economic afterthought. From the oil bust onward, tourism became the 800-pound gorilla that nobody could ignore.

Tourism began to make serious impacts on the city's landscape. Enlargement of the Morial Convention Center went ahead at flank speed. At a price of $121 million, Phase I of the Center was finished in 1991, and by 2000 Phase III had turned it into one of the largest convention facilities in North America, half a mile long, with more than a million square feet of contiguous exhibit space. (It was, in fact, so big that residential neighbors had begun to complain that the Center—despite its economic benefits—was a barrier that separated Orleanian citizens from their newfound river—almost as bad as the old docks and railroad lines had been in earlier times.) And as of 2002, the city was seeking $455 million from the state in order to build Phase IV, which would add another half-million square feet of space. As a city for conventioneers, New Orleans was plainly running in the big time, in the same league with Orlando, Las Vegas, and San Francisco.[2]

The combined efforts were hugely successful, according to the NOMCVB, which books the Convention Center. In the 1970s, tourists to New Orleans were counted in the thousands. By 2000, the count had risen to something between eight and eleven *million* tourists per year, and their expenditures were estimated at $4.78 *billion*—income to the city and its residents, in one form or another. Even juicier, conventioneers commonly pay premium prices for hotel

---

[2] This elite group of cities was identified by David Hyatt, director of Public Affairs for the enormous National Automobile Dealers Association, whose conventions commonly attract upwards of 25,000 attendees. These were the only cities that met the NADA's requirements for "exhibit space, hotel rooms, and 'general desirability' (of the city's environment)."

accommodations: $200 per night is a common price for a room at a convention hotel, and suites for officers and special gatherings go for much more.

Enumerations of tourist volume may be a trifle on the optimistic side; they were generated by the NOMCVB, which is not an institution to hide its light under a bushel. But the numbers are in the right ballpark. Tourism is the biggest act in town, and the tourists evidently are happy. In a poll commissioned by the Convention Bureau, an overwhelming majority of visitors to the French Quarter declared themselves to be "very satisfied" with their experience, and nine out of ten said the same thing about the riverfront.

Aside from the Brobdingnagian Convention Center and the handsome new riverfront, the exploding tourist industry had also profoundly changed the appearance of the central business district. Most of that change has come through the building of large new hotels which now dominate the city's skyline. In 1960, when the tourist bureau was founded as a branch of the Chamber of Commerce, it counted 4,160 hotel rooms in the entire metropolitan area. At the turn of the twenty-first century, the total had risen to more than 33,000 rooms—with more than 7,000 added since 1996.

The hotel building business did not always create big new buildings, although it often did. By contrast, several hotel chains joined hands with preservationists and converted distinguished old business buildings into upmarket hotels. Perhaps the most striking of these conversions saw the splendid old Maison Blanche Department Store on Canal Street become the New Orleans Ritz-Carlton—acclaimed by both the AAA and Mobil Travel Guide with a "coveted 5-star" rating.[3] The conversion was much admired, and helped buttress the architectural integrity of lower Canal Street, which was badly in need of help as downtown stores had drifted to the suburbs in the 1970s and 80s.

Whatever else can be said about the tourist industry in New Orleans, tourist promotion served as a major economic shot-in-the-arm for a badly depressed city. According to data from the Louisiana State Labor Department, 67,300 people in the metropolitan area worked in hotels, bars, and restaurants—an increase of thirty-five percent in the 1990s alone. According to the U.S. Census, nearly half of the entire work force was employed in the "service sec-

---

[3] The adjective "coveted" is apparently obligatory when talking about 5-star hotel or restaurant ratings. But stars did not protect the hotel against financial troubles. Shortly after it was finished, the Ritz-Carlton sued for bankruptcy. The hotel management explained that it had spent too lavishly on the conversion and, despite income from astronomical room rates, was unable to pay the bills. The hotel stayed open for business, however, although it presently lost one of its coveted stars.

tor" — more than all the jobs in manufacturing and the oil and gas industries combined. The total annual payroll came to more than a billion dollars.

And, to cap the triumphant story, tourists were spending more than they had in former times—considerably more. In 2000, the Convention Bureau announced with ill-concealed delight that the government-allowed per diem for federal employees traveling on government business in New Orleans had been raised from $89 to $139 per day. In its announcement, the Bureau boasted that this was the largest per diem increase anywhere in the nation. It was evident that New Orleans was not to be seen as a sleepy southern town where travelers could rent hotel rooms for a pittance; the city was a place where big spenders could feel at home, and Uncle Sam would accept their receipts. This was success, indeed.

But amid the official rejoicing, there were critics who argued that tourism was not the triumph claimed, but instead was a weak and unsatisfactory reed for a big city's fortunes to lean on. The critics cited a long bill of particulars.

To begin with, said the critics, the claims of job creation were grossly inflated. The majority of jobs in tourism were not very good (to put it politely), paying minimum wage or less, for housekeepers in hotels, busboys in restaurants, garbage collectors, and similar jobs that offer little chance of promotion to more skilled and more rewarding positions.

Furthermore, the critics continued, jobs in tourism were notoriously uncertain, just as the industry itself is uncertain. Tourism is a fragile business, extremely susceptible to unexpected exogenous events. That fragility was cruelly demonstrated on September 11, 2001, when the terrorist attacks in New York City, Washington, D.C., and rural Pennsylvania sent the tourist business all over the nation (and world) into a tailspin. In New Orleans, uncounted service employees were fired, and it was little comfort to know that bartenders, taxi-drivers, and waitresses in Orlando and Las Vegas had also lost their jobs.[4] But the cancellation of several large conventions led to the cancellation of thousands of hotel and restaurant reservations, not to mention reservations for ballrooms, convention exhibitors, restaurant reservations, and kindred enterprises. All kinds of innocent people suffered the impact: concessionaires at the airport, limousine drivers, janitors at the convention center, checkroom attendants at Lakefront restaurants, travel agents, and host of others, who felt the effects like falling dominos.

---

[4] In fact, the tourist industry in New Orleans fared better than that in Honolulu, largely becasue almost all visitors to Hawaii come by plane, whereas a large proportion of New Orleans's tourists drive to the city from nearby areas of Mississippi, Alabama, Florida, and East Texas.

The critics also noted problems arising from attitudes and policies of large tourist-oriented corporations. Among them was the notorious practice of big hotel and restaurant chains to bring in top-paying management from the home office, leaving the locals to pick up lower positions on the corporate pecking order. Then, to rub salt in the wound, when it came time for promotions to managerial positions, top brass would bring in people from the home office in Dallas or Chicago, rather than entrust authority to local people, who were less known and less trusted. It was little comfort to know that Orleanians were not special victims of such corporate discrimination; the same practice occurred (and occurs) in tourist destinations all over the world.

Many Orleanian critics, however, argued that the worst feature of tourism as a basis of the city's economy was the damage it did to the ambience and texture of the oldest parts of the city—especially the French Quarter. In a poll commissioned by the NOMVCB, the Quarter was found to be the No. 1 destination of some ninety-eight percent of all tourists questioned. This came as a surprise to nobody, but it served to remind the tourist establishment of the unique importance of the Quarter to New Orleans's image. Given the very large increase in the total number of tourists in New Orleans, however, it also served to remind the city that the Quarter requires constant maintenance to make up for the increasing wear and tear—not to mention the necessity of huge, new parking lots, and the elementary matter of cleaning up debris left by bibulous visitors. But cleaning up debris did nothing to reduce the increasingly noisy and rowdy crowds that disturbed the peace at all hours, and contributed heavily to driving out much of the Quarter's resident population. Meantime, commercial establishments, which had formerly catered to those residents, gradually changed their market from the dwindling number of locals and turned their attention to tourists. Thus, the wonderful old French Market of earlier times had been a place where farmers, butchers, and fishermen peddled their products from carts and sold them to locals, who took the food home and cooked it. The new improved French Market gave all that up. Tourists, it was believed, did not wish to step on the occasional discarded fish head or sidestep scavenging dogs, cats, and occasional rats. So the French Market became, in effect, a collection of boutiques, where tourists could "get what they wanted": T-shirts, bamboo bar furniture from Thailand, scented candles made in China, cute umbrellas to decorate summer drinks, and the predictable assortment of other knick-knacks to be found in identical places from Hong Kong to Niagara Falls. The Café du Monde, across Decatur Street from Jackson Square, a place famous for its *beignets*, chicory coffee, and a relaxed open-air atmosphere, began to urge its customers not-so-subtly to finish their coffee and donuts and move on so that their table could be 'turned over' quickly to somebody else in the crowds of waiting tourists.

A good share of such "improvement" derives less from consumer demand than it does from the preconceptions about tourists that seem implanted in the minds of those who cater to visitors. It is the same mentality that has caused builders in Santa Fé—another major tourist destination in the U.S.A.—to cover everything with adobe, including such ancient monuments as gas stations and stalls for parking lot attendants. ("You want adobe? We'll give you adobe!") And that mentality, charge the critics of booster tourism in New Orleans, has turned much of the French Quarter from a genuine community, made up of resident Orleanians and the commercial establishments that served them, into a tarted-up 24-7 hurdy-gurdy that some have unkindly dubbed "Creole Disneyland." The comparison to Disneyland is unfortunately apt: parts of the Quarter are genuinely fake and make only the thinnest pretense of being a real place. A century ago, Creole Orleanians perceived the Quarter as their *centre ville*—a place where they lived, shopped, worshipped, and went out to eat and drink. No more. Many (if not most) Orleanians, irrespective of ethnic origin, rarely go near the Quarter, except when houseguests come to town and ask to be shown it. To be sure, most of the old buildings are still there, but in the view of many old-time Orleanians, the qualities that made it a magical place are vanishing. It is no accident that the National Trust for Historic Preservation has repeatedly listed the French Quarter on its élite annual list of "America's 11 Most Endangered Places"—not for fear that its ancient buildings are in danger of demolition, but rather that its *genius loci* is being grossly and permanently disfigured.

The tourist business is mainly focused on a strip of territory that stretches from the Quarter upriver to the Convention Center and the Warehouse District—and then up St. Charles Avenue into and beyond the Garden District. As far as most tourist agencies know, that is all there is to New Orleans. (Tourists on the streets of the Quarter are routinely quoted as saying that they've never heard of the St. Charles streetcar, or Algiers Point, or the newly created Jazzland, a 140-acre theme park in eastern New Orleans.) Not surprisingly, the traditional tourist district receives disproportionate attention from city services: it is heavily policed, most of its streets are well-paved, and the city tries (with mixed success) to keep the area free of litter and homeless people. It is an area where tourists are supposed to feel happy and comfortable—

which is, of course, just the point. Attention to the tourist district encourages neglect of nontourist parts of the city, however picturesque they may be. In ordinary neighborhoods, potholes go unfilled for years on end, in spite of despairing wails from residents. And the police presence, ubiquitous in tourist districts, is too often lacking in parts of the city that badly need it.

A good many responsible Orleanians are seriously unhappy about the disproportionate reliance on tourism. Scorching articles have appeared in *The Times-Picayune* and elsewhere, criticizing the way that tourism has eroded the quality of life, especially in the Quarter, and warning that the qualities that attracted tourists in the first place are being degraded to the point that the Quarter will eventually no longer be the Quarter.[5]

But the city and its residents are in a Catch-22 situation. The city will not fare better economically unless solid commercial or manufacturing enterprises can be enticed to the city, bringing with them a substantial number of skilled, well-paying jobs. But that will not happen as long as the city's working population is perceived to be undereducated and unfitted for skilled jobs. Tourism does little to break into that circle of causation—and, in fact, perpetuates it by offering largely pointless and poorly paid jobs to the city's work force. It is little comfort to know that distinguished old southern cities such as Charleston and Savannah find themselves in very similar kinds of traps.

Yet, despite legitimate worries about the tourist industry and its effects, the juggernaut rolls on. And it will continue to roll until New Orleans finds another substantial means of support in industry or commerce. Meantime, failing any alternative, it will remain the biggest act in town. As long as that is so, nobody, but nobody in the city's Establishment would dream of doing anything to stem the increasing flow of tourists into the Big Easy.

[5] See, especially, Coleman Warner's newspaper article in a 1999 issue entitled "The Tourist Trap." In Warner's words: "the quality of residential life in the Quarter seems to wane by the year, residents say. Longtime Quarter residents continue to complain about rowdy drunks, T-shirt shops, crowded sidewalks, loud bar music and a pervasive loss of privacy."

Chapter 8
The Rising Water: The Threats
of Floods and Hurricanes

*I*T CAN BE ARGUED that most of New Orleans's human problems might eventually be solved—or at least ameliorated—by the application of careful study, hard work, good will, and a fair dose of luck. After all, the city has found solutions to a variety of human problems in the past, and each time it has survived to celebrate a new day.

But there are permanent physical threats to the city that simply will not go away. They have menaced the city since the time of Bienville: floods on the Mississippi River and hurricane-driven tidal surges from the Gulf of Mexico.[1] Each has visited the city in the bygone past, and each has left ruin in its wake. Within recent time, however—that is, within the memory of living Orleanians —there have been close calls (Betsy was the closest) but no real calamities.

As a result, a good many residents take a relaxed attitude toward environmental hazards in general, assuming they have always been under control and, therefore, that they will remain under control. Such insouciance may be justified when it come to threats of river flooding. It is emphatically *not* justified

---

[1] Flooding occurs after major rainstorms, of course, but the city's pumping system rapidly gets rid of the unwanted water.

when it comes to the matter of hurricanes, and the murderous tidal surges that accompany them.[2]

Mississippi River Flooding

After the epochal flood of 1927, Congress assigned responsibility for controlling floods on the Mississippi to the U.S. Army Corps of Engineers. Since that time, the Corps has built an elaborate and integrated system of levees and other structures to keep the river within prescribed limits. Most of the time those structures have done the job they were assigned to do. One of the highest priorities, of course, was to keep floodwaters from spilling over the levees into New Orleans.

It was no small task. As we have seen, the Corps managed the job by building high protection levees around the city, on all sides, so that New Orleans came to resemble a large shallow saucer, with its center below sea level. The levees kept the city safe from the annual spring flooding of the Mississippi, but it did not allay the threat of what hydrologists call "the hundred-year flood"—much less the cataclysmic 200-year or 500-year floods.[3] If one of those huge floods topped or breached the levee, much of the old backswamp, the geographic center of the present city, would end up under many feet of water, doing massive damage and very likely drowning a good many people.

To avert such a catastrophe, the Corps had built spillways upriver from New Orleans so that peak floods could be diverted before they reached the city. The main spillway was, in fact, a complex of spillways, controlled by a network of floodgates, severally called the Morganza Spillway and the Old River

---

[2] A tidal surge (also called a storm surge) behaves like a tidal wave, or tsunami. A surge can occur when hurricane winds drive ocean (or lake) waters to abnormally high levels against a coast. The storm surges are further heightened when the water is forced into a narrow embayment—such as Mississippi Sound—or when it occurs at the same time as high tide. (A full moon adds to the consequence.) One storm surge from Hurricane Camille roared inland near Gulfport, Mississippi, measuring 22.6 feet high. After the hurricane had passed, it turned out that the storm surge had literally erased all sign of habitation and vegetation where it crossed an offshore barrier island in its path.

[3] "Hundred-year flood" is a statistical term, and simply means that a storm of a certain magnitude is likely to occur on an average of once every century. In a statistical sense, it is quite possible that such a flood might occur more than once, or not at all, during that same period. It emphatically does *not* mean that such floods occur, like clockwork, every hundred years, nor does it mean that, once such a storm has occurred, a particular place is immune for another century.

Spillways—or, simply, the Old River Structures. Both Morganza and Old River were designed to let surplus Mississippi River water flow into the Atchafalaya River in case the big river rose to dangerous levels.[4] In times of flood, the Old River and Morganza structures could be opened to carry as much of the Mississippi's flow as was necessary to keep the river from inundating New Orleans. In fact, in the record-breaking flood of 1973, the water rose so high at Old River that it overflowed the massive concrete structures, undermined their foundations, and very nearly destroyed them. Had the Old River structures failed, the Mississippi would have poured out to the Gulf of Mexico by way of the Atchafalaya; in effect, it would have changed and shortened its course, as it has done repeatedly in the past. And if that had happened, the most serious problem would not have been protecting New Orleans against flood; rather, the Corps would have been faced with the challenge of getting the Mississippi out of the Atchafalaya and back into its present channel.[5]

So the threat of Mississippi River flooding has not disappeared, but it seems to be more or less under control. Not so the threat of hurricanes. During the same period that the risk of river flooding has diminished (thanks to the Corps of Engineers), the danger from hurricanes has grown steadily more deadly. There are two prime reasons why that is so.

Hurricanes and Storm Surges

In the first place, there are ways to divert the Mississippi River's waters in case of flood. To date, nobody has discovered a way to divert hurricanes from their paths, nor are they likely to.

Secondly, there is always plenty of advance warning of a flood on the Mississippi, and plenty of time either to move people to high ground or to evacuate the city should that become necessary. That is not the way with hurricanes. According to Colonel Thomas Julich, commandant of the New Orleans District of the Corps of Engineers: "it would take sixty hours' advance notice to get everyone out of the danger zone." That kind of advance notice does not (and will never) exist.

---

[4] Even in normal times, about a third of the Mississippi's volume is diverted to the Gulf by way of the Atchafalaya—thus converting that little-known slough into what has been called "the shortest of the world's great rivers."

[5] For an entrancing account of the battles the Corps has had with the Mississippi, Old River, and the Atchafalaya, not to mention its sedulous courtship of Louisiana politicians, see John McPhee's "Atchafalaya," in *The Control of Nature*, 1989.

Hurricane paths in the Gulf are notoriously erratic. If the city were evacuated every time a hurricane was within sixty hours of the coast and heading in the general direction of the city, evacuation orders would be frequent events—and nearly all of them false alarms. Evacuating hundreds of thousands of people on even a sixty-hour notice is a very expensive and extremely disruptive event—as experience in New Orleans and elsewhere has demonstrated vividly. And one does not need to be a social psychologist to predict what would happen to public reactions if the Corps gained a reputation for crying wolf every few years. The hard fact is that, despite improvements in forecasting, hurricanes do not allow time for large numbers of people in their paths to reach safety. That is especially true in places such as New Orleans, where the number and capacity of escape routes is limited.[6]

But the danger is very real. During the eighteenth, nineteenth , and early twentieth centuries, the city was hit head-on by hurricanes, whose winds and floodwaters did extensive damage. But the city was smaller then, and nearly all of it built on the elevated ground of natural levees. Furthermore, extensive deltaic wetlands south of New Orleans helped to reduce the force of tidal surges, the cause of most hurricane damage.

The twentieth century has brought major scares, however. Hurricanes Camille and Betsy both came perilously close to New Orleans, and both wrought major damage east of the city where they finally made landfall. But the real wake-up call was Hurricane Georges of September 27-29, 1998. From 15:00 to 21:00 on the 27th, Georges was heading directly for New Orleans, with peak winds of 110 miles per hour. Then, at the last moment, during the night of the 27th–28th, the storm unexpectedly veered slightly eastward. It was not much, but it was enough. Georges roared ashore as a category 2 hurricane, just east of Gulfport, Mississippi.[7] Even though it was then downgraded to the status of 'tropical storm', it caused considerable havoc.

Hurricane Georges helped rouse Orleanians to face a question that had lurked in the wings for a long time: what would happen if a major hurricane hit the city dead on? Prognoses were dismal. In the words of Al Naomi, of the Corps of Engineers: "Had (Georges) hit us directly, our levees would not have protected

---

[6] The Louisiana Highway Department has sought to increase the capacity of I-10 west and northeast of the city by building crossover lanes to enable traffic to flow one-way. This helps, but does not solve the problem.

[7] Hurricanes are rated on a scale from 1 to 5, the latter being the most violent. Camille was a category 5, Betsy a category 4.

us . . . A tidal surge from such a storm would have topped (the levees) by several feet." And that would have spelled catastrophe for much of New Orleans.

Perhaps the most ominous warning came in a carefully documented report by Mark Fischetti in the journal, *Scientific American,* for October, 2001. *Scientific American* is a highly respected and cautious journal, not given to alarmism or hysteria. But Fischetti's language is hair-raising:

> "New Orleans is a disaster waiting to happen. . . . If a big slow-moving hurricane crossed the Gulf of Mexico on the right track, it would drive a sea surge that would drown New Orleans under 20 feet of water . . . Scientists at LSU [Louisiana State University] who have modeled hundreds of possible storm tracks on advanced computers predict that more than 100,000 people could die."

That would be the worst natural disaster in all of U.S. history—the death toll surpassing the Galveston hurricane of 1900, the San Francisco earthquake of 1906, and the Johnstown flood of 1888, all rolled into one. Fischetti added, almost as an afterthought, that, given the statistical record of hurricanes in the Gulf of Mexico, "a direct hit is inevitable."

If one accepts Fischetti's dire prognosis as plausible, it is natural to ask: why is the city so seriously threatened now, but much less so in the past? There are two basic answers, and both point to possible solutions to the threat.

First of all, New Orleans is not only bigger, but also lower than it has ever been before. That is partly because the entire Mississippi Delta is gradually sinking under the accumulated weight of sediments, carried to the delta over thousands of years from a drainage basin that stretches halfway across North America. But there are human agencies at work, too, and they operate at a local level. Ever since Baldwin Wood's great pumps began to drain the city's backswamps, the organic material of those former swamps has been shrinking and settling like a drying kitchen sponge. As a result, only two sizable parts of New Orleans remain above sea level: filled areas such as Lakefront and the natural levees of the Mississippi and its old distributaries. Most of the city's inhabited areas lie dangerously below sea level. Furthermore, a major tidal surge from the Gulf of Mexico could easily inundate much of the metropolitan area—not just areas below sea level. And if the National Academy of Sciences is right, sea levels are rising all over the world. In effect most of the world's seacoast cities are in danger of coastal flooding. It is small comfort to Orleanians to learn that other coastal cities are in peril, too.

The second cause of New Orleans's increased peril—and a much more important one—results from erosion of the delta itself by waves from the Gulf of Mexico. Only within recent time has it become known that the wetlands south of the city are valuable for more than catching crayfish and drilling for oil; they also serve as a buffer against tidal surges from the Gulf. The crucial statistic seems to be this: *every four miles of marshland will reduce the height of a storm surge by one foot.*[8] Given the fact that a storm surge from Hurricane Camille in 1969 measured 22.6 feet above sea level, it follows inexorably that preserving and enlarging the deltaic marshland south of New Orleans is very literally an issue of life or death for the city. For almost a century, however, that marshland has been disappearing into the Gulf at the insupportable rate of between twenty-five and thirty square miles per year. It is a sour joke among local hydrologists, that unless something is done before the twenty-first century is gone, New Orleans will become a seaport on the Gulf of Mexico.

The immediate cause of the wetland loss is erosion by storm waves along the Gulf shore. But that erosion has been hugely accelerated by two things that human beings have done to the delta over the century or so: building levees next to the Mississippi and building canals through the delta.

The purpose of a levee seems obvious: to keep the Mississippi River water from spilling over its banks. There is, however, a deadly side effect that is far less obvious: those same levees prevent the river's load of silt and clay from being deposited into the backswamps where, absent human intervention, the sediments would accumulate to build new deltaic wetland. People have been building serious levees along the lower Mississippi (below the city, that is) for well over two centuries, with the result that the river, instead of building its delta the way a well-behaved river normally does, carries most of its sediments all the way to the Gulf of Mexico, where most of it disappears into deep water—out-of-sight, out-of-mind. And there, thanks to Colonel Eads's famous jetties, even sand bars are carried away by the river water. In prelevee times, just as now, the Gulf storms eroded the delta's wetlands, but the river promptly restored them during times of flood. Today, marine erosion continues as before, but the delta is no longer rebuilding itself—thanks to the levees. The delta is like a bank account where there are constant withdrawals, but nobody is making deposits any more. Unless something is done to restore the deposits, the account—and the delta—will eventually disappear. It is a great irony: the very

[8] These and other data about the hurricane menace come either from Fischetti's report in *Scientific American* or from reports by the U.S. Army Corps of Engineers.

levees that were built to protect life and property in southern Louisiana are potential agents of their destruction.

The digging of canals is the second major cause of wetland erosion. The whole delta is crisscrossed with canals; deep-water navigation canals such as MR-GO are only the most conspicuous. But there are innumerable smaller canals, most of them slashed through the marshes to give access to oil or gas rigs. People have been drilling for oil in the Mississippi Delta ever since the early twentieth century, which sounds innocent enough, but it is not. Road building across the delta's mucklands is prodigiously costly, and oil drillers quickly learned that an easier and cheaper way to bring heavy machinery to a delta drill site was to dig a canal in the wetlands and float the machinery to the site. Later on, the same canal might be used occasionally to remove drilling equipment, to bring in gear for repairs or maintenance, or simply to barge out oil taken from the well. Ordinary maps of Louisiana do not show those small canals; there are simply too many of them.[9]

But many of those innumerable canals—whether big ones such as MR-GO or smaller ad hoc canals to the oil rigs—can and do allow salt water to make its way into wetlands where it can kill the freshwater biota that normally would flourish there. Without the root mat of those freshwater plants, the wetlands disintegrate and become easy prey for marine erosion. In sum, canal-borne salt water is literally killing off the delta—and with it, New Orleans's best protection from hurricane-driven storm surges.

Plainly, correcting the causes of shoreline erosion should be a matter of first priority, but it is equally plain that there is no quick way to do it. It is obviously impossible to block all the canals (although it is likely that MR-GO will be abandoned and allowed to silt up), and equally impossible to tear down all the levees. The Corps of Engineers has embarked on an "experimental program" whereby floodgates are inserted into the levee so that river water can be allowed to flow into planned sections of the backswamp, as it did in prehistoric days. As of this writing, one such site is now operative and, *mirabile dictu*, it seems to be working—replacing salt water with fresh and creating new delta land, just as it did in days before levees were built, but on a vastly smaller scale.

---

[9] It is hard to appreciate the sheer number of these canals unless one sees them from the air– or at night. One might suppose that the delta at night would be a place of lonely darkness. In fact, the oil rigs, each with its own flare-like illumination, create a panoply of brilliant light which, from a ship on the river, looks for all the world like an endless amphibious city.

Given the need to rebuild deltaic wetlands, and given that there are means to do it, common sense would seem to dictate that the levees along the river should be cut in many places—especially on the right bank below New Orleans. While wholesale levee-cutting might have been possible in the past, it is no longer—thanks largely to opposition from residential builders and the seafood industry, both powerful in the legislative halls at Baton Rouge. (Neither oysters nor crayfish take kindly to sudden changes in salinity.) Meantime, however, the Corps continues to build more and more "experimental" floodgates and rebuild deltaic wetlands as fast as politics and available budgets allow. It is, alas, not as fast as many would wish.

Other means to protect New Orleans against storm surges have been suggested. Some are palliative, such as dredging the floor of the Gulf to create new barrier islands offshore to help subdue the violence of tidal surges. Others projects are simply gigantic—among them a proposal to build an enormous floodwall across the eastern entrance of Lake Pontchartrain, to bar storm surges from entering the lake and flooding Lakeside New Orleans. Another is to build a number of "islands" within the city, surrounded by very high levees, to create havens of refuge during the worst hurricanes. Another is to breach the levee and divert the river permanently, some tens of miles below New Orleans, thus allowing the Mississippi to reach the Gulf of Mexico by a new and much shorter route. That Draconian measure would allow the present river channel to silt up, and start creating a new delta that would eventually fill Barataria Bay and extend beyond it into the Gulf. It is a radical proposal, but no more outlandish than building a large city below sea level in the potential path of frequent hurricanes. Like the British Empire, New Orleans seems to have been built in a fit of absentmindedness.

Any of those measures would help, but all of them range from very expensive to ferociously (and probably prohibitively) expensive. Louisiana's congressional delegation has traditionally exercised powerful clout in the halls of Congress, and it seems likely that some help is on the way. Whether that money will build enough structures or buy enough time to avert disaster is quite a different question, and nobody knows the answer to it. What is known, however, is that the city is in great danger, and that common sense would dictate extreme measures to avert it.

Epilogue to Book Two
WHERE NOW, THE FINE CITY?

NEW ORLEANS is a city with a good many defects, and this book has enu-
merated more than a few of them. The worst problems — such as
threats from hurricanes and the consequences of racial divisions — have been
with the city for a long time, and it is improbable that they can be solved
quickly — if, indeed, they can be solved at all. Some of the worst afflictions —
such as execrable schools and sinking backswamps — seem to be getting worse,
rather than better. But it is not necessary to sound like Pollyanna to suggest that
many of those problems were created by human beings, and that human beings
are capable of correcting them, given the right ingredients: time, money,
intelligence, technical competence, and a great deal of good will. All of those
ingredients are abundantly available in New Orleans, and there are men and
women who have shown themselves willing to take action to improve their
beloved city. But those problems cannot be addressed unless they are given
blinding and continuing publicity — unless a new generation of Muckrakers
arises in New Orleans and identifies the problems and possible solutions, shows
the way to bring the city back to its former glory and shorn of its former
defects, and then sticks with it.

Some have asked if it is even worth trying. Why should the nation bother, say,
to invest many billions of dollars to build the devices necessary to divert the
tidal surge that will someday surely come with a devastating hurricane? How is
it possible to introduce high-quality public education for a population where

there is no tradition of decent public education? How is it possible to break down racial barriers that were entrenched centuries ago, and are today reinforced by divisions of class, income, and accent? The question is simple and unanswerable: New Orleans was, once upon a time perhaps, a fine city—and much of it remains very fine. It is worth trying because it is one of the few cities in the United States with a special *genre de vie*—a special *genius loci*—that sets it apart from all others.

As Coleman Warner once said to me, New Orleans is a "very rich place." There are simply very few places in North America that are like New Orleans in its wealth of sybaritic delights—a *tout ensemble* of handsome architecture, world-famous indigenous music, superb regional cuisine, and a host of urban delights that are peculiar to this special city. And New Orleans is not lacking in citizens who are passionately in love with the city. In Richard Campanella's heartfelt words, New Orleans is "one of the world's few truly beloved cities." And on those grounds alone, it is worth cherishing—worth the effort of trying to correct its worst iniquities.

That will not happen, however, unless men and women of good will, both black and white, are willing to reach out their hands and work together for the common cause of civic betterment. And that cannot be done until the people of New Orleans collectively agree that they cannot have a fine city unless they, *as Orleanians,* are willing to do battle with the city's cruelest problems: racial discrimination and intolerance, wretched public schools, miserable housing, and grinding poverty, especially among black citizens. All these problems are intimately related, and all are deeply rooted in the past. But New Orleans cannot truly be called a fine city while a large part of its population lives in physical and intellectual privation, and has little hope of escaping.

Human beings created that situation, and they can correct it. If Orleanians can begin to do that, their beloved New Orleans might again rightly be called a fine city, and a beacon not just to tourists, but to the whole nation.

Appendix A
CONCERNING DIRECTIONS IN NEW ORLEANS

AMERICANS, accustomed to grid pattern towns with streets that run north-south and east-west, are often lost in New Orleans. They will remain lost until they relax and remember that conventional compass directions mean nothing and the Mississippi River means everything.

The river divides the metropolitan area into two unequal parts called "East Bank" and "West Bank." This locution causes confusion immediately, since the Mississippi has perversely turned eastward through New Orleans, so that "East Bank" is really north of the river and "West Bank" is south of the river. Never mind. Remember that "East Bank" is where travelers from the Atlantic Coast would first arrive, and that is where most of the city is located. "West Bank" is where visitors from California come from, with a lot of swamps and new suburbs. Keep in mind, too, that Orleanian directions ignore convolutions of the river, and for a short distance opposite the central business district it is flowing due north; thus, East Bank is really west, and vice versa. It is a helpful concept to remember when one is driving across the Greater New Orleans Bridge, heading west with the sunset behind. It is a mere detail; Orleanians look at the big picture.

On the East Bank, where most people live, there are four cardinal directions: "Riverside," which means toward the river (no matter where the river is), and "Lakeside," which is the direction toward Lake Pontchartrain, and generally north. The other two directions are "Uptown" and "Downtown." Uptown is upriver from Canal Street and is roughly equivalent to the old American city. Downtown is downstream from Canal Street, including the French Quarter and so on. Visitors beware: "Downtown" does not necessarily mean the central business district to an Orleanian.

Finally, some streets are labeled with compass directions. In the Lakeside areas with a conventional grid pattern, there is no problem. In Riverside, however, such directions cause mass confusion until one notes that streets receive their directional labels where they cross Canal Street. Thus, "South Claiborne" heads northwest in the Uptown area, but is so designated because it *started* from Canal Street heading southwest.

Appendix B

A Pronouncing Gazeteer
of South Louisiana Names

Note: This abbreviated list of Louisiana pronunciations reflects the fact that, in southern Louisiana, things are *sui generis*—often more American than French, but not recognizably either. There are no general rules of pronunciation, therefore, and the visitor simply must memorize the commonest aberrations. The closest thing to a rule, perhaps, is that southern Louisiana pronunciations of French words sound like a Deep Southerner who has had a bad course in French a long time ago. Indian words are pronounced like a Deep Southerner who has never had a course in Indian at any time.

AMITE: AY-meet (sometimes AH-meet)

ATCHAFALAYA: 'chah-fah-LAH-yah

BIENVILLE: BYEN-vill (no trace of French pronunciation)

BONNET CARRÉ: Bonny Carry

BURGUNDY: bur-GUN-dee

CAJUN: KAY-jun

CONTI: KON-tie

IBERVILLE: IH-bur-vil (not EE-bur-vill)

LAFOURCHE: La-FOOSH

MANCHAC: MAN-shack

MELPOMENE: MEL-po-mean

METAIRIE: MET-urry (or MET-ry)

MICHOUD: MEE-shoe

NEW ORLEANS: A complicated business. Note to begin with that few cultivated southerners would pronounce "New" as the Yankee "NOO." It is always "NYU," as the British commonly do it. As for the "Orleans," "AW-lens" is the way well-spoken natives do it. "ORluns" or "OR-lee-uns" will pass for Yankees and radio announcers. A.J. Liebling's sensitive ear also heard "NOO WAW-luns," but that is more commonly heard upstate than in the city. But "or-LEENS" is forbidden when talking about the city. "Orleans Street," however, is pronounced just that way: "or-LEENS." Also, the exclusive Uptown "Orleans Club" makes a stab at French locution, where it comes out, "or-lee-AHN." In summary, try it as "nyu AW-lens." If your tongue is Yankee and you can't cope, try "nyu OR-luns."(Incidentally, "NO-luns" or "NAW-luns" are often heard but considered hicky.)

PLAQUEMINES: PLACK-a-minn

TCHOUPITOULAS: chop-a-TOO-lus

THIBODAUX: TIB-ah-doe

VIEUX CARRÉ: vee-YOU ka-RAY (this pronunciation approximates French more closely than most other Orleanian words or phrases, but a Parisian still recoils to hear it spoken); also, sometimes VOO Ka-RAY.

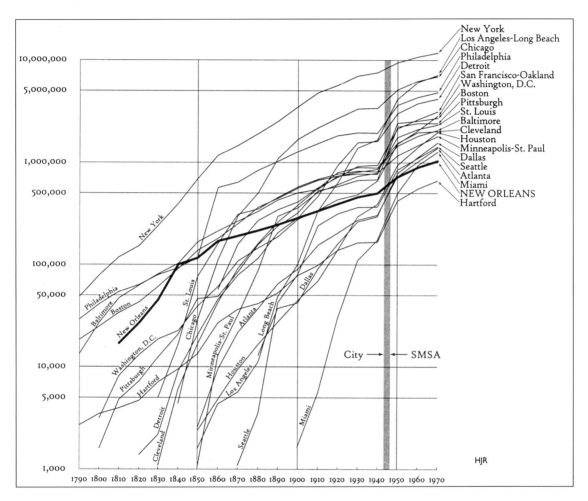

Figure 64. **Population growth of America's twenty largest cities, from the earliest census to 1970.**
New Orleans joined the Union as the nation's fifth largest city and was on the verge of becoming the second city in the cotton boom of the 1850s. Growth slackened abruptly after 1860, less the result of the Civil War than of railroad competition for the upper Mississippi Valley's hinterland, which greatly lessened the value of the river shipping that nourished the city's economy. Thereafter, with slower growth, the city was, in turn, overtaken by two groups of cities—first the railroad-industrial centers of the North and East, between 1850 and 1940; subsequently by the sun-and-space cities of the West and South, mainly between 1940 and 1970. (The abrupt jump in all cities between 1940 and 1950 is a statistical aberration, resulting from the redefinition in the census of cities as Standard Metropolitan Statistical Areas.)

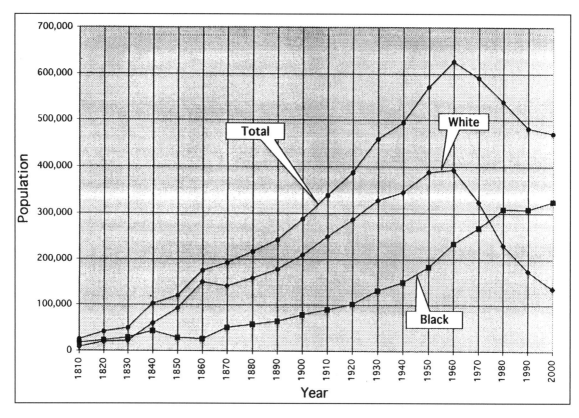

Figure 65. **New Orleans's population, 1810–2000, showing racial composition.**

1810–1830: Blacks slightly outnumbered whites in the first two American decades, although the total population was small. The black-to-white ratio reflected the booming slave trade as the Cotton Belt exploded across the Upland South, and then across the Mississippi. During that time, New Orleans was one of the main slave-trading centers in the entire South—hence, the colloquial expression, being "sold down the River." During this period, the black population of New Orleans was largely slave, but there was also a substantial free-black population. A certain proportion of those free blacks had come from the West Indes, and some from Haiti after the bloody revolution of the late 1790s. Some scholars believe that the design for "shotgun" houses was brought from West Africa to New Orleans by way of those Haitian refugees.

1830–1860: The white population skyrocketed, as steamboat traffic on the Mississippi turned New Orleans into one of America's major ports—and the only important ocean port to serve the huge region of Mississippi River drainage. Contributing to the large increase in the white population was the construction of major canals in the city, which attracted considerable numbers of Irish immigrant labor. By 1840, New Orleans had become the fourth largest city in the United States.

1860–1870: The white population declined, as the Civil War choked off shipping on the Mississippi. Meantime, the exploding railroad network of the upper Midwest began to divert river cargo away from New Orleans and redirect it eastward by rail to large northern cities such as Chicago, Cincinnati, and New York City. Although mainline railroads eventually made their way to New Orleans, the city never recaptured the losses of this period.

1870–1950: As the Port of New Orleans was rebuilt and modernized, and as the city simultaneously turned itself into a major railroad terminal, the local economy recovered. A moderate but solid prosperity ensued, and lasted through World War II. New Orleans continued to attract whites and blacks at a rate somewhat higher than natural increase, the result of continued prosperity in the city. And while New Orleans was no model of racial tolerance, it was considerably more hospitable to blacks than the rural areas of the old Cotton Belt. As cotton production in the Deep South waned from the 1920s onward, field jobs were lost, and increasing numbers of blacks migrated into nearby cities. New Orleans, the nearest big city to major cotton-producing areas of the Delta and Black Belt districts of Mississippi and Alabama, was a major destination of those migrants. Throughout that whole period, New Orleans's white population continued to exceed the black population by a ratio of about 2:1, suggesting that whites were also moving to New Orleans from less-favored areas. Thus, during the whole period, the city remained dominantly white.

1950s: The decade was a great watershed in the racial composition of New Orleans. Although black population increased substantially—the result of natural increase and continuing immigration from rural areas—white population remained numerically static, but not stable. Heretofore, natural increase (excess of births over deaths) had led to an increase of about 40,000 whites per decade. In the 1950s, however, the increase was only about 5,000. These numbers reveal the beginning of large-scale net outmigration by whites—the inception of "white flight." The graph suggests that, perhaps, 35,000 whites left New Orleans City in the last half of the 1950s.

1960–2000: White flight shifted into high gear. White population plummeted, at the same time that black population continued to increase. By about 1974, for the first time since 1830, the numbers of blacks in New Orleans exceeded that of whites. By 2000, blacks outnumbered whites by a ratio of well over 2 to 1. Throughout this period, the rate of white flight was such that the city's white population dropped from almost 400,000 to fewer than 140,000. Simultaneously, the city's total population of about 625,000 in 1960 had dropped to fewer than 500,000 in 1990. By the year 2000, the total white population of New Orleans was smaller than it had been since before the Civil War. New Orleans had been converted from a white city with black enclaves, to a black city with white enclaves—mostly upper-income.

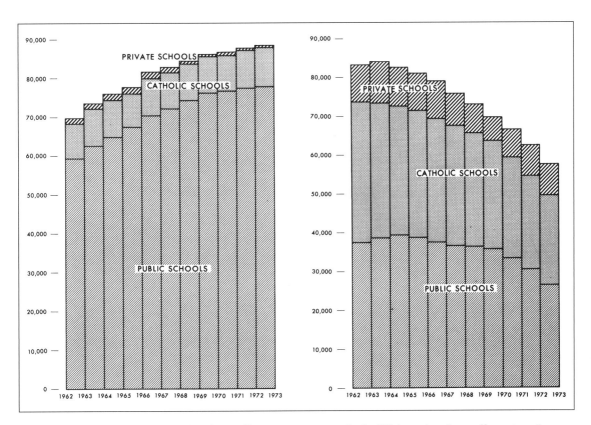

Figures 66 and 67. Left: **Black school enrollment, 1962-1973.** Right: **White school enrollment, 1962-1973.** These two graphs show the epochal shift in school enrollment at the moment that New Orleans was in the process of converting from a majority-white city, to one that was majority-black. Compare the simultaneous increase in black enrollment; change is especially drastic in public schools, which most blacks attend. Note, also, the relative increase but absolute decline in white enrollment in private and Catholic schools. Source: Stanley Fitzpatrick. *Facts and Finances 1972-1973* (New Orleans: New Orleans Public Schools, Orleans Parish School Board, 1973.)

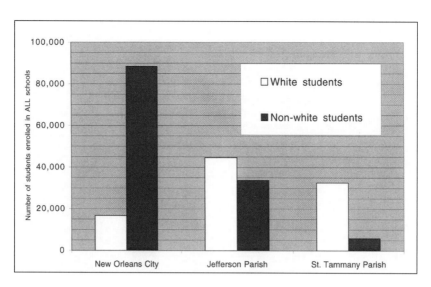

Figure 68a. **Race in public, private, and parochial schools, 1999–2000** (New Orleans Metro Area: City v. Inner and Outer Suburbs). The "City" is Orleans Parish; East Bank Jefferson Parish, largely populated between 1950 and 1980, is the "inner" suburb; and St. Tammany Parish, north of Lake Pontchartrain, is the "outer" suburb. When the data for these figures were gathered in the year 2000, St. Tammany was growing faster than any parish in Louisiana. This figure shows the combined school enrollment in both public and private schools. In effect, it is a surrogate for the number of families with children of school age. In New Orleans City, the ratio of black to white population is about 2.5:1, but the ratio of black *children* to white *children* is more than 5:1. White flight has deprived the city of most of its white families with children. A similar tendency occurs in Jefferson Parish, where whites far outnumber blacks, but the number of *children* is close to equal. There are obviously very few blacks in St. Tammany Parish.

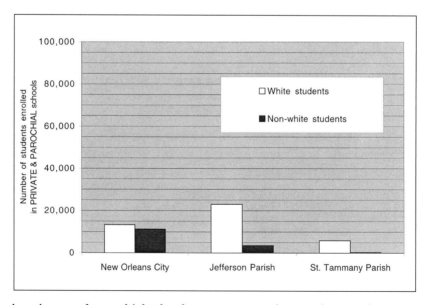

Figure 68b. **Race in private and parochial schools, 1999-2000**, in the same three parishes. Nearly all of New Orleans's white students are enrolled in private schools, generally of much higher quality than the public schools. Black families who can afford to do so send their children to private schools as well. The large enrollment of white students in Jefferson's private schools represents a kind of white flight from the public schools, presumably anticipating what has already happened in Orleans Parish. Even in St. Tammany Parish, however, private and parochial schools are well-supported, mainly by whites.

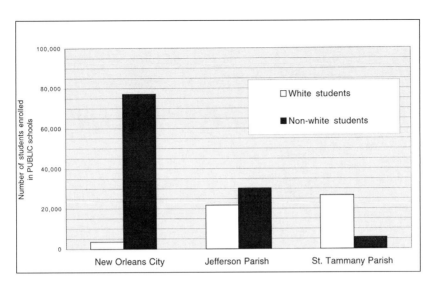

Figure 69a. **Race in public schools, 1999–2000,** in the same three parishes. In New Orleans, whites have virtually abandoned the public school system; the few white children who remain are enrolled in exclusive magnet schools (not shown on the graph). The process of abandonment of public school by whites is well under way in the inner-suburb Jefferson, but hardly noticeable in the outer-suburb of St. Tammany.

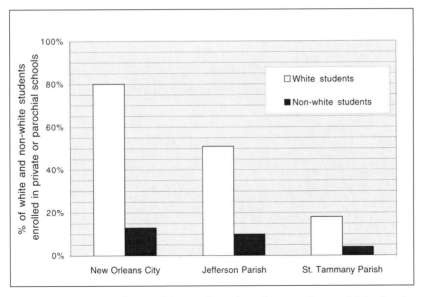

Figure 69b. **Percentage of white and nonwhite students in private and parochial schools, 1999–2000.** The graph reflects a dismal educational situation throughout the metropolitan area. Of New Orleans's small number of white children, eighty percent attend private schools—mainly Catholic. Fewer than fifteen percent of black children are so enrolled, presumably because of the high cost of private education. In the inner suburb of Jefferson, more than half of the white children but only about ten percent of the black children are in private schools. Even in distant St. Tammany, nearly one out of five white children are in nonpublic schools.

BIBLIOGRAPHY TO BOOK ONE (1976)

Adams, John S. "The Geography of Riots and Civil Disorders in the 1960's." *Economic Geography* 48 (January, 1972): 24–42.

Arellano, Richard G., and Manuel M. Alarcon. "New Orleans and Visitors from Latin America." *Louisiana Business Survey* 2, 1 (January, 1971): 14–15.

Ayers, H. Brandt, and Thomas H. Naylor, eds. You *Can't Eat Magnolias*. New York: McGraw-Hill, 1972. (A publication of the L.Q.C. Lamar Society.)

Baughman, James P. "Gateway to the Americas." In Hodding Carter, ed., *New Orleans, 1718–1968*. New Orleans: Pelican Publishing House, 1968, pp. 258–87.

Bechtel Corporation. *New Orleans Centroport, U.S.A., Master Plan for Long Range Development*. A report prepared for the Board of Commissioners of the Port of New Orleans, an Agency of the State of Louisiana. New Orleans: March, 1970.

Blassingame, John W. *Black New Orleans, 1860–1880*. Chicago: University of Chicago Press, 1973.

Burck, Charles G. "It's Promoters vs. Taxpayers in the Superstadium Game." *Fortune* 87,3 (March, 1973): 104–13, 178–82.

Bush-Brown, Albert. "Your Right to a Fine City." *House and Garden,* March, 1968, pp. 118ff.

Calhoun, James, ed. *Louisiana Almanac, 1973–74*. Gretna, LA: Pelican Publishing Company, 1973.

Carter, Hodding, ed. *The Past as Prelude: New Orleans, 1718–1968*. New Orleans: Pelican Publishing House, 1968. (A Tulane University publication.)

Chai, Charles Y. W. "Who Rules New Orleans? A Study of Community Power Structure. Some Preliminary Findings on Social Characteristics and Attitudes of New Orleans Leaders." *Louisiana Business Survey* 2 (October, 1971): 12–16.

Chamber of Commerce of the New Orleans Area. *The New Orleans Area Story*. New Orleans: Flambeaux Publishing Company, n.d. [but probably 1972].

Chase, John. *Frenchmen, Desire, Good Children . . . and Other Streets of New Orleans*. 2nd ed. New Orleans: Robert L. Crager & Co., 1960.

————— *Louisiana Purchase*. New Orleans: The Hauser Press, 1954, 1960.

Christovich, Mary L.; Roulhac Toledano; Betsy Swanson; and Pat Holden. *New Orleans Architecture. Vol. 2: The American Sector.* Gretna, LA: Pelican Publishing Company, 1972.

Chubbuck, James; Edward Renwick; and Joe Walker. "An Analysis of the 1970 New Orleans Mayoral Election." *Louisiana Business Survey* 1,3 (July, 1970): 6–12.

Collin, Richard H. *The New Orleans Underground Gourmet.* 2d ed., rev. New York: Simon and Schuster, 1973.

Davis, Jack. "Can Anybody Save the Business District?" *Figaro* (New Orleans) 2, 19 (May 12, 1973): 1,6–9.

Dufour, Charles L. *Ten Flags in the Wind: the Story of Louisiana.* New York: Harper and Row, 1967

Farrier, Dean Grimes. "Impact of Environmental Legislation on the Transportation Decision-Making Process in New Orleans: The Derailment of the 1–310 Riverfront Expressway." *Journal of Urban Law* 51 (1974): 687722.

Federal Writers' Project of the Works Progress Administration for the City of New Orleans. *New Orleans City Guide.* American Guide Series. Boston: Houghton Mifflin Company, 1938.

Feibleman, Peter S. *American Cooking: Creole and Acadian.* New York: Time-Life Books, 1971. (Time-Life *Foods of the World* series.)

Filipich, Judy A., and Lee Taylor. *Lakefront New Orleans: Planning and Development, 1926–1971.* New Orleans: Urban Studies Institute, Louisiana State University in New Orleans, 1971.

Fisk, H.N. *Geological Investigations of the Alluvial Valley of the Lower Mississippi River.* Vicksburg: Mississippi River Commission, 1944.

————*Geological Investigation of the Atchafalaya Basin and the Problem of Mississippi River Diversion.* Vicksburg: Mississippi River Commission, 1952.

Fitzpatrick, Stanley. *Facts and Finances, 1972–1973.* New Orleans: New Orleans Public Schools, Orleans Parish School Board, 1973.

Fleishman, Joel L. "The Southern City: Northern Mistakes in Southern Settings." In H. Brandt Ayers and Thomas H. Naylor, eds., *You Can't Eat Magnolias*, New York: McGraw-Hill, 1972, pp. 169–94.

Gagliano, Sherwood M., and Johannes L. van Beek. *Geologic and Geomorphic Aspects of Deltaic Processes, Mississippi Delta System.* Report no. 1, Hydrologic and Geologic Studies of Coastal Louisiana. Baton Rouge: Coastal Resources Unit, Center for Wetland Resources, Louisiana State University, February, 1970.

Gallup, George, and the American Institute of Public Opinion. Reports of a poll on American attitudes toward particular cities. *The New York Times,* September 7, 1969, p. 59; and September 8, 1969, p. 25.

Gilmore, H.W. "The Old New Orleans and the New: A Case for Ecology." *American Sociological Review* 9(1944): 385–94.

Glaab, Charles N., and A. Theodore Brown. *A History of Urban America.* New York: Macmillan, 1967.

Glazier, Captain Willard. *Peculiarities of American Cities.* Philadelphia: Hubbard Brothers, 1883. (Especially Chapter XX, "New Orleans," pp. 264–80.)

Greater New Orleans Tourist and Convention Commission. Annual reports.

Hammer, Greene, Siler Associates. "An Economic and Social Study of the Vieux Carré, New Orleans, Louisiana." Technical Supplement to *Plan and Program for the Preservation of the Vieux Carré.* New Orleans: Bureau of Governmental Research, December, 1968.

Hansen, Harry, ed. *Louisiana: A Guide to the State.* Rev. ed. New York: Hastings House, 1971. (From the *American Guide* series, originally compiled by the Federal Writers' Project of the Works Progress Administration of the State of Louisiana.)

Hayward, John. *A Gazetteer of the United States of America. . . .* Hartford, CT: Case, Tiffany, and Company, 1853.

Hilliard, Sam Bowers. *Hog Meat and Hoecake: Food Supply in the Old South, 1840–1860.* Carbondale: Southern Illinois University Press, 1972.

Housing Authority of New Orleans. Monthly memoranda from the deputy executive officer to the executive director concerning occupancy of St. Thomas, Iberville, and Florida Avenue projects. January 2, 1968–September 4, 1973.

Huber, Leonard V. *New Orleans: A Pictorial History.* New York: Crown Publishers, 1971.

Jefferson Parish Planning Department. "Residential Construction Trend in Jefferson Parish, Louisiana, excluding Kenner, Gretna, Westwego and Grand Isle, 1960–1971." Metairie, LA, March 21, 1973. (Mimeographed.)

Juhn, Daniel S. "Managerial Thinking in the New Orleans Area." *Louisiana Business Survey* 2 (October, 1971): 12–16.

Kenyon, James B. "Elements in Inter-Port Competition in the United States." *Economic Geography* 46, 1 (January, 1970): 1–24.

Key, V.O., Jr. "Louisiana: The Seamy Side of Democracy." In *Southern Politics in State and Nation,* Chapter 8. New York: Alfred A. Knopf, 1949.

King, Grace E. *New Orleans, the Place and the People.* New York: The Macmillan Company, 1895.

Kniffen, Fred B. *Louisiana, Its Land and People.* Baton Rouge: Louisiana State University Press, 1968.

Kolb, Carolyn. *New Orleans: An Invitation to Discover One of America's Most Fascinating Cities.* Garden City, NY: Doubleday and Company, 1972.

Kolb, Charles R. *Distribution of Soils Bordering in the Mississippi River From Donaldsonville to Head-of-Passes.* Vicksburg, MS: U.S. Army Waterways Experiment Station, Technical Report no. 3–601, April, 1962.

Kolb, Charles R., and J.R. Van Lopik. *Geology of the Mississippi River Deltaic Plain, Southeastern Louisiana.* 2 vols. Vicksburg, MS: U.S. Army Engineer Waterways Experiment Station, Technical Report no. 3–483, July, 1958.

Liebling, A.J. *The Earl of Louisiana.* New York: Ballentine Books, 1961.

Morse, Jedidiah, and Richard C. Morse. *A New Universal Gazetteer . . .* 4th ed. New Haven: S. Converse, 1823.

New Orleans, City of. City Planning and Zoning Commission. *Major Street Report,* 1927.

Community Renewal Program. New Orleans: City Planning Commission, n.d. [but apparently 1970].

Newsom, Robert T. "Worker Mobility in New Orleans, 1960 to 1965." *Louisiana Business Survey* 1, 1 (January, 1970): 1–4.

Newton, Milton B., Jr. *Atlas of Louisiana: A Guide for Students.* Baton Rouge: Louisiana State University, School of Geoscience, 1972. (Miscellaneous Publication 72–1.)

Official Guide of the Railways and Steam Navigation Lines of the United States. New York: National Railway Publication Company. (Published monthly.)

Patton, Donald J. "General Cargo Hinterlands of New York, Philadelphia, Baltimore, and New Orleans." *Annals of the Association of American Geographers* 48, 4 (December, 1958): 436–55.

Patton, Donald J. *Port Hinterlands: the Case of New Orleans.* College Park: University of Maryland, February, 1960. (Office of Naval Research, Contract 595 [05] NR 388–033.)

Peirce, Neal R. "Louisiana: An evocation." In *The Deep South States of America: People, Politics, and Power in the Seven Deep South States.* New York: W. W. Norton, 1974., pp. 13–122.

Price, Reynolds. "Dodo, Phoenix, or Tough Old Cock?" In H. Brandt Ayers and Thomas H. Naylor, eds., You *Can't Eat Magnolias.* New York: McGraw-Hill, 1972.

Plan and Program for the Preservation of the Vieux Carré: Historic District Demonstration Study. New Orleans: Bureau of Governmental Research, December, 1968. See, also, the following Technical Supplements:

1. Environmental Survey (Marcou, O'Leary and Associates)

2. Legal and Administrative Report

3. Economic and Social Study (Hammer, Greene, Siler Associates)

4. The Vieux Carré, New Orleans, Its Plan, Its Growth, Its Architecture (Samuel Wilson, Jr.)

5. New Orleans Central Business District Traffic Study (Louisiana Department of Highways)

6. Summary Report: Evaluation of the Effects of the Proposed Riverfront Expressway (Marcou, O'Leary and Associates)

7. Technical Report on the Effects of the Proposed Riverfront Expressway on the Vieux Carré, New Orleans, Louisiana (Marcou, O'Leary and Associates)

Regional Planning Commission. *History of Regional Growth of Jefferson, Orleans, and St. Bernard Parishes, Louisiana.* New Orleans, November, 1969.

Reissman, Leonard, et al. "Housing Discrimination in New Orleans: Summary and Recommendations." Based on a series of reports prepared for the New Orleans City Planning Commission. New Orleans: Tulane University Urban Studies Center, April, 1970. (Mimeographed.)

"Sociological Components of Community Renewal in New Orleans." A report prepared for the City Planning Commission of New Orleans. New Orleans: Department of Sociology, Tulane University, c. 1965.

Rushton, Bill. "The Damned Stadium: Blueprint of a Scandal." *The Courier: The Weekly of New Orleans 10*, 17 (August 31–September 6, 1973): 1, 12–18.

Sanford, Terry. "The End of the Myths: The South Can Lead the Nations." In H. Brandt Ayers and Thomas H. Naylor, eds., You *Can't Eat Magnolias.* New York: McGraw-Hill, 1972, pp. 317–29.

Saucier, Roger T. *Recent Geomorphic History of the Pontchartrain Basin, Louisiana.* Technical Report no. 16. Baton Rouge: Louisiana State University Coastal Studies Institute, June, 1963.

Saussy, Gordon A. *The Dynamics of Manufacturing Employment Location in the New Orleans Metropolitan Area.* Research Study no. 16. New Orleans: Division of Business and Economic Research, College of Business Administration, Louisiana State University in New Orleans, 1972.

Slusher, David F.; W.L. Cockerham; and S.D. Matthews. "Mapping and Interpretation of Histosols and Hydraquents for Urban Development." Alexandria, LA: U.S. Department of Agriculture, Soil Conservation Service. Paper presented before Soil Science Society of America, Miami, Florida, October 30, 1972. (Mimeographed.)

Smith, Robert J., ed. 1973 *Annual Directory, Port of New Orleans.* New Orleans: Board of Commissioners of the Port of New Orleans, 1973.

Smith, T. Lynn, and Homer L. Hitt. *The People of Louisiana.* Baton Rouge: Louisiana State University Press, 1952.

Somers, Dale A. "Black and White in New Orleans: A Study in Urban Race Relations, 1865–1900." *The Journal of Southern History* 40 (1974): 19–42.

Taeuber, Karl E., and Alma F. Taeuber. *Negroes in Cities: Residential Segregation and Neighborhood Change.* A Population Research and Training Center Monograph. Chicago: Aldine, 1965.

Thornbury, William D. *Regional Geomorphology of the United States.* New York: John Wiley & Sons, 1965. (See, especially, Chapters 2 and 3, "The Continental Margins" and "The Coastal Plain Province.")

Trollope, Frances. *Domestic Manners of the Americans.* London: Whittaker, Treacher & Co., 1832. (There are numerous reprintings and revisions. Among the best is Donald Smalley, ed., for Vintage Books. New York: Alfred A. Knopf, 1949.)

U.S. Army Corps of Engineers. *Report on Hurricane Betsy, 8–11 September* 1965, *in the U.S. Army Engineer District, New Orleans*. New Orleans: U.S. Army Engineer District, November, 1965.

———*Report on Hurricane Camille, 14–22 August* 1969. New Orleans: U.S. Army Engineering District, May, 1970.

U.S. Bureau of the Census. *Census of Housing: 1970. Block Statistics, New Orleans, La., Urbanized Area*. Final Report HC[3]–101. Washington, D.C.: U.S. Government Printing Office, September, 1971.

———*Census of Population and Housing: 1970. Census Tracts, New Orleans, La., Standard Metropolitan Statistical Area*. Final Report PHC[1]–144. Washington, D.C.: U.S. Government Printing Office, February, 1972.

———*Statistical Abstract of the United States: 1972*. 93d ed. Section 33, "Metropolitan Area Statistics." Washington, D.C.: U.S. Government Printing Office, 1972. pp. 837 ff.

U.S. Census Office, Department of the Interior. "New Orleans, Louisiana." In *Report on the Social Statistics of Cities*, compiled by George E. Waring, Jr. Part II, "The Southern and Western States." Washington, D.C.: U.S. Government Printing Office, 1887.

U.S. Department of Commerce. Environmental Science Services Administration, Environmental Data Service. *Climatic Atlas of the United States*. Washington, D.C.: U.S. Government Printing Office, June, 1968.

Vance, Rupert B. *Human Geography of the South*. Chapel Hill: The University of North Carolina Press, 1935. (See, especially, Chapter XI, "The Delta Plantation Heritage," pp. 261–74.)

"Vieux Carré Commission, Its Purpose and Function." New Orleans, n.d.

Williams, T. Harry, *Huey Long*. New York: Alfred A. Knopf, 1969.

Wilson, Samuel, Jr. "The Vieux Carré, New Orleans, Its Plan, Its Growth, Its Architecture." Technical Supplement to *Plan and Program for the Preservation of the Vieux Carré*. New Orleans: Bureau of Governmental Research, December, 1968.

Wilson, Samuel, Jr., and Bernard Lemann. *New Orleans Architecture. Vol. 1: The Lower Garden District*, Mary L. Christovich and Roulhac Toledano, eds. Gretna, LA: Pelican Publishing Company, 1971.

Woodward, C. Vann. *Origins of the New South, 1877–1913*. Baton Rouge: Louisiana State University Press, 1951; paperback reprint, 1970.

Bibliography to Book Two (2003)

(The following citations complement the original bibliography of 1976.)

Access New Orleans. New York: Harper Collins, 1999.

Aiken, Charles S. *The Cotton Plantation South since the Civil War.* Baltimore: Johns Hopkins University Press, 1998; paperback edition, 2003. (Part of the *Creating the North American Landscape* series, and winner of the 1999 J.B. Jackson award of the Association of American Geographers.)

Barone, Michael, and Grant Ujifusa. *The Almanac of American Politics.* Washington, D.C.: The National Journal, 1976–2001. (Published biennially since 1972.)

Baumbach, Richard O., Jr., and William E. Borah. *The Second Battle of New Orleans: A History of the Vieux Carré Riverfront Expressway Controversy.* University, AL: University of Alabama Press, 1981.

Bell, Natalie Whitman. "The Metropolitan New Orleans Economy, 1976–1995," *Louisiana Business Survey* 27, 1 (Spring, 1996): 7–12.

Black, Dan; Gary Gates; Seth Sanders, and Lowell Taylor. "Demographics of the Gay and Lesbian Population in the United States: Evidence from Available Systematic Data Sources." Syracuse, NY: Center for Policy Research, Syracuse University, October, 1999.

Britton, Robert. "The Dark Side of the Sun." *Focus* (a journal of the American Geographical Society of New York City) 32, 2 (November-December, 1980): 10–16.

Bourne, Joel. "Louisiana's Vanishing Wetlands: Going, Going . . . ." *Science* 289 (15 September 2000): 1860–63.

Calhoun, Milburn, ed. *Louisiana Almanac: 2002–2003 Edition.* Gretna, LA: Pelican Publishing Company, 2001.

Campanella, Richard, and Marina Campanella. *New Orleans: Then and Now.* Gretna, LA: Pelican Publishing Company, 1999.

Darcé, Keith covers business affairs for the *Times-Picayune.* Like those of Coleman Warner (q.v.), his writings are substantial, detailed, and highly reliable. The volume of his newspaper reporting makes it impossible to cite individual writings, but any serious student of New Orleans (and especially the Port of New Orleans) should pay careful attention to what Darcé has to say.

DeVore, Donald E., and Joseph Logsdon. *Crescent City Schools: Public Education in New Orleans, 1841–1991.* New Orleans: Orleans Parish School Board, 1991.

Dunne, Mike. "Divert a River, Save a Marsh: Protecting Louisiana's coastal wetlands is a never-ending battle." *Planning* 76, 2 (February, 2001): 12–17.

"Economic Impact: New Orleans port creates jobs at all levels of business." *PortRecord: The Worldwide Publication of the Port of New Orleans.* New Orleans: Board of Commissioners for the Port of New Orleans (July-August, 1999): 8, 12–13.

Fischetti, Mark. "Drowning New Orleans." *Scientific American* 285, 4 (October, 2001): 76–85.

Fish, Jamie. "Economic impact of gambling in Louisiana." *Louisiana Business Survey* 30, 2 (Fall, 1999): 2–4.

Foley, Ludivine Dorée. "The 1998 economic Impact of domestic travel in Louisiana." *Louisiana Business Survey* 30, 2 (Fall, 1999): 7–9.

Friends of the Cabildo. *New Orleans Architecture. Vol. 1, The Lower Garden District; Vol. 2, The American Sector (Faubourg St. Mary); Vol. 3, The Cemeterie; Vol. 4, The Creole Faubourgs; and Vol. 5, The Esplanade Ridge.* Mary Louise Cristovich et al., eds. Gretna, LA: Pelican Press, 1971–1977.

Hagan, Peter Edward, III. "The history and impact of the 1984 Louisiana World Exposition." An unpublished Master of Liberal Arts thesis, Tulane University, New Orleans, LA, December 2, 1994.

Hart, Katherine. "Ports and promenades: New Orleans to Toronto: Waterfronts are getting lots of respect." *Planning* 67, 2 (February, 2001): 20–22.

Heard, Malcolm. *French Quarter Manual: An Architectural Guide to New Orleans' Vieux Carré.* New Orleans: School of Architecture, Tulane University, 1997.

Jordan-Bychkov, Terry G. *The Upland South: The Making of an American Folk Region and Landscape.* Santa Fe, NM: Center for American Places, 2003.

Kane, Harnett Thomas. *Louisiana Hayride: the American Rehearsal for Dictatorship, 1928–1940.* New York: W. Morrow & Co., 1941.

Kimbrough, Julius E., Jr. "The nature of poverty in New Orleans: A closer look at the 1990 Census," *Louisiana Business Survey* 28, 2 (Fall, 1997): 7–11.

Klumpp, Scott. "Louisiana annual net migration, 1969–1992." *Louisiana Business Survey* 24, 2 (Fall, 1993): 5–9.

Liebling, A. J. *The Earl of Louisiana*. New York: Ballentine Books, 1961.

Magruder, Harriet. *A History of Louisiana*. Boston: D. C. Heath & Company, 1909.

McPhee, John. "Atchafalaya," Chapter 1 in *The Control of Nature*. New York: Farrar Straus Giroux, 1989, pp. 3–92.

McLain, James J. "The economic impact of Mardi Gras, 1998." *Louisiana Business Survey* 30, 1 (Spring, 1999): 10–12.

Metrovision Economic Development Partnership. *Perspectives 2001: The Economic Development Factbook and Guide to Business Investment in Southeast Louisiana and the New Orleans Region.* Metairie, LA: New Orleans Publishing Group, 2001.

Moody, Marlise, and Frédéric Dimanche. "New Orleans Area visitors: A closer look." *Louisiana Business Survey* 29, 1 (Spring, 1998): 5–11.

New Orleans Metropolitan Convention and Visitors Bureau, Inc. *1999 New Orleans Area Visitor Profile: Annual Report.* New Orleans: College of Business Administration, University of New Orleans, 1999.

Nelson, Kristin. "The last three blocks of Market Street." An unpublished seminar paper, Department of Geography, University of California, Berkeley, 1976.

Niehaus, Earl F. "The new Irish, 1830–1862." Reprinted in *The Louisiana Purchase Bicentennial Series in Louisiana History, Volume X: A Refuge for All Ages: Immigrants in Louisiana History*, 1966, p. 388.

"Planning February 2001: Special conference issue on New Orleans." *Planning* (Journal of the American Planning Association): 67, 2. (A special conference issue was also issued in connection with the APA's meeting in New Orleans, February, 1991.)

Ray, Scott. "The economic impact of the 1993 New Orleans Jazz and Heritage Festival." *Louisiana Business Survey* 25, 1 (Spring, 1994): 6–9.

Rehder, John B. *Delta Sugar: Lousiana's Vanishing Plantation Landscapes*. Baltimore: Johns Hopkins University Press, 1999. (Part of the *Creating the North American Landscape* series, and winner of the 2000 Abbott Lowell Cummings Award of the Vernacular Architecture Forum.)

Rusk, David, et al. *The New Regionalism: Planning Together to Reshape New Orleans' Future.* (An advertising supplement to *The New Orleans Times-Picayune,* September 8, 1999. Paid for by the Regional Cooperation Fund of the Greater New Orleans Foundation.)

"Strategic policy plan for the New Orleans Riverfront" (Draft). New Orleans: City Planning Commission, 1991.

Steinbeck, John. *Travels with Charley: In Search of America.* New York: Viking Press, 1962.

University of New Orleans (in partnership with Dillard, Loyola, Southern, Tulane, and Xavier universities). "The effects of land-based and riverboat gaming in New Orleans." *Louisiana Business Survey* 28, 1 (Spring, 1997): 2 ff.

Vlach, John M. "The shotgun house: an African architectural legacy." *Pioneer America* 8 (1, 2): 47–56, 57–70.

Warner, Coleman. "A blight on the City." *New Orleans Times-Picayune,* May 9, 1999. (Note: Coleman Warner covers urban affairs and higher education for the *Times-Picayune,* the newspaper of record for New Orleans. Warner has written voluminously and perceptively about the city. He knows the city intimately, and his essays are clear-eyed and hard-hitting. To cite even the best of his essays and articles would overwhelm this bibliography. My advice to any serious student of the city is to pay close attention to anything that appears under Coleman Warner's byline.)

———— "Freret's Century: Growth, Identity, and Loss in a New Orleans Neighborhood." *Louisiana* History XLII, 3 (Summer, 2001): 323–358.

———— "The nontourist's guide to New Orleans: What's behind the mask." *Planning* 67, 2 (February, 2001): 4–11.

———— "The tourist trap." *The New Orleans Times-Picayune,* May 11, 1997.

Williams, James L. "Oil price history and analysis." *Energy Economics Newsletter.* London, AR: WTRG Economics, 1996. Web site: www.wtrg.com/prices

Index

ABOUT THE AUTHOR

Peirce F. Lewis is professor of geography, emeritus, at the Pennsylvania State University in University Park, where he taught in the Geography Department from 1958 to 1996.

Mr. Lewis is a student of American physical and human landscapes—especially the ordinary urban and rural landscapes created by ordinary Americans. His writings on these subjects have been published widely and have received awards from the Association of American Geographers and the Pennsylvania Geographical Society.

His numerous publications include "Axioms for Reading the Landscape," "Small Town in Pennsylvania," "America's Natural Landscapes" (for the *Encyclopaedia Britannica*), "America between the Wars: the Engineering of a New Geography," and "The Urban Invasion of Urban America: the Galactic City." He has also helped design educational films for the *Encyclopaedia Britannica* and for Pennsylvania Public Television.

Mr. Lewis has served as president of the Association of American Geographers, the nation's primary organization of professional geographers. He has been awarded fellowships by the John Simon Guggenheim Memorial Foundation, the Woodrow Wilson International Center for Scholars at the Smithsonian Institution in Washington, D.C., and the National Science Foundation. He has held visiting appointments at the University of California in Berkeley, Concordia University in Montréal, and Michigan State University, where he held the first appointment as John Hannah Visiting Professor of Integrative Studies.

As a teacher, Mr. Lewis is a recipient of the Lindback Foundation Award, Penn State's highest award for distinguished teaching, the Wilson Teaching Award from the College of Earth and Mineral Sciences at Penn State, and a national award as a teacher at the college level by the National Council for Geographic Education. *New Orleans: The Making of an Urban Landscape*, *Second Edition* won the 2004 J. B. Jackson Prize of the Association of American Geographers for the best book in American geography.

Mr. Lewis is a native of Michigan. He lives in the Borough of State College, Pennsylvania.

THE CENTER FOR AMERICAN PLACES is a tax-exempt 501(c)(3) nonprofit organization, founded in 1990, whose educational mission is to enhance the public's understanding of, and appreciation for, the natural and built environment. It is guided by the belief that books provide an indispensible foundation for comprehending—and caring for—the places where we live, work, and explore. Books live. Books endure. Books make a difference. Books are gifts to civilization.

With offices in Santa Fe, New Mexico, and Staunton, Virginia, Center editors bring to publication as many as thirty books per year under the Center's own imprint or in association with publishing partners. The Center is also engaged in numerous other educational programs that emphasize the interpretation of *place* through art, literature, scholarship, exhibitions, lectures, curriculum development, and field research. The Center's Cotton Mather Library in Arthur, Nebraska, its Martha A. Strawn Photographic Library in Davidson, North Carolina, and a ten-acre reserve along the Santa Fe River in Florida are available as retreats upon request. The Center is also affiliated with the Rocky Mountain Land Library in Colorado.

The Center strives every day to make a difference through books, research, and education. For more information, please send inquiries to P. O. Box 23225, Santa Fe, NM 87502, U.S.A. or visit the Center's Web site (*www.americanplaces.org*).

About the Book:
The text for *New Orleans: The Making of an Urban Landscape, Second Edition* was set in Perpetua and Syntax. The paper for the second paperback printing is 140 gsm Thai A.

FOR THE CENTER FOR AMERICAN PLACES:

George F. Thompson, president and publisher

Randall B. Jones, associate editorial director

Lauren A. Marcum, editorial assistant

Purna Makaram, manuscript editor

David Skolkin, designer and typesetter